F

THE OVER-
EDUCATED
AMERICAN

THE OVER-EDUCATED AMERICAN

Richard B. Freeman

Department of Economics
Harvard University
Cambridge, Massachusetts

RECEIVED

JUN 1 2 1978

MANKATO STATE UNIVERSITY
MEMORIAL LIBRARY
MANKATO, MN.

ACADEMIC PRESS

New York   San Francisco   London

A Subsidiary of Harcourt Brace Jovanovich, Publishers

ACADEMIC PRESS, INC.
111 Fifth Avenue, New York, New York 10003

United Kingdom Edition published by
ACADEMIC PRESS, INC. (LONDON) LTD.
24/28 Oval Road, London NW1

Library of Congress Cataloging in Publication Data

Freeman, Richard Barry,   Date
      The overeducated American.

      Includes bibliographical references.
      1.   College graduates–Employment–United States.
2.   Labor supply–United States.   I.   Title.
HD6278.U5F73   1976   331.7′1   75-36646
ISBN 0–12–267250–X (cloth)
ISBN 0–12–267252–6 (paper)

PRINTED IN THE UNITED STATES OF AMERICA

This book is dedicated to my parents,
Herbert J. and Sylvia F. Freeman

Contents

Acknowledgments

I received both direct and indirect aid from a large number of people in writing this book. Alan Garber, Jonathan Leonard, and Peter Meyer were valuable research assistants. Zvi Griliches discussed numerous issues with me. Martin Feldstein, James Medoff, David Riesman, Herbert Hollomon, and Jacob Mincer, among others, provided useful comments verbally or in writing. More indirectly, the book owes much to the pioneering work of T. W. Schultz, J. Mincer, and G. Becker who made analysis of "human capital" an area of research for labor economists. Unfortunately, blame for errors of omission or commission rest solely with me.

Introduction

College education has traditionally been a major route for social and economic advance in the United States, providing individuals with training that promised high earnings and occupational status, in addition to a broad liberal arts education, and providing the nation with scientific and technical specialists and skilled white-collar workers. Viewed as an economic investment in skills, college training has been highly profitable to individuals and to society, and an integral part of the American dream of success and the good life. Indicative of the desire of Americans for college education is the television advertisement of the Negro College Fund, which shows a black mother scrubbing an office floor so that her son can go to college.

In the 1950s and 1960s the United States took major steps toward making the goal of college a reality for millions. The proportion of GNP allocated to higher education, including junior and community colleges, doubled. The number of college students tripled; the number receiving bachelor's degrees increased by 91%; the number receiving master's and doctoral degrees jumped more than threefold. By 1969, nearly half of white men of college age (18 to 19) were enrolled in colleges and universities of some type. Employment in higher education reached 1,669,550 in 1970, considerably more than in either the automobile or the steel industry—two of the most important industries of the twentieth century. The

1

number of workers with at least one year of college training surpassed both the number of union members and the number of manufacturing production workers in the mid-1960s, substantially altering the nature of the American labor market.[1]

National policy encouraged the growth of the college-educated work force. Subway, bus, radio, and television advertisements trumpeted the fact that college graduates typically earned $100,000 more than high school graduates in the course of their working life. Federal support of higher education grew from virtually nothing in 1962 to over $6 billion in 1972. Following Sputnik (October 1957) and related Soviet technological successes, President Kennedy declared that "the shortage of Ph.D.'s constitutes our most critical national problem" and initiated major federal scholarship and fellowship programs, which were further expanded by President Johnson. State and local governments created hundreds of new colleges, junior colleges and community colleges. From 1800 in 1950 the number of public and private institutions of higher education grew to about 2600 in 1972.[2]

Economic analysis of higher education supported the notion that "more is better." The "human capital" school initiated by Schultz and Becker found that—treated as an investment in work skills similar to investments in income-producing machines—education had a substantial payoff. Indeed, despite the increased supply of college-educated workers, the rate of return on investment in a college education remained high compared to other potential investments of national and private resources. Production function studies, which analyze output in terms of such inputs as labor, land, and

[1] The proportion of GNP allocated to higher education was obtained from U.S. Office of Education, *Digest of Educational Statistics 1974*, Table 27, p. 26. Numbers of college students and degree recipients from *Digest*, Table 87, p. 75 and Table 115, p. 101. The proportion of 18 to 19-year-old men in college in 1969 was 47.3%, according to the U.S. Bureau of the Census, "School Enrollment," *Current Population Reports*, Series P–20, No. 206, p. 8. Employment in higher education, automobile, and steel from U.S. Bureau of the Census 1970 Census of Population , *Industrial Characteristics*, PC(2)–7B, Table 1, pp. 1–4. Number of union workers from U.S. Department of Labor, *Handbook of Labor Statistics 1974*, Table 152, p. 366 and number of production workers from Table 41, p. 106.
[2] Federal funds for higher education from *Digest*, 1974 Table 138, p. 126. The number of colleges from U.S. Bureau of Census, *Historical Statistics of the United States*, p. 210 and U.S. Office of Education, *Digest of Educational Statistics 1972*, Table 110, p. 93. The figures refer to all institutions of higher education, including junior colleges. President Kennedy's quotation is from his news conference on 15 January 1962.

capital, showed that education substantially raised productivity in the economy. Upward of 30% of the increase in per capita income since the Great Depression was attributed to increased schooling. A rising share of the nation's capital stock—goods that produce other goods and services—came to be held in the form of human skills, produced by education rather than by machines.[3]

Nonorthodox economists also stressed the socioeconomic importance of college and university training in the postwar years. The New Left argued that schools were the prime mechanism for reproducing the class system, allowing the wealthy to pass on their status to their children in the form of a good college education. They argued that the burgeoning junior and community college movement served the purpose of teaching persons of lower social origin the skills needed for paraprofessional jobs, without increasing their ability to think independently. Galbraith, on the other hand, fastened on the growth of the college-trained technostructure as the essential feature of the "New Industrial State," claiming that corporate power had passed into the hands of highly trained managerial and technical experts whose decisions dominated the economy. His hope was that the "Scientific–Educational Elite," consisting of college professors and researchers, would use their role as producers of human skill and knowledge to institute Galbraithian changes in the nation.[4]

In short, there was a general consensus among policymakers and analysts, supported by available data, that college training was a

---

[3] The initial papers on human capital by T.W. Schultz are found in *Investment in Human Capital* (New York: The Free Press, 1971). G. Becker's contribution is *Human Capital* (New York: Columbia University Press, 1964). The major production function study is by Z. Griliches, "Notes on the Role of Education in Production Functions and Growth Accounting," in W. L. Hansen (ed.) *Education, Income, and Human Capital* (New York: Columbia University Press, 1970), pp. 71–127. Estimates of the impact of schooling on the increase in per capita income are given in E. Denison, *Accounting for United States Economic Growth 1929–1969* (Washington D.C.: The Brookings Institution, 1974). The rising share of capital held in human form is documented in T.W. Schultz "Reflections on Investment in Man," *Journal of Political Economy* (supplement, Oct. 1962), pp. 1–8.

[4] For the work of the New Left economists, see S. Bowles "Unequal Education and the Reproduction of the Social Division of Labor," *Review of Radical Political Economics* (Fall, 1971), Vol. 3, No. 3, pp. 1–30. Also, H. Gintis, "Education, Technology, and the Characteristics of Worker Productivity," *American Economic Review* (May 1971), pp. 266–279. Galbraith's assertions are given in *The New Industrial State* (New York: New American Library, 1972).

fruitful economic investment, both to the individual and to society—
one leading to a vastly different type of work force than in the
traditional industrial society.

What went wrong? In the mid-1970s a very different picture of
the college worker in the labor market seems to emerge. For the first
time since the Depression, newspapers report new graduates having
difficulty in obtaining college-level jobs. For prospective schoolteachers, primarily females, jobs in elementary and secondary schools are
especially scarce. Doctoral graduates face the less severe but still
substantial problem of a collapsing academic job market. In some
graduate areas, such as physics or English, the situation deteriorated,
at least in some years, to virtual crisis proportions. Recipients of
bachelor's, master's and doctoral degrees in most fields accepted
salaries in the early 1970s at real rates of pay far below those of their
predecessors—and often in jobs quite divorced from their field of
study and well below their levels of aspiration.

How significant was the 1970s downturn in the labor market
for college-educated manpower? Has the United States produced so
many graduates that the college-trained worker is, in fact, *overeducated* in the marketplace? What does the future hold—continued
depression in employment opportunities for the college-educated or
a revival of the job market to the level of previous decades? What are
the potential effects of a depressed college job market—on the
educational sector, on the role of formal education in society, on the
nation's social system as a whole? What are the economic mechanisms that connect the labor market and the educational system?
How can these mechanisms be used by policymakers to ameliorate
the problem? *What should be done?*

These questions constitute the subject matter of *The Overeducated American*, which analyzes, within the limits of available data
and knowledge of market processes, the turnaround in the college
job market and seeks to determine whether it constitutes a relatively
long-term or merely a temporary change in the economic status of
graduates. *Overeducated* relates in this context to the connection
between years and type of college studies and labor market earnings
and opportunities, not to the broader cultural aspects of higher
education. I use the term to denote a society in which the economic
rewards to college education are markedly lower than has historically
been the case and/or in which additional investment in college

training will drive down those rewards—a society in which education has become, like investments in other mature industries or activities, a marginal rather than highly profitable endeavor.[5] The book identifies the occupations that have been the most and the least affected by the market decline; examines how minority and other discriminated-against groups, such as women, have fared; and considers the implications of the changes for students choosing a career, for guidance and placement directors, for university administrators, and for governmental decision makers—for the American dream of success via a college education.

To answer such questions and to explore feasible policy alternatives, an analytic model of how the college labor market functions has been constructed and is used to diagnose past and current developments and to forecast the future. Such an analysis requires a detailed examination of the available statistical evidence on the supply of and demand for college-educated workers, and of the interaction of supply and demand in the marketplace.

The book begins with a careful examination of the depressed state of the college market in the 1970s, the rapid change from the boom conditions of the 1960s, and the past and present course of salaries and job opportunities. Following this is an evaluation of the way in which young persons have altered their education and career plans in response to the decline and the impact of the prevailing buyer's market on colleges and universities, and on employers.

The analytic core of the book is contained in Chapter 3, which analyzes the operation of the college job market, explains the reasons for its sudden collapse, and presents a forecast of future employment and income prospects, using the Recursive Adjustment Model that has been employed for several years at the Massachusetts Institute of

---

[5] The definition is designed to cover two possible economic situations. The first and most clear-cut case of "overeducation" with respect to the job market occurs when the economic rewards of college are driven down by continued increases in the number of graduates relative to demand and in which the rewards remain at historically low levels due to continued growth of graduates. The second, and possibly more realistic situation, relates to a society in which reductions in the supply of new graduates restores much of the traditional economic advantage enjoyed by graduates but where moderate increases in supply could not be "absorbed" without substantial declines in relative incomes and job position. The unifying feature of both economic worlds is that—in sharp contrast to the past—college education offers only limited opportunities for economic advancement, with increased investment yielding rapidly declining relative incomes.

Technology's Center for Policy Alternatives and elsewhere to analyze supply and demand in college-level professions.

Chapters 4 and 5 look at the differential experience of several important college-level professions in the 1960s and 1970s. Certain professional areas—the physical sciences and all levels of teaching (university, high school, and elementary school)—enjoyed exceptionally strong markets in the 1960s and exceptionally weak ones in the 1970s, while several others—law, medicine, master's level business administration, accounting, and engineering—were only moderately affected by the downturn and experienced quite different patterns of market ups and downs.

One of the most heartening developments in the late 1960s was the beginning of a serious effort to improve the economic status of groups that had traditionally been discriminated against—first blacks and then women. Chapters 6 and 7 examine how black and female graduates have fared in the falling market, whether or not equal employment opportunity practices have shifted demand in their favor and provided a countervailing force to the overall market decline.

The last chapter examines the implications of "overeducation" in the job market for such important social issues as intergenerational mobility, income distribution, and the relation between education and work, and considers how different groups of decision-makers might best respond to new market realities.

The most difficult problem faced in the book is the attempt to predict how long the depressed market for college graduates is likely to continue. Forecasting the future is a hazardous business in the social sciences, for two reasons. First and most obviously, the model used as a basis for forecasts may be faulty. A model that "fits" one period and seems valid may—because of omitted factors or changes in the social system—turn out to be inapplicable in another. Even with a correct model, moreover, forecasts can err because exogenous factors—those aspects of the world not analyzed in the model—differ from expectations, falsifying otherwise correct inferences about the future. For example, the federal government may suddenly embark on a major new space program or push energy research and development (R&D) beyond the levels that seem plausible today. If these events occur, an anticipated relative surplus of graduates may be turned into a shortage, a modest shortage into a serious deficit, and so forth. Given the true future values of governmental expenditures, the model might be able to predict market conditions perfectly, but, alas, the true future values of exogenous factors are, in the absence of clairvoyance or telekinesis, unknown. The only way to handle this problem is to make several forecasts, each dependent on "reasonable" expectations of the future state of the world, and then to evaluate the robustness of the forecasts to changes in state. A prediction is robust if it does not hinge critically on any one of a set of plausible projections of exogenous factors.

Even robust forecasts must be treated cautiously. Social scientists do not have an admirable record of peering accurately into the future. At the end of World War II, most expected a return to the Great Depression; in the mid-1960s, few, if any, anticipated that the civil rights movement would produce noticeable economic gains for blacks; *no* analyst predicted the collapse of the college labor market of the early 1970s. With respect to college workers, moreover, the only serious social science forecasts made in the past turned out to be completely wrong. In 1949, Professor Seymour Harris, then of Harvard, predicted a substantial market glut for the 1950s and 1960s—decades that were a veritable "golden age" for the college trained. Despite the dangers of forecasting and the dismal record of past forecasters, predictions are needed to guide current decisions about the allocation of resources to higher education and to alert us to possible future social problems. Accordingly, I have made forecasts in this book and offer them to the reader, though with a number of provisos and equivocations.

Because the questions considered here are of importance to persons outside of economics, the material is presented in as nontechnical a manner as possible. Figures and graphs are used extensively in place of tables of statistics or econometric regressions. The recursive market adjustment model is described verbally, rather than in algebraic formulae. The basic hypotheses and dynamics of the model are relatively simple, and little is lost in such a presentation. More technical analyses are contained in the scholarly articles and books cited in the text and briefly in the technical appendixes.

The Depressed College Labor Market

After years in which a college education was trumpeted as the sure route to a good job and high income ($100,000 more than the income expected by a high school graduate in the course of a working life, according to government sources) reports suddenly appeared in the early 1970s that graduates were experiencing serious employment problems. For the first time in recent history, questions began to be raised about the economic value of a degree. To what extent do these reports and questions reflect economic reality? To what extent do they exaggerate the state of affairs? Did a new world of employment develop for college graduates in the 1970s—a world significantly different from that of the past—a world in which the college worker was overeducated in the marketplace?

This chapter outlines the basic changes in the job market of the 1970s. It examines relevant statistical evidence on the salaries and jobs obtained by graduates, and compares employment experiences in the downturn with those in the boom of the preceding decade. Attention is given here mostly to male graduates, leaving for Chapter 7 a detailed analysis of the economic status of female graduates.

INDICATORS OF MARKET CHANGE

Because of the distinctive way in which the college job market functions, the analysis focuses on two indicators of market conditions: (1) salaries—an especially good measure of the college job market because college rates are set directly by supply and demand, rather than, as in unionized blue-collar markets, by collective bargaining; and (2) job opportunities—broadly defined as the availability (number) of positions at given salaries *in the area for which an individual has been trained*. Opportunities are important because educated workers invariably find some sort of employment, making the quality of jobs, not the number employed or unemployed, the principal nonprice mode of adjustment. In addition, however, some attention is given other indicators of labor market conditions—rates of unemployment, recruitment visits of companies to campuses, and the like. To minimize the dangers of misreading cyclical or temporary changes in employment conditions in the 1970s for the type of long-run climacteric that merits serious concern, comparisons are made with the situation in earlier decades.

The most sensitive indicator of market reality, given great stress in this book, is the economic status of new graduates—determined by what amounts to a national bourse every spring, when thousands of companies and hundreds of thousands of individuals are respectively engaged in an active search for appropriate employees and employment. Economic changes are likely to show up most dramatically and rapidly among new graduates, for several reasons. First, all new graduates but only a few older workers are on the active job market in a given period, making the position of the former more immediately sensitive to recent fluctuations in the supply—demand balance. Second, firms will generally find it easier to alter new hiring patterns and starting salaries than to adjust the position of experienced personnel already in positions. Transaction costs are clearly greater in the latter case, making the young the initial "margin of adjustment" to change. Third, companies and individuals are likely to obtain more accurate and rapid information about economy-wide developments from the regular spring and summer graduate bourse than from intermittent changes in the status of the experienced, and will react accordingly. Once companies learn the appropriate rates of pay in the market for new workers, they will gradually alter their overall salary structure, either moderating or intensifying planned changes, to preserve internal parity. In industrial relations terminology, new graduates are an "entry port" linking an enterprise's internal college manpower policy to the external market. Changes in the employment status of new graduates are thus a key "leading indicator" or warning device of supply–demand imbalance and are likely to be followed in time by similar changes for all college-trained workers.

What Happened to the High Salaries?

Evidence that the salaries or income of college-trained workers, particularly those just beginning their careers, underwent a major and

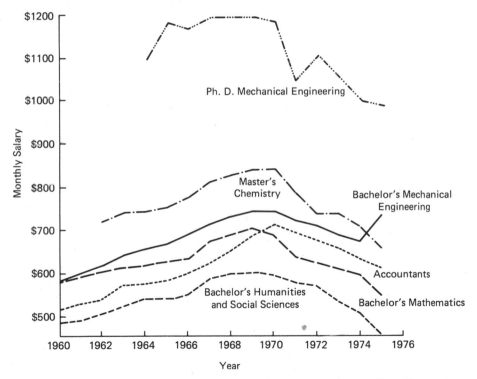

Figure 1. Real starting salary of college graduates, 1960–1975 (from College Placement Council, *Salary Surveys, 1960–1975*; price deflator from U.S. Bureau of the Census, *Statistical Abstract, 1973*, Table 568, p. 346; updated with figures from *Monthly Labor Review* (July 1975), Tables 22, 33, p. 83).

unprecedented downturn in the 1970s is impressive. By all relevant indicators, the income position of young graduates deteriorated sharply relative to that of other workers. From 1970 to 1975 the spring and summer bourse yielded to new graduates in most specialties substantially lower real salaries (money salaries adjusted for the consumer price index) than had been attained in the past. Figure 1 records the starting pay, *deflated by the consumer price index*, of male graduates employed in industry from 1960 to 1975. It covers science, business administration, bachelor's, master's, and doctoral graduates in the humanities, the social sciences, and applied and physical sciences. What stands out in the figure is the dramatic fall in the real salaries of new graduates, which began at the turn of the decade and continued through 1975. Whereas in the 1960s new college graduates obtained large gains in real salaries, generally above those of the other workers, they experienced a striking real and relative decline in the 1970s. From 1961 to 1969 humanities and social science graduates, for example, enjoyed a sizable increase in real pay, 2.7% a year, exceeding the rate of gain in average hourly earnings (2.6%), in annual full-time earnings (2.1%), and in other wage series in the economy. Then, from 1969 to 1975, their pay dropped precipitously—from $608 per month (in 1967 dollars) to just $470 per month—below the level obtained by similar graduates 15 years earlier. This sharp downward alteration in the salaries of new graduates in the 1970s was a major break with past economic developments.

Not surprisingly, the drop in real salaries dashed the earnings expectations of the vast majority of graduates. Figure 2 shows that for the class of 1972 actual earnings on the first job were frequently, often substantially, lower than expected and quite rarely above expectations. While evidence on the relationship between actual and expected earnings in earlier years is unavailable, it is implausible that anywhere near 45% of bachelor's graduates obtained earnings below their expectations during the previous strong market. The drop in real income clearly produced a situation in which many graduates— who had opted for college during the booming 1960s—were severely disappointed with their economic status.

The downward movement in real rates of pay—the classic free market response to a manpower surplus—was effectuated, it must be stressed, by the concurrence of rapid inflation and rough stability in

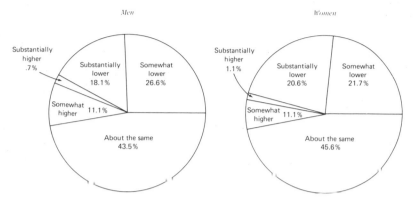

Figure 2. Earnings of degree recipients compared with earnings expectations (1972) by sex (From U.S. Bureau of Labor Statistics, *Employment of Recent College Graduates* (October 1972), Special Labor Force Report 169, Table F, p. A-12).

money salaries, rather than by decline in actual salary levels. This, however, does not mean that general inflation, as opposed to the specific situation of college-trained workers, caused the decline. The wages of most workers, including blue-collar production workers, employees in government, and so forth, more or less kept pace with inflation in the period. Those of college graduates did not. Because of the general downward rigidity of salaries, inflation may have made the adjustment quicker and possibly easier than would otherwise have been the case, but it did not cause the decline in real college starting rates.

The income of male college graduates as a whole also evinced some weakness in the early 1970s, falling relative to that of high school or grade school graduates, though not as rapidly or sharply as starting salaries. Figure 3 depicts the course of the annual income of year-round, full-time employed college men relative to that of high school and grade school men from 1968, when the graduate market was still strong, through 1974, when the market was substantially depressed. The income of year-round, full-time personnel is relatively immune to cyclical ups and downs in unemployment and time spent at work, and is thus the best available measure of rates of pay. The figure shows the college premium dropping substantially from 1969 to 1974. Among all men in 1969, college graduates earned 53% more than high school graduates and 99% more than grade school graduates; in 1974, the premiums stood at 35% and 74% respectively.

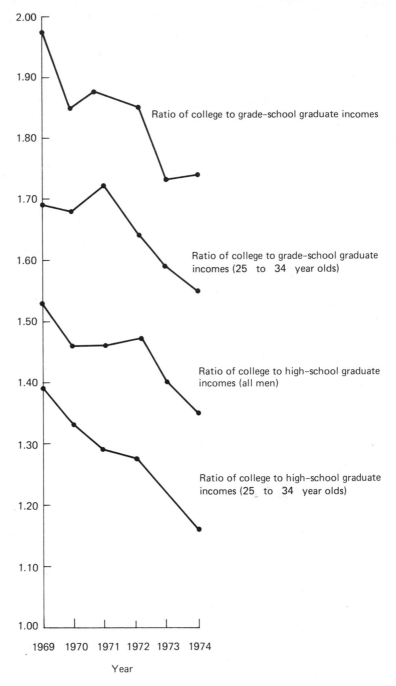

Figure 3. The falling relative income of year-round, full-time, employed, male college graduates, 1969-1974 (From U.S. Bureau of the Census "Consumer Income," *Current Population Reports,* Series P—60, Nos. 66, 75, 80, 92, 97, 101. Note: Incomes refer to the mean incomes of year-round, full-time workers).

14

Among the young (aged 25 to 34) the fall is, as would be expected by the active market argument, steadier and stronger. Here, the college advantage dips from 39% to 16% relative to high school men and from 69% to 55% relative to grade school men.[1] The 1974 ratios were the lowest in the post–World War II years for which comparable data exist. Income figures for all workers, including those employed only part of the year or employed part-time, tell a similar story—drops of 15 points (college–high school) and 17 points (college–grade school), respectively, for all male workers from 1969 to 1974, for example.[2]

Because the 1960s were a decade of relative economic advance for college workers, the decline of the 1970s should not be exaggerated. Part of the drastic picture of decline in the college job market is due to the comparison with a period of exceptional boom. Even so, however, the rate of decline is impressive. By 1975 the gains of college workers in the preceding decade were "undone" and then some. It is clear that with lower real starting salaries, lower average incomes, and lower rates of increase, the college graduate of the 1970s faced a job market very different from that in the historic past.

The sharp decline in the college income premium was not anticipated by conventional economists working in the "human capital" or economics of education framework of analysis. At the outset of the 1970s, human capital analysts believed that the relative income of the educated would be maintained in the future, as in the past, and developed subtle explanations as to why the growth of supply would not reduce the premium. According to one expert, there was a special relation between education and capital, which meant that as new machines were introduced into the economy, demand for educated workers would grow, relative to that for the less educated. According to another, it was the rate of technological

[1] More detailed analysis of the income of college and high school men in 1968 and 1973, using the computer tapes from the U.S. Bureau of the Census *Current Population Survey* (March), indicate that virtually all of the decline in income ratios for all college men is concentrated among those with less than 5 years of work experience or below 30 years of age. This provides striking support for the "active labor market hypothesis" that change occurs largely among the young. See R. Freeman, "The Decline in the Economic Rewards to College Education," *Review of Economics and Statistics* (forthcoming).

[2] These data are from U.S. Bureau of the Census, "Consumer Income," *Current Population Reports*, Series P–60, No. 75, p. 101; No. 97, p. 122; No. 101, p. 116. They relate to mean earnings of four-year college graduates.

advance, induced by R&D and related factors, that would increase the demand for college workers, who had a special advantage in understanding and adjusting to change.[3] While there is probably some truth in both of these arguments, the decline of the 1970s shows that more basic supply–demand forces ultimately dominated the market. The issue is no longer why college salaries remained high relative to high school salaries but why they declined so sharply, rather than more gradually over time, and whether the decline will be maintained in the future. Reasons for the sudden turnaround and forecasts of future possibilities are given in Chapter 3, which seeks to explain the changing labor market in terms of changes in the critical determinants of supply and demand.

WHERE HAVE THE GOOD JOBS GONE?

There was a time, in the 1950s and 1960s, when the college graduate had a choice of numerous good jobs upon receipt of the diploma. Thousands of companies recruited at the major campuses, searching for desired specialists. Even graduate students without a completed dissertation obtained good academic positions in the late 1960s—for instance, assistant professorships with salaries as high as $15,000. This golden age of employment opportunities, in which *jobs sought graduates*, was transmogrified in the 1970s. In the new, depressed market, graduates sought a relatively shrinking number of high-level jobs and were lucky to obtain positions in their area of study. The collapse of employment opportunities forced an unprecedented number into noncollege-level jobs, often very different from those for which they had prepared in school.

Figure 4 examines the dimensions of the 1970s drought in employment opportunities. It graphs the ratio of professional and managerial (college-level) jobs to total jobs in the economy and the ratio of such jobs to the stock of graduates—perhaps the best measure of the availability of high-level employment to individuals. To

---

[3] Z. Griliches, "Notes on the Role of Education in Production Functions and Growth Accounting," in *Education, Income, and Human Capital*, ed. W. Lee Hansen, *National Bureau of Economic Research Studies in Income and Wealth*, Vol. 35 (New York: Columbia University Press, 1970); F. Welch, "Education and Production," *Journal of Political Economy* (January–February 1970).

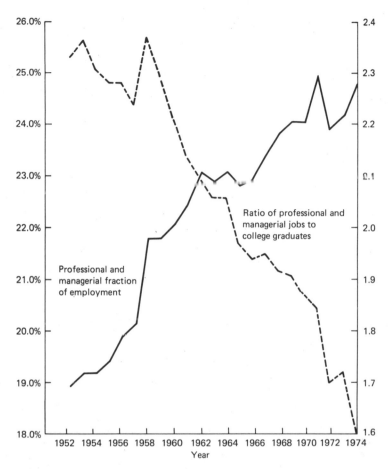

Figure 4. Professional and managerial jobs, 1952–1974 (data on professional and mana-gerial employment from U.S. Department of Labor, *Manpower Report of the President* (1974), Table A-11, p. 267, *Manpower Report of the President* (1963), Table A-7, p. 143; updates from U.S. Department of Labor, *Employment and Earnings* (June 1975), Vol. 21, No. 12, Table 1, p. 7; data on college graduates, *Manpower Report of the President* (1974), Table B-9, p. 299, with interpolations; updates from U.S. Bureau of Labor Statistics, *Educational Attainment of Workers* (March 1974), Special Labor Force Report No. 175, Table 1, p. A-17).

provide historic perspective, the figure treats the entire post–World War II period. According to the figure, the professional–managerial share of the work force, which had been growing rapidly since the Census Bureau first began to collect occupational statistics in 1870, leveled off in the 1970s, despite continued increases in the number of college graduates. In 1950, 18.3% of jobs were in college-level categories; in 1969, 24.0%; and in 1974, 24.8%. Adjusted for the fact that the economy entered a major recession in the mid-1970s, the data tell a more dramatic story because, typically, the share of high-level employment rises when unemployment rises. Had the number of professional and managerial jobs increased at the same rate as in the past, 27.5% of the work force would have been so employed in 1974. With educational attainment rising over the entire postwar era, moreover, the number of "good" jobs per graduate trended downward, at a modest rate in the 1950s and 1960s but at a rapid pace in the 1970s. In 1952, 18.4% of American workers were professionals or managers, while only 7.9% had a college degree— which implies that there were 2.33 college-level jobs available per graduate workers; in 1969, prior to the downturn, with the fraction of graduates having risen to 12.6%, the ratio of college-level jobs to workers dropped to 1.90. Finally, as a result of the slowdown in the growth of professional and managerial jobs in the 1970s, the number of high-level positions per college graduate plummeted even further; by 1974 the college graduate share of the work force had risen to 15.5%, reducing the ratio of jobs to workers to 1.60.

The more rapid increase in the number of graduates than of professional or managerial employment in the 1950s and 1960s did not, however, adversely affect the job distribution of the college trained. Instead, the college graduate's share of such employment rose, as young graduates replaced older, less-educated personnel. Between 1960 and 1970, for example, the fraction of professional and managerial jobs held by graduates rose from 35% to 45%. The probability that a male graduate would be employed in a college-level job rose from 0.75 to 0.80 over the decade, while that of a female graduate went up from 0.79 to 0.88.[4]

When the share of high-level jobs began to stabilize and the drop in professional and managerial employment available per graduate began to accelerate in the 1970s, however, there was a marked worsening in the levels of jobs obtained by graduates, particularly those starting their careers.

The deterioration in employment opportunities for the young is examined in Figure 5, which compares the experience of graduates in

[4] Calculated from data in U.S. Bureau of the Census 1960 Census of Population , *Educational Attainment*, PC(2)-5B, Table 8, pp. 136, 137; and 1970 Census of Population, *Educational Attainment*, PC(2)-5B, Table 11, pp. 213, 217.

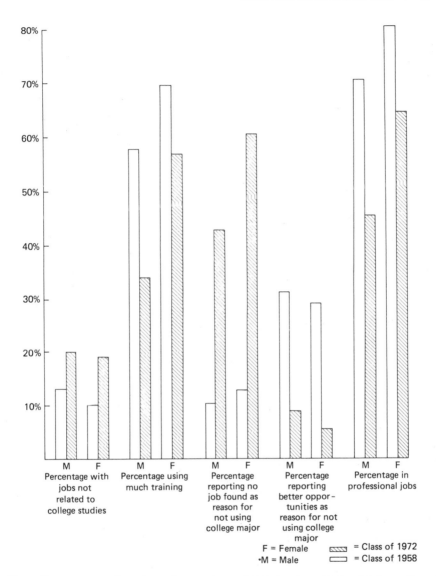

Figure 5. Job status of starting college graduates (1958 data from National Science Foundation, *Two Years after the College Degree* (1963), NSF 63-26, Tables A-35 M, W, pp. 234–226; Tables A-37 M, W, pp. 240–241; Tble 32, p. 46. 1972 data from U.S. Bureau of Labor Statistics, *Employment of Recent College Graduates* (October 1972), Special Labor Force Report No. 169, Table C, p. A-9, Table 3, p. 36.) Note: 1958 data for "not related" include following categories: no use, college irrelevant, and inadequate preparation; 1958, "considerable use" used for used much training; 1972 data for percentage in professional jobs relate to bachelor's degrees only.

the class of 1972 with those in the class of 1958. By every indicator, the graduates of 1972 were worse off than those of 1958, despite relatively better overall labor market conditions in the latter year. First, an exceptionally large number of persons in the classes that entered the market in the 1970s were forced into jobs outside of the professional areas. In the class of 1972, for example, only 46% of males with bachelor's degrees obtained professional jobs, compared to 71% of comparable men in the class of 1958; 65% of women in the graduating class of 1972 were employed as professionals, compared to 81% of women in the class of 1958. Additional data on bachelor's and master's graduates from the survey reveal that in 1972 over 30% of men and 25% of women ended up employed in nonprofessional, nonmanagerial jobs. By contrast, just slightly over 5% of 1958 recipients of bachelor's and master's degrees were so employed at a similar period in their working life. Second, many graduates of the early 1970s reported that they were employed in positions not related to their fields of study. Twenty percent of employed male and female graduates in these classes ended up in areas "not related" to their college studies, compared to about 10% of the graduates starting work a decade or so earlier (class of 1958). Just 34% of the men and 57% of the women were using "much of their training" in 1972, compared to 58% and 70% of those in the class of 1958. The absence of jobs, rather than the existence of better opportunities in other fields, was given by the graduates of 1970–1971 as the principal reason for working in jobs not directly related to field of study—which contrasts sharply with the reasons given by the class of 1958. One-third of the male graduates and nearly two-thirds of female graduates who were not working in their field in the early 1970s cited lack of jobs as the reason, compared to 10% and 13% in the early 1960s; less than one in five men and virtually no women moved to new areas because of better opportunity in 1971, in contrast to about three in ten in the 1958 graduating class.[5]

Experienced graduates also found it difficult to obtain good jobs in the declining market, with the result that a markedly smaller fraction

[5] The two surveys compared in this monograph report the status of graduates at different times in their work history. The 1958 data relate to 2 years after the degree; the 1972 data, to 6 months afterward. This is unlikely to bias the results substantially, as 6 months is a reasonable time to find the type of job graduates have normally held.

of all college graduates ended up in professional or managerial positions than in the past. Between 1969 and 1974 the proportion of men with 4 years of college working as professionals or managers dropped from 76% to 68%, while the percentage of women graduates so employed fell from 81% to 71%. At the opposite end of the spectrum, the proportion of male graduates working as salesmen increased by 23%, and the proportion of female graduates employed in clerical positions, by 26%.[6]

All told, our second major indicator of the state of the college job market—employment opportunities—confirms the picture of depressed conditions given in the salary statistics. However measured, the job situation for graduates by the mid-1970s was bad.

GRADUATE UNEMPLOYMENT: MYTH OR REALITY?

Although unemployment is not a major mode of adjustment in the college labor market, it is still a valuable indicator of the supply–demand balance. Here, as in other aspects of market performance, there has been a marked deterioration in the status of college workers, with young graduates having an increasingly difficult time obtaining jobs. In October 1972, the rate of unemployment for graduates in the class of 1972, for example, stood at 11.7%, far in excess of the national average for workers (5.1%) and above that for high school graduates of about the same age (7.7%). Persons who had majored in the humanities or social sciences faced "double digit" unemployment rates, 15.4% and 16.0%, respectively. Although less dramatic, there was an analogous worsening in the rate of unemployment among all college graduates and among professional and managerial workers. In 1968, 0.7% of college graduates, 1.2% of professionals, and 0.8% of managers lacked employment, compared to an

---

[6] Date from the U.S. Bureau of Labor Statistics, *Educational Attainment of Workers,* Special Labor Force Report, (March 1974 and March 1969, 1970) No. 175, Table I, p. A-17, 18; and No. 125, Table I p. A-28, 29. Investigation of the March 1969 and 1974 *Current Population Survey* tapes, focused on the *difference* between the probability of college and high school men obtaining professional or professional and managerial jobs, shows, once again, that most of the deterioration in the position of college workers occurs among those with less than 5 years experience. R. Freeman, "The Decline in the Economic Rewards to College Education," Table 3.

economy-wide male average of 3.1%. Between 1969 and 1974, these rates rose to 2.3% (college graduates), 2.3% (professionals), and 1.8% (managers). While the overall rate of unemployment remained much above that for graduates, it increased proportionately less rapidly from 3.6% to 5.6%.[7] Because rates of unemployment vary over the business cycle, however, a proper comparison of rates requires some adjustment for cyclical changes. Corrected data show that the increased ratio of professional to other rates of unemployment was not due to normal market developments, as it is even more pronounced than in the raw figures. Under normal cyclical patterns the professional rate would, for example, have averaged 1.9% from 1970 to 1974, 0.5 points below the actual average of 2.4%.[8]

In short, the unemployment of college graduates worsened substantially in the downturn and attained levels among new graduates that made the problem of finding a job—much less a good job—a reality, not a myth.

RISING COSTS AND FEWER FELLOWSHIPS

While job opportunities and salaries declined, the costs of college rose unabated in the 1970s, at rates far above the average rate of inflation. In private, high-quality institutions, increases of $300–

[7] The unemployment data in this paragraph are from the U.S. Bureau of Labor Statistics, *Employment of Recent College Graduates*, Special Labor Force Report (October 1972), No. 169, Table I, p. 34, for data on the class of 1972; U.S. Bureau of Labor Statistics, *Employment of High School Graduates and Dropouts* Special Labor Force Report (October 1972), No. 155, Table A, p. A-10, for data on high school graduates (I have used the figure for the high school classes that graduated before 1970, for approximate age comparisons); U.S. Department of Labor, *Handbook of Labor Statistics 1974*, Table 66, p. 156, for 1969 rates by occupation and Table 60, p. 144 for totals in October 1972. *Monthly Labor Review* (April 1975), Table 4, p. 94, for 1974 rates by occupations and the total rate; U.S. Bureau of Labor Statistics, *Educational Attainment of Workers* Special Labor Force Report (March 1968), No. 103, Table B, p. A-6, for data on all college graduates; and (March 1974) Special Labor Force Report, No. 175, Table B, p. A-10, for data on all college graduates.

[8] Adjustment based on multiple regression of professional unemployment (PU) on total unemployment (U) for 1947 to 1974. The predicted average of *PU* is given in the text. The actual regression is

$$PU = .29 + .30\,U \qquad R^2 = .51$$
$$(.06)$$

where the number in parentheses is the standard error.

$400 in tuition and other charges in a given year have been common. In 1976 it cost $7000 per year to attend a prestigious Ivy League school. In 1958, tuition, fees, and room and board at a private university stood at 15% of the income of families likely to have youngsters of college age (those headed by men aged 45 to 54). By 1974 the figure was 22%.[9] If the black mother in the advertisement scrubbed floors for 10 years, she still could not have afforded 4 years of college for her child at that price. Most private institutions did, however, award sizable scholarships to youngsters from poor families, placing much of the burden of the higher costs on the middle class.

Public colleges and universities, which expanded rapidly in the postwar period, provided something of a damper on costs, although their rates also increased rapidly. Because public institutions charged less, the average annual cost of higher education to individuals and their families in 1974–1975 was $2100, although the total cost, borne by all taxpayers, was nearly as high as for private institutions. Between 1969 and 1974, tuition costs increased at both public and private institutions much more rapidly than the rate of inflation (an increase in tuition and fees of 42% in public and 51% in private institutions versus a 35% rate of inflation).[10]

At the graduate level, there was, in addition, a tremendous cutback in federal fellowships, making it much more difficult to continue studies. Under the Nixon administration the number of fellowships—which had increased greatly in the 1960s—was substantially reduced. In 1968, there were 51,446 graduate students receiving federal fellowships and traineeship support; in 1974, just 6,602. [11]

[9] Tuition, fees, room, and board in 1958 were $1767; in 1974, $3811. The income of families headed by 45- to 54-year-old men in 1957 was $11,712; in 1973, $16,976. U.S. Office of Education, *Report of Educational Statistics, 1974*, Table 127, p. 113. U.S. Office of Education, *Projections of Educational Statistics to 1978–9*, Table 49, p. 104. U.S. Bureau of the Census, "Consumer Income," *Current Population Reports* Series P–60, No. 66, Table 22, p. 52; No. 97, Table 36, p. 78.

[10] In 1969 the Consumer Price Index was 109.8; in 1974, 147.4. In 1969 public institutions charged $1206 in tuition fees; private institutions, $2532; in 1974, the public institutions charged $1710; private institutions, $3811. 28% of students attended private institutions in 1969, and 20% in 1974. U.S. Office of Education, *Digest of Educational Statistics 1974*, Table 127, p. 113. Note that these calculations excluded charge for board.

[11] R. Freeman and D. Breneman, *Forecasting the Ph.D. Labor Market*, (Washington, D.C.: National Board of Graduate Education, 1974), Technical Report No. 2, Table 6, p. 13.

According to the National Science Foundation survey of graduate science education, 42% of students in the sciences were supported, in some fashion, by the federal government in 1967 compared to 26% in 1973. Only 18% of the first-year students in graduate science programs received federal support in 1973.[12] The attraction of graduate studies leading to a master's or doctoral degree was accordingly reduced.

THE $100,000 PIPE DREAM

It *never* was true that the college graduate obtained $100,000 more in life's earnings than the high school graduate. Not that the statisticians who made the estimate counted wrong; they erred by failing to take account of the fact that much of the higher income of the college graduate is received later in life when dollars are worth less than dollars received today. During the 4 or so years of college study, the college student earns relatively little while the high school graduate holds down a full-time job with substantial earnings. Since a dollar today can be invested in the bank, in the stock market, or in real assets, and earn a return by tomorrow, it is more valuable than a dollar tomorrow. Simply adding up differences in cumulative income over the years exaggerates the advantage of a college training.

There are two related ways to summarize the overall income difference between college and high school graduates and thus evaluate the extra financial value of college training. The first is to calculate a rate of return analogous to the percentage rates used by banks, businesses, and individuals to estimate the value of investments. The second is to compare the present value of college and high school incomes with future earnings discounted at an appropriate rate. In general, these two techniques yield the same results. When the rate of return is above that from alternative investments, going to college is an economically wise investment; similarly, when earnings are discounted at the return of alternatives, a positive present value tells the same story. There are, of course, numerous

[12] Data for 1967 from National Science Foundation, *Graduate Student Support and Manpower Resources in Graduate Sciences Education* (Fall 1969), NSF 70–40, Table C–15a, p. 56. Data for 1973 from National Science Foundation, *Graduate Science Education Student Support and Postdoctorals* (Fall 1973), NSF 74–318, Table IV–1, p. 57.

problems in evaluating the pecuniary worth of college. Not all of the difference in income between college-trained and high school workers is due to education; some can be attributed to differences in ability or drive or in initial family wealth. For the purpose of analyzing changes over time, however, neither of these factors is likely to bias results to any serious extent.

While the $100,000 computation exaggerates the dollar value of a college training, estimates of rates of return and discounted present values of the extra income accruing to graduates in the 1960s indicate that it was, in fact, a good investment for individuals and for the nation as a whole. Private rates of return, based on the after-tax incomes of college and high school workers and the private costs of college, averaged 11% to 12%, which is good, relative to most investments; social rates, based on before-tax incomes and the total cost of college, were modestly smaller, 10% to 11%. Estimates of the extra income from college, net of the costs of 4 years of school discounted at a 10% rate, yielded positive present values, as is to be expected given higher rates of return. Various studies found that between 1959 and 1969, the rate of return to college investments by men either rose modestly or stayed fairly constant.[13]

The fall in the salaries of college graduates relative to those of other workers plus the increased tuition and related charges that characterized the market turnaround clearly operated to reduce the pecuniary value of college training. The precise quantitative effect of the downturn on rates of return is, however, difficult to assess because it depends on how *future* income streams will be altered. Rates of return are *forward-looking* concepts, which require implicit or explicit forecasts of future possibilities, a risky and uncertain endeavor of the type in which economists have not excelled in the past. If the graduates of the mid-1970s recoup the relative salary losses experienced in the downturn and obtain income advantages comparable to those of older college men compared to older high school men, the rate of return will fall moderately. If, on the other hand, income differentials remain compressed over the life cycle, the

[13] R. Freeman, "Overinvestment in College Training?" *Journal of Human Resources* (Summer 1975), pp. 287–311. W. McMahon, N. Hoang, A. Wagner "Returns to Invesment in Higher Education," mimeo (University of Illinois, October 1975), and F. Welch and J. Smith, "Black-White Male Earnings and Employment," U.S. Department of Labor, R-1666-DOL-(June, 1975). All show increases in the rate of return in the 1959–1969 period.

estimated return will fall considerably from past values. In period of change, like the 1970s, when the past may no longer be a good guide to the future, forward-looking rates are difficult to determine.

To deal with this problem, I have made estimates of the return to college under several alternative postulates about the future earnings of persons graduating in the 1970s and compared them to those of graduates in 1968, when the college marketplace was still strong. The details of the estimating procedure are given in Appendix A. The results are summarized in Table 1, which displays rates of return for 1968 and 1973 under two postulates about the future earnings of young persons (those aged 25 to 29). The first postulate (A) assumes that young college graduates enjoy exceptional income gains in the future so that when they reach the ages 30 to 40 and thereafter, they have an income advantage over high school graduates as large, in percentage terms, as that of older college graduates. This assumption tends to minimize the downturn in the college job market, and I regard it as too conservative. The B calculation assumes that the graduates of the 1970s obtain income increases in the future equal to those of persons in the relevant age groups during the 1963 to 1973 decade, a period covering both the 1960s boom and the 1970s bust. I regard this estimate as more realistic and moderate.

Both sets of figures show a noticeable fall in the rate of return to 4 years of college education, with returns dropping in the

Table 1. Estimates of the Private Rate of Return and Discounted Present Value of Investing in College under Alternative Assumptions of Future Lifetime Incomes, 1968–1973

	Rate of return		Net discounted income with 10% interest rate (in thousands of 1973 dollars)	
	Assumption A	Assumption B	Assumption A	Assumption B
1968	12.5%	11.0%	$6.4	$4.0
1973	10.0%	7.5%	−1.4	−7.0
Change, 1968–1973	−2.5%	−3.5%	−7.8	−11.0

Note: Assumption A: Future incomes of college and high school graduates follow cross-section profiles, with 1.5% additional increase per year due to overall economic growth. Assumption B: Future incomes obtained by applying *actual* 1963 to 1973 cohort income gains to the income of 25- to 29-year olds in 1968 and in 1973.

Source: See Appendix A. Also R. Freeman "The Decline in the Economic Rewards to College Education," *Review of Economics and Statistics* (forthcoming).

span of 5 years from 12.5% to 10.0% under postulate A and from 10.5% to 7.5% under postulate B. Calculations based on somewhat different data from the Bureau of the Census *Current Population Reports* surveys for 1975 suggest a further moderate drop of about one percentage point through that year.[14] Columns 3 and 4 of the table tell a similar story with respect to the "net discounted income of college graduates"—the difference between the lifetime income of college and high school graduates, minus the direct costs of college, discounted with a 10% interest rate. Here the economic advantage of college graduates in discounted 1973 dollars falls from $6400 (1968) to −$1400 (1973) under postulate A, and from $4000 (1968) to −$7000 (1973) under postulate B. Of course, lower interest rates will yield different numeric results, since they would value income in the later years, when college graduates do better, more heavily. What is important is not the precise estimates but rather the finding that, however calculated, the statistics show declines in the monetary return to college investments in the 1970s.[15]

SYMPTOMS OF THE DOWNTURN[16]

The decline in the job market has had, according to various reports, a devastating effect on various campuses and in particular fields.

[14] These figures are based on the May 1975 and May 1973 *Current Population Survey*, which reports usual weekly earnings rather than total yearly income. See Appendix A for further details.

[15] My previous estimates, given in Freeman, "Overinvestment in College Training?" were based on different calculating procedures. They used 1970 Census lifetime income figures, extrapolated to 1972 and 1974, rather than the more up-to-date current population data figures. Despite these differences the picture of declining returns is quite similar. Moreover, as noted in "Overinvestment in College Training?" published Census estimates of lifetime income tell a similar story for the 1969–1972 period, although their procedure, which involves estimation of the income of young persons of curve-fitting, is suspect among persons less than 25 years of age. See U.S. Bureau of the Census, *Current Population Reports* Series P–60, No. 62. All of the five estimating procedures used in Appendix A also show a similar pattern of decline in rates of return.

[16] See R. Rapaport, "New Myth on Campus," *Esquire* (September 1974), pp. 93–94, 182, for University of California at Berkeley Department of English data; *New York Times* (2 February 1975), p. 8, for report of a Council of Graduate Schools survey giving experience of history graduates; *NBC Nightly News* (5 March 1975), for recruitment at Illinois; *Harvard Crimson* (11 February 1975), pp. 1, 6, for Harvard career interviews; *Bergen Evening Record* (20 Feb. 1975) p. A-29, for Montclair State experience.

• In 1973, only 24 of 55 graduates and doctoral candidates from the University of California at Berkeley English Department searching for college teaching jobs found them; in 1974, only 15 of 62.

• Of 1225 history graduates and doctoral candidates in the United States seeking jobs as academics in 1973, just 182 found them.

• 18% of the graduates of the 1973 class of the College of Arts and Letters at one of the "big ten" universities who entered the labor market were still unemployed 6 months after graduation. Another 15% were working as receptionists, clerks, laborers, factory workers, and janitors.

• At the University of Illinois, students slept overnight in front of the placement office to sign up for interviews with firms in the spring of 1975. The job situation was so bad that the university sent out recruiters to bring in more employers.

• At Harvard, students lined up outside the Office of Career Services in February 1975 for interviews with banks, with nearly twice as many seeking interviews than there were available time slots, leading one placement director to remark, "The only time I've seen more people in this building is when they're demonstrating."

• A questionnaire sent to 1800 graduates at Montclair State asking about the jobs they had obtained elicited a poor response, with only 289 replying that their jobs were commensurate with their education. Unemployment averaged 13% in the class of 1970.

THE DOWNTURN IN PERSPECTIVE

There appears to be no historical antecedent to the sharp and extended downturn in the college labor market. In the Depression, college graduates suffered, to be sure, but their position relative to others improved rather than worsened. In particular, although graduates were forced, as in the 1970s, into jobs that were below their skills and expectations, so too were other workers; the salaries of the college trained did not fall relative to others; and, most importantly, rates of unemployment by education show graduates least injured by the prevailing socioeconomic ills of the day. Similarly, while college graduates in India typically are unemployed for several months (an average of 6 months in 1967) before finding a suitable job, the return on their training remains high—as high as 17% or so.[17] Latin American graduates in some fields, such as law or psychology, have often experienced difficulties in the labor market, but, as in India, these problems could be resolved by taking general white-collar administrative jobs at quite high pay. The only potentially comparable historical experience to the U.S. downturn appears to be a similar though less pronounced development in Japan and Western Europe, which also began in the 1970s and has attracted some attention from the Organization of European Cooperation and Development (OECD). As no detailed investigations have been made, however, the extent of the college market problem in Western Europe and in Japan remains to be seen. Presumably, because the United States is the most technically advanced country, with the most highly educated work force, the problem is of less serious dimensions elsewhere.

Even with the fall in the economic value of a college education, though, it is useful to remember that graduates still earned considerably more and had much greater chances of obtaining high-level professional and managerial jobs than did nongraduates in the early 1970s. Moreover, in some fields the fall in the economic rewards of higher education has been relatively slight—as will be shown later in this book. Despite the great variation in high-level labor markets in the 1970s, however, the overall pattern is one in which the economic rewards to college diminished relative to the booming 1960s.

Finally, while this book is concerned almost exclusively with the payoff of a college education in the job market, it should not be forgotten that college offers substantial other rewards. Students attend not only to obtain good jobs and high incomes but also "to gain a general education" (cited as very important by over one-half of the freshmen in the class of 1975), "meet new and interesting people," "become more cultured," and so on.[18] Society subsidizes higher education in order to transmit cultural values and produce better-educated individuals, as well as for purely economic reasons.

[17] M. Blaug "The Unemployment of the Educated in India," in *Third World, Employment,* ed. B.R. Jolly, E. Dekadt, H. Singer, and F. Wilson (Penguin, 1973), Table 1, pp. 206—207. I report the figure for private rates, unadjusted.
[18] American Council on Education, "The American Freshman: National Norms for Fall 1971," *ACE Research Reports* (1971), Vol. 16, No. 6, p. 43.

Studies of the impact of college on students suggest that the noneco-
nomic effects may be substantial; while the evidence is not unequiv-
ocal, attending college appears to be associated with (and a possible
cause of) such attitudinal changes as increased open-mindedness,
increased intellectual orientation, and a decrease in authoritarian
attitudes. In the Trent and Medsker study, which compared the
changes in attitude of young persons who had been to college and
those who, instead, had worked the 4 years, using a large sample of
10,000 it was found, for example, that the college group had greater
relative gains in scales of nonauthoritarian attitudes, "thinking intro-
version" (defined as a liking for reflective abstract thought), "com-
plexity of outlook" (independence and creativity in views), and so
forth.[19] On the other hand, however, the experience of the late
1960s with student revolution, and Lewis Feuer's study of student
movements showing totalitarian biases among students, raise some
questions about these attitudinal changes.[20]

A college education, and years of schooling in general, is also
associated with such phenomena as lower fertility rates, increased
labor participation of women, and a greater propensity to vote.
Recent economic studies of the household have examined the impact
of education on the efficiency of the family to combine goods and
services purchased in the market with household activities to produce
desired "final" commodities. More educated women, for example,
appear more adept at educating children at home, with consequences
for social mobility and the transmission of status across generations.[21]

If the labor market rewards of college continue to decline, we
will undoubtedly see greater stress placed on the cultural and nonjob
benefits of college, which are unlikely to experience a comparable
decline. The rewards are real and valuable. They should not be
overlooked. Nor, however, should they be stressed to the extent that
changing economic rewards are downplayed.

---

[19] See K. Feldman and T. Newcomb, *The Impact of College on Students* (San
Francisco, Calif.: Jossey-Bass, 1969), Vol. 2, pp. 45 and 53, for a summary of the relevant
data from Trent and Medsker, *Beyond High School: A Psychological Study of 10,000
High School Graduates* (San Francisco, Calif.: Jossey-Bass, 1958).

[20] L. Feuer, *Conflict of Generations* (New York: Basic Books, 1970).

[21] See G. Becker and R. T. Michael, "On the New Theory of Consumer Behavior,"
Swedish Journal of Economics (1973), 75, pp. 378–396

SUMMARY

The statistics examined in this chapter show that there has been a major decline in the college market in the 1970s, breaking sharply with previous historical patterns and having an especially severe impact on new entrants into the labor market. For the graduates of the mid-1970s, falling salaries, scarce job opportunities, and dwindling career prospects are the new reality.

Responses to the Depressed Market

When the economy collapsed in the 1930s, men were reported to have jumped out of hotel windows, left their homes to wander as hobos, or ·simply sat and wept. Nothing so melodramatic occurred in response to the decline of the college job market in the 1970s. Still, there was a marked reaction to the new market reality by students, colleges, and employers that represented a break with past patterns of behavior.

- Many young persons, especially white males, decided against going to college, reversing the historic upward trend in the percentage enrolled.
- Career decisions were altered, with the students of the 1970s moving from academic and scientific fields into business-oriented vocational fields.
- Relatively fewer bachelor's graduates chose to continue their studies in graduate school, and those taking additional studies shifted from academic to professional curricula.
- A new study ethic replaced the social activist ethos on campuses, as students competed for the favor of employers or professional schools.
- Programs in higher education were cutback, several colleges were closed, and efforts were made to begin to change traditional modes of operation and to enroll older persons.

● Employers substituted low-paid college graduates for less-educated workers on some jobs, and reduced their visits to campuses as well as the number of jobs offered.

THE DECISION *NOT* TO GO TO COLLEGE

In the 1970s, for the first time in recent history, the proportion of young persons enrolled in college declined sharply, reversing a historic upward trend. Whereas going to college had been the norm for most graduates of suburban and quality high schools in the 1960s, it became increasingly acceptable to say "I'm not going" and to seek alternative career paths in the falling market. This development may herald the end of an era of increasing educational attainment and of significant economic growth via additional schooling.

The reversal in the trend of college enrollments among men is displayed in Figure 6, which graphs the proportion of 18- to 19-year-old men and women enrolled in college from 1951 to 1974, and the percentage of each year's high school graduating class that enrolled as freshmen in the following year. What stands out is the sudden and sharp fall in the relative number of male college students, beginning in 1969 (1968 in the high school graduate data), when the labor market took a downward turn after more than a decade of steady and substantial increases. In 1969, 44% of all 18- to 19-year-old male civilians were enrolled in college, and 60% of male high school graduates elected to become freshmen (down from 63% in 1968). Five years later, just 33.4% of 18- to 19-year-olds and 49% of male high school graduates were enrolled in college—declines of 10.6 and 11 percentage points, respectively. The decline proceeded so rapidly that by the mid-1970s the proportion of males in college had fallen to the levels of the late 1950s. Despite a 20% increase in the number of persons of college age, enrollment of 18- to 19-year-old men fell from 1,397,000 in 1969 to 1,262,000 in 1974.

Among women the situation changed less drastically. The proportion of young women (18 to 19 years old) enrolling in college roughly stabilized in the 1970s, a sharp divergence from previous increases but not a reversal of trend. In 1951, 14.6% of 18- to 19-year-old women were in college; in 1969, 34.4%; and in 1974,

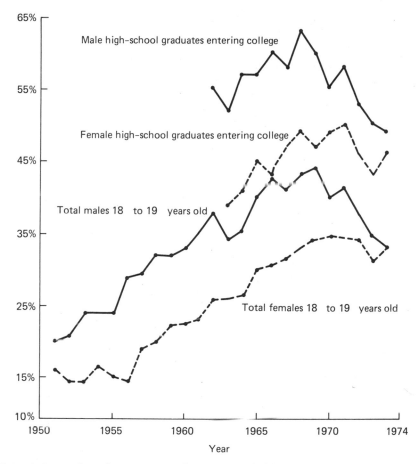

Figure 6. Proportion of young men and women enrolled in college, 1951–1974 (from U.S. Bureau of the Census, "School Enrollment," *Current Population Reports*, Series P-20; various editors, 1950–1974; U.S. Bureau of Labor Statistics, *Employment of High School Graduates and Dropouts*, Special Labor Force Report, No. 168, (Oct. 1973) p. 50; *Monthly Labor Review* (Aug. 1974), p. 35; with 1974 update).

33%. With the proportion of young men enrolled falling sharply and the proportion of young women holding steady, the likelihood of going to college converged between the sexes in the 1970s. By 1974, there was very little difference in female–male ratios of enrollment—a far cry from the situation in 1969, when the ratio for 18- to 19-year-old men was 10 percentage points above that for women (44% versus 34%), though some differences were still found in the high school graduate figures. With male enrollments down and female enrollments steady, the net effect was a downward trend in educational attainment among all young persons. For the first time in American history, cohorts of college-age youth were less likely to obtain a college education than the cohorts before them.

Declining Enrollments and Family Background

It is perhaps surprising that the going-to-college norm weakened even at suburban and quality high schools, among youngsters from middle- and upper-class backgrounds. In New Trier East High School of Wilmette, Illinois, the proportion of graduates going on to college dropped from 92% in 1968 to 85% in 1973; in Wellesley, Massachusetts, there was a comparable fall, from 78.4% (1969) to 73.5% (1974); in Hanover, New Hampshire, where many of the students are the children of Dartmouth faculty, from 85% (1969) to 80% (1974).[1] National data from the Census Bureau on the family income of college students show that these declines are not unique. As the estimates in Table 2 indicate, the proportion of young persons attending college full-time dropped throughout the income distribution, even in the upper quartile of the distribution. More importantly in terms of social mobility, the data reveal that the drop in enrollments was least severe among youngsters from families in the lower income brackets and greatest among middle-class youngsters. Aided by scholarships, and possibly more motivated than their peers, the disadvantaged—whose opportunities to go to college had increased greatly in the 1960s—appear to have been less discouraged by the depressed market than the advantaged. For many of those from lower-income backgrounds, college still represented their best opportunity for socioeconomic advancement. By contrast, the burden of meeting the increased costs of tuition at a time when the payoff from higher education was dropping apparently deterred exceptionally large numbers of middle-class families from sending their children to college. One consequence of the drop in enrollments from the middle and upper classes is that unprecendented numbers of young persons from advantaged backgrounds appear likely to receive

---

[1] Data obtained by telephone interviews.

Table 2. Estimates of the Relative Probability of Attending College Full-time, by Income Class

Income of family (in dollars)	Estimated probability		Change in probability %
	1969 %	1973 %	
< $3000	.16	.13	−19
$3000–4999	.22	.17	−23
5000–7499	.31	.22	−29
7500–9999	.40	.27	−34
10,000–14,999	.45	.33	−??
15,000 +	62	.50	−21

Note: Probabilities are estimated from data on number of members of family 18- to 24-years old, with families reporting two or more members 18 to 24 treated as if they had just two members.

Source: U.S. Bureau of the Census, "School Enrollment," *Current Population Reports,* Series P-20, Nos. 206, 272.

less schooling, and presumably to achieve lower occupational status, than their parents. The long-standing pattern of upward mobility across generations, with children doing better than their parents, may thus be in the process of being replaced by a period of downward generational mobility for a not inconsiderable number of families.

Some Exceptions to the Trend[2]

The trend of enrollments in the 1970s was not uniform among all groups. Young black men, who first began attending college in large numbers in the 1960s, continued to increase their representation in higher education in the 1970s and thus to narrow substantially the black–white gap in ratios of attendance. In 1969, there were 236,000 black men enrolled in college; by 1974, the number was 422,000, raising the black representation among male students from 5.3% to 8.6%. In percentage terms, the number of 18- to

[2] The data in this section come from U.S. Bureau of the Census, "School Enrollment," *Current Population Reports,* Series P-20: No. 278, Tables 4, 5; No. 206, Table 1 and No. 260, Table 19. Figures for older persons are also given in U.S. Bureau of Labor Statistics, *Going Back to School at 35,* Special Labor Force Report, No. 159, and in *The New York Times,* (20 April 1975), p. 9.

19-year-old black men enrolled rose slightly over the same period, from 23.1% to 24.5%, which, given the drop in white male enroll-ments, reduced the white advantage in the probability of going to college substantially. The reasons for the differential enrollment behavior of young white and black men are explored in Chapter 6, which examines the effect of reductions in discrimination against college-educated blacks on the value of their obtaining a degree.

Enrollments also increased among older men and women aged 30 to 34 or 35+ who had previously attended college in relatively small numbers. In 1969, 536,000 persons aged 30 to 34 enrolled in college; in 1974, 720,000. In relation to the number of persons of that age, 5.1% of 30- to 34-year-old men attended in 1969 compared to 6.5% in 1974. As for those 35 and over, between 1972 (when data were first obtained for this age group) and 1974, enrollments jumped by 30%, to about 1 million. The majority of these persons attended part-time, as might be expected given their likely family responsibili-ties, and enrolled primarily in vocational programs designed to help them in their careers. There are several factors behind the move toward college attendance of older persons: increased recognition of the need for retraining in fields of rapid technological progress, giving companies an incentive to provide special programs and funds for occupational education; a decline in the number of children per family, freeing time for other activities; special recruitment efforts by colleges hard pressed for students; possible changes in attitudes toward education; the shorter working hours and increased unem-ployment resulting from the recession of 1974–1975, which made it less costly to switch from work to study or retraining. To the extent that long-run, rather than cyclical, factors underlie the observed changes, the rise in adult enrollments may portend a major change in the age distribution of college students, particularly in the 1980s, and, more importantly, could buffer the higher education system from the anticipated precipitous fall in enrollment of 18- to 21-year-olds in the next decade, due to demographic trends. However, because of the comparative numbers involved—the fact that persons aged 30 to 34 constituted just 8% of students in the peak year of 1974—a sizable increase would be required to save colleges and universities from the crisis of falling enrollments. According to Cartter, student enrollments are likely to drop by 1.1 million between 1982 and 1990; the 1974 number of older persons in college would have to nearly double, in order to maintain zero growth.[3]

SHIFTS IN OCCUPATIONAL CHOICE

Because the collapse of the college manpower market had a differential impact on various specialties, there were significant changes in the fields of study and the careers chosen by students. Previously glamorous areas, such as physics or aeronautical engineering, were shunned in favor of business or the professions; among women, there was a striking movement away from teaching toward the health professions and several traditional male specialties.

Some of the important changes in career plans are examined in Table 3, which compares the probable occupations of entering freshmen in 1974 with those entering in 1966. The former were making their plans in the midst of the market decline, while the latter chose occupations on the basis of the strong market of the early 1960s. Perhaps the most remarkable shift shown in the table is the precipitous drop in the number expecting to teach, both at the elementary–secondary level and at the college level. In 1966, 13.4% of male freshmen and 35.6% of female freshmen anticipated teaching careers; in 1974, just 4.5% and 12.7%, respectively. Another response to the rapidly deteriorating market is the large increase in the proportion of students in the "undecided" category who appear to be in a "holding pattern" because of uncertainty about career prospects. Among male students, the prospective number of engineers and scientists fell, while the prospective number headed for farming and the health professions rose, as did the proportion expecting to work in "other" jobs—presumably outside the traditional college-type professions. Among women, the proportion intending to work in such "male-oriented" occupations as business, medicine, law, engineering, and even farming rose—presumably as a result of women's liberation, affirmative action, and related social changes.

The pattern of enrollments in particular types of schools and curricula provides a further indicator of changes in vocational orienta-

[3] A. Cartter, "Scientific Manpower for 1970–1985," *Science* (April 1971), Vol. 172, p. 133, Table 1.

Table 3. Changes in Freshman Career Plans in the Declining Market, Distribution by Probable Career Occupations

	Male		Female	
	1966	1974	1966	1974
Business	18.5	17.6	3.3	8.5
College professor	2.1	0.7	1.5	0.8
Doctor	7.4	6.9	1.7	3.5
Elementary, secondary school teacher	11.3	3.8	34.1	11.9
Engineer	16.3	8.5	0.2	0.8
Farmer	3.2	6.2	0.2	1.3
Health profession, including nurse	3.2	5.8	11.9	22.7
Lawyer	6.7	5.3	0.7	2.3
Scientist	4.9	2.7	1.9	1.4
Other	15.8	24.5	31.0	26.9
Undecided	5.0	12.3	3.6	12.6

Source: American Council on Education "National Norms for Entering College Freshmen—Fall 1966," *ACE Research Reports,* Vol. 2, No. 1, pp. 6, 13, and (with University of California Graduate School of Education, Los Angeles): *The American Freshmen: National Norms for Fall 1974,* pp. 20, 32.

tion. The agricultural colleges, for example, experienced a boom due to the potentially strong market for agricultural experts. According to the National Association of State Universities and Land Grant Colleges, total enrollments in the 70 colleges increased from 54,000 in 1969 to 82,000 in 1974, including an increasing proportion of women. First-year enrollments in engineering curricula, which had dropped greatly in the late 1960s and early 1970s, jumped by an astounding 20% in 1973–1974, as the market for B.S. engineers improved because of a relative shortage of new graduates.[4] By contrast, enrollments in education curricula fell through the 1970s. In the junior colleges, vocational programs, including secretarial and commercial courses, became more attractive than liberal arts, causing some schools that had previously stressed transfer to four-year colleges to shift their emphasis in the direction of the job market.

While it takes some time for the full impact of a market swing to affect the number of graduates in a particular specialty because of

[4] The data on land grant colleges appeared in *The New York Times* (17 January 1975); the data on engineers is taken from Scientific Manpower Commission, *Manpower Currents* (May 1975), Vol. 12, No. 4, p. 20.

the 4- to 5-year lag between enrollment and completion of a degree program, the number of degrees granted in various fields began changing in the early 1970s. Between 1969 and 1972, for example, the number of bachelors degrees awarded men in mathematics and languages declined by 15% and 20%, respectively, while degrees in computer sciences, psychology, and health sciences were up substantially. Among women, the pattern was similar: gains in psychology, health sciences, computer science, and business and declines in degrees in mathematics, languages, and physical sciences. Enrollments in business and energy-related courses tended to increase in the mid-1970s at the expense of liberal arts fields. Pennsylvania State University's College of Earth and Mineral Sciences received more liberal arts transfers in 1975 than in the previous 20 years. At other institutions, enrollments in economics, business, and accounting courses skyrocketed—a development examined further in Chapter 6. Overall, increases in the number of degrees granted and in enrollments tended to be in those fields continuing to offer reasonable job prospects, while declines were concentrated in the scientific and academic fields which had experienced the greatest market bust.[5]

For many students, the shift in career plans, while attuned to economic reality, involves painful decisions. Especially hard hit are those who have trained to be schoolteachers; their chances for a job are small, yet they have no other salable skills. At some graduate schools, students were reported to be delaying completion of their degrees so as to postpone entrance into a dismal market. The B'nai Brith Career and Counseling service began advising collegians to shift from such desired fields as fashion design to those with some job prospects. "A couple of years ago," said one career officer, "no one came here for career help. Now kids ask where the jobs are."[6]

In short, the career and study plans of young persons underwent a major reorientation in the 1970s—one that is not yet complete. The emerging trend appears to be away from the academic and

[5] Degree data for 1969 are from U.S. Bureau of the Census, *Statistical Abstract 1970*, Table 204, p. 130; degree data for 1972 are from xeroxed sheets provided by the U.S. Office of Education. Evidence on enrollment patterns in schools from *The New York Times* (2 November 1975).

[6] The B'nai Brith quote from *The New York Times* (17 January 1975).

the "pure" scientific or intellectual—the glamorous areas of the 1960s, toward the applied and business-oriented specialties.

THE DECLINE IN GRADUATE STUDIES

At the graduate level, too, there was a significant response to the depressed market, with enrollments in graduate school falling relative to the size of the prospective population. Between 1968 and 1971, for example, the ratio of the number of first-year graduate students enrolled for master's or doctoral degrees to the number of bachelor's graduates dropped by over 10%, from 0.72 to 0.63. Since many graduate students are older persons, rather than newly graduated from college, these figures do not, of course, mean that 72% of the graduating class in 1968 or 63% of the class in 1971 chose to go on to graduate studies, but rather that for every 100 new bachelor's graduates, 72 or 63 persons reentered academia to seek a higher degree. By contrast, the relative number of new enrollments in professional schools actually rose slightly, from 7.4% in 1968 to 8.3% in 1971. Reduction in enrollments was most severe in fields oriented toward the declining academic market or in those that were experiencing well-publicized job shortages; increases in enrollments were greatest in applied and professional areas, where job markets were continuing to expand, particularly law, medicine, and "applied" social sciences—such as urban studies and city planning. Even at an institution like MIT, there was a remarkable change in postgraduate study plans. In the early 1970s more MIT students applied to take the law school and medical school entrance exams than had ever been the case before.[7]

STUDY—YES! RADICALISM—NO![8]

"The bad job market has really depressed students on this campus." "People are just stepping all over each other to get these

[7] Numbers of enrolled students, from R. Freeman and D. Breneman, *Forecasting the Ph.D. Labor Market.* (1974 Technical Report No. 2), Table 9. Number of bachelor's graduates, from U.S. Office of Education, *Earned Degrees Conferred* 1967-8, Table 2, p. 4; and *Digest of Education Statistics, 1972*, Table 114, p. 98.

[8] These developments and quotations are from *Bergen Evening Record* (20 Feb. 1975), p. A-26, pp. 93–94, 182; and personal discussions.

grades." "The kids are worrying about jobs this year." "The competition is fantastic." "Chemistry classes are jammed with premed kids who are willing to cheat, steal, sabotage, or do anything else it takes to get into medical school." These are some typical comments from students and faculty on campuses around the nation in the mid-1970s.

Economic depression has historically been the bane of radical and protest movements. When jobs are hard to find, social concerns disappear and individuals concentrate on their own economic security. The seventies downturn in the college labor market was no exception While other factors—the end of American involvement in Vietnam and the draft—were important, the depressed job situation produced a major change in the mood on campuses. A new study and work ethic replaced the radical activist social concerns that had characterized the late 1960s. Where students had once demanded pass—fail options in place of grades, they now chose to be graded, since good grades raised prospects for professional schools or jobs. At Harvard, so few freshmen law students signed up for pass—fail that the system was dropped. Competition for grades and jobs became so severe that some faculty and students began to worry about the quality of "intellectual life on campus." Colleges, such as Johns Hopkins or Barnard, were forced to give up honor systems because the desire for good grades led to cheating.

Attitudes toward industry also changed. Campuses that had greeted industrial and government recruiters with hostile demonstrations now laid down the red carpet for them. Said one recruiter, "You wouldn't believe it's the same place. I spoke with six students in 1970 and had to 'sneak' on campus to avoid the SDS. Last week (1975), I spoke with 75 students who wanted to work for us. No troubles." Another put it this way, "It's a buyer's market. It's no longer a matter of what we can offer them. The question is what they can do for us."

The change in student attitudes has shown up in a variety of ways. In the annual American Council of Education survey of freshmen, the proportion interested in politics fell in the 1970s, as did the number wanting to abolish grades (Figure 7). The desire to "be well off financially," on the other hand, appears to have increased, presumably as a result of the new economic insecurity facing graduates. Reserve Officers' Training Corps (ROTC), which had generated

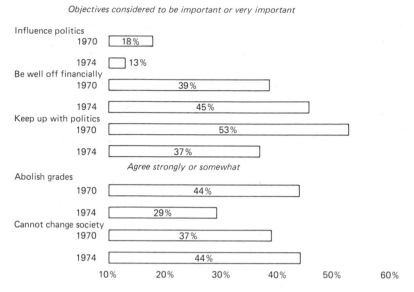

Figure 7. Changes in student attitudes, 1970–1974 (from American Council on Education, *National Norms for Entering Freshmen, Fall 1970,* ACE Research Reports, pp. 42–43; and (with University of California Graduate School of Education, Los Angeles) *The American Freshman: National Norms for Fall 1974*, p. 48).

riots on many campuses in the 1960s, became more popular, with the prospect that it offered financial support for schooling and an army job as an officer upon completion. Total enrollment in ROTC increased, from 1973 to 1974, by about 8%—the first such rise since 1965. No longer did anyone seek to "kick ROTC off campus"; several prestigious schools that had done so began thinking about inviting its return.

Among law students, the change in attitude was reflected in a change both in clothes and in employment demands. "At Columbia, those who wear jeans are the ones who have jobs; the students who wear suits or dresses are still looking for work." A few years ago the first thing students asked major firms was how much *pro bono publico* work it did. "Now they politely ask about our corporate clients."[9]

Within the span of a single student generation, the prophecies of "youth revolution" and "the greening of America," and fears that

[9] *Newsweek* (9 December 1974), p. 74.

totalitarian leftist student groups might shut out intellectual freedoms have been disproved. What is remarkable, and worth remembering, is *the rapidity with which the atmosphere on the campuses and the behavior of the young has so dramatically changed.*

THE RESPONSE OF COLLEGES AND UNIVERSITIES

What does one do in the face of a precipitous fall in the demand for one's product?

Like the railroads and aerospace companies before them, colleges and universities have been forced by the depressed market to initiate substantial changes in their mode of operation. These changes took two basic forms: efforts to save on expenses and efforts to expand the market by finding new clientele.

At one extreme a nonnegligible number of institutions folded up in the early 1970s. Between 1972 and 1974, the American Council of Education reported that 18 four-year accredited institutions of higher education and 7 two-year colleges closed.[10] Private colleges faced the greatest difficulties; some, like the University of Pittsburgh, were amalgamated into state systems; others had such financial problems that in New York the State Department of Education estimated that as many as 80 of the state's 120 private colleges would fold, in the absence of additional public funding. More common than the closing of institutions was the curtailment of programs. New York put a moratorium on new master's and doctoral programs in 1974 and, in the name of "quality control," began to consider the elimination of many existing programs in the state system. The University of Vermont gave up its football program. Virtually all institutions were unable to carry out the plans for expansion they had projected in the 1960s.

Widespread staff reductions, mostly by attrition and a drop in the employment of young, nontenured faculty, caused a major problem in the academic job market (see Chapter 4). The University of Florida imposed a freeze on hiring; Harvard planned to reduce faculty by attrition. Some schools sought to fire tenured faculty as

---

[10] From *Accredited Institutions on Higher Education 1974–75*, (Washington, D.C.: American Council on Education, 1975). pp. 211–212.

well but ran into legal problems (Bloomfield College in New Jersey), which left the burden of adjustment on the young. Others, such as MIT and Stanford, tried to reduce employment by the early retirement of senior faculty. Teaching loads and class sizes, which had been reduced in the previous decade's boom, were increased, to cut the cost of instruction per student.[11]

In their efforts to expand the market, many institutions altered their programs so as to attract those young people who were concerned with the falling value of a traditional college training and those older persons who had previously not thought of attending college. To appeal to the new vocationally concerned student, small liberal arts schools initiated career programs. Cazenovia College in upstate New York, for instance, staked its future in such career-oriented areas as fashion design, and museum studies. "We'll be involved in a long-term guessing game, trying to keep one jump ahead of the competition in guessing on the careers students will be pursuing. We're no longer in the position of telling students what the requirements are if they want a Cazenovia degree. Now we say: 'You tell us what you want, and we'll provide it.' " Other campuses, ranging from Brigham Young University (Utah) to Oklahoma City University to Massachusetts State College at Boston, began experimenting with new technologies of education. With federal support, these schools sought to redefine the goals of liberal education in terms of practical "marketable" skills, often patterned after the training that companies provide for executives. Even graduate schools and professional academic associations, particularly in history and English, began to consider "what we might teach master's and Ph.D.'s that will be valuable in business employment." Whether these program changes will prove effective or not remains to be seen; their initiation indicates the response of educational institutions to the depressed job market.[12]

In an effort to attract more "paying customers," many colleges wooed older adults by advertising in newspapers and magazines and

---

[11] Many of these developments are described in *The New York Times* (15 Jan. 1975), p. 89.

[12] *New York Times* (15 January 1975), p. 90; (1 April 1975), pp. 1, 20. The Cazenovia quotation is from *The New York Times*, (15 January 1975), p. 88. The changed attitude of the history and English professional societies has led to a large study of career opportunities and job experience of doctorates in the humanities by the Higher Education Research Institute of the University of California at Los Angeles.

tailoring programs to suit those who could attend only part-time. Some gave credit for nonacademic activities, reducing the number of credits, and hence the time and cost, needed for a degree. Since only older persons have accumulated the type of experience that can reasonably be given credit, the result is a bifurcated market, with 18- to 19-year-olds paying more in time and money for their degree than older persons. Such "price discrimination" is, of course, a classic business method for increasing revenue. Several institutions offered courses off-campus to reduce the transportation and time costs of college attendance. In New York: Adelphi University put professors on railroad trains to teach credit courses to commuters; LaGuardia Community College sent professors to teach courses to employees at branch offices of First National City Bank; Staten Island Community College sent faculty to lecture at plants and offices of Consolidated Edison; and Queensborough Community College offered courses at Pan Am's cargo building at Kennedy Airport. Caldwell College of New Jersey set up a daycare center to attract housewives. Queens College of the City University of New York instituted a special Adult Collegiate Education program limited to persons over the age of 30.[13]

Various other recruiting techniques were resorted to. Testing organizations, such as the College Entrance Examination Board, have sold names and addresses to college administrators who used them to solicit applicants. The Riverside campus of the University of California sent out 12,000 oversized decks of playing cards carrying campus facts on the back. Some colleges pressure prospective students with the type of hard sell once associated only with profit-making proprietary schools or business colleges—mailing out slick brochures, conducting telephone canvasses, and giving out such gimmicks as free T-shirts, bumper stickers, and so on. In some cases, public relations firms have been hired to take over the whole admissions operation, receiving substantial fees for recruiting. While apparently still rare, the tactic of bounty hunting—for which proprietary schools have earned much opprobrium—has appeared, with recruiters paid on the basis of the number of students "delivered." The job of admissions officers, particularly at weaker institutions, is

---

[13] These developments are described in *The New York Times* (15 January 1975), p. 90 and (20 April 1975), p. 9.

no longer to weed out unsuitable applicants but to find warm bodies.[14]

Despite these efforts, however, the fraction of young people opting for college has fallen, and the proportion of older persons in college has increased only modestly. The schemes to expand the market have as yet had a minimal impact on individual decisions. There is no way to hide the fact that the degree no longer carries the job value it once did.

A BUYER'S MARKET

For employers, the depressed job market offers more, rather than fewer, opportunities—a larger number of applicants for jobs, a chance to exercise greater selectivity, and the sudden possibility of hiring relatively low-cost graduates for what have traditionally been noncollege-level jobs.

The ease of obtaining specialists has led to a significant curtailment of recruiting visits and interviews. As Figure 8 shows, even at MIT the number of companies seeking workers fell sharply, as did the number of interviewers and number of students interviewed, with companies seeking fewer graduates in 1974 than in 1970.

Companies also responded to the surplus of graduates and lower relative salaries by substituting college for less-educated workers in certain types of jobs: sales and managerial positions for men, clerical positions for women. When graduates were hard to obtain and cost 40% more than high school workers, enterprises preferred the latter for these white-collar jobs. Now, with graduates plentiful and costing, on average, just 25% more than their high school competitors, it became profitable to substitute the former. Between 1969 and 1974, while the number of male college graduates relative to high school graduates increased by 20%, the ratio of college to high school salaried managers jumped 48%, and the ratio of college to high school salesmen by 63%. In 1969, college men constituted 17% of salesmen, high school men 40%; in 1974, the college share had risen to 24%, the high school share had fallen to 34%. Similarly, among

[14] See *The New York Times* (2 February 1975), Rapaport, "New Myth on Campus," p. 94.

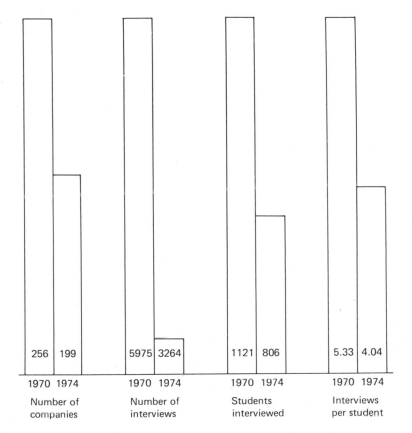

256	199		5975	3264		1121	806		5.33	4.04
1970	1974		1970	1974		1970	1974		1970	1974
Number of companies			Number of interviews			Students interviewed			Interviews per student		

Figure 8. Recruiting at the Massachusetts Institute of Technology, 1970–1974 (from MIT, "Report of the Career Planning and Placement Office, 1973–1974," Table V, p. 14.)

women, the college share of clerical workers increased by 94% in the period, while the high school share fell by 8%.[15] In many cases, employers were shocked by the level of education of applicants for their jobs. The principal of a private school in Massachusetts reported, for example, letters from Ph.D.'s in physics and mathematics seeking positions as grade school teachers. "I am struck by the very high overall quality of the applicants." While formal educational requirements are not being raised for jobs, the competition is such that college graduates are pushing the less educated out of their

[15] Calculated from data in U.S. Bureau of Labor Statistics, *Educational Attainment of Workers,* (1969 and 1974) Special Labor Force Report, No. 175, Table I, p. A—18.

traditional white collar areas. "It isn't that we don't consider high school applicants," said one employer seeking a secretary, "but so many good college girls apply that the high school kids just can't compete."[16]

SUMMARY

The important finding of this chapter is that the depressed job market has caused students, colleges, and employers to alter long-standing attitudes and "patterns of behavior" in response to the new economic reality.

[16] See *The New York Times* (15 January 1975), p. 83, for the quotations from the Massachusetts school principal. The second quotation is from personal interviews. For an econometric analysis of the impact of the large number of college graduates on high school workers in white collar employment, see R. Freeman, "Youth Employment Opportunities: Changes in the Relative Position of College and High School Graduates," in S. Wolfbein (ed.), *Labor Market Information for Youth* (Philadelphia: Temple University Press, 1975).

The Way It Works: Why the Booming Sixties Bust and What the Future May Bring

3

Why did the college job market deteriorate so greatly in the 1970s? What caused the labor shortages of the late 1950s and early 1960s to become the surpluses of the 1970s? How long will the depressed market last? What lies ahead for college graduates?

To pin down the causes of the depressed market of the 1970s and predict the period of "overeducation," it is necessary to examine the operation of the job market for educated workers—to understand the way in which individuals, enterprises, and institutions respond to economic developments and the way in which their behavior interacts in the marketplace. In this chapter, which constitutes the analytic core of the book, are set out what I believe to be the critical elements in the college job market. The resultant analytic framework is used to explain the sharp deterioration in the supply—demand balance of the 1970s and to forecast the future. The forecasts are derived from a formal model of supply and demand for graduates— the *recursive adjustment model*—which has been used with some success to analyze developments in several high-level occupations at

MIT's Center for Policy Alternatives and elsewhere in recent years. Market models of this type received considerable support as the appropriate tool for forecasting at the 1974 National Science Board Manpower Forecasting Conference.[1] Because realistic analysis depends not on specific techniques or models but on correct specification of the actual behavior of individuals in the job market, the chapter concentrates on the forces that influence individual decisions and market dynamics, relegating technical details to Appendix B.

FUNCTIONING OF THE COLLEGE JOB MARKET

To understand the operation of a complex social system like the labor market for college graduates, in which numerous individuals and institutions interact to determine employment and wages, it is necessary to simplify reality and focus on the salient features of the system.

There are, according to my analysis, four key elements in the operation of the market for college graduates, whose interplay determines its dynamic operation over time.

Responsive Supply Behavior on the Part of Young Students

The career and educational decisions of young persons and their families are critical in the operation of the market because these decisions ultimately determine the long-run supply of graduates to the economy. If the supply behavior of the young is highly sensitive to such economic incentives as salaries and job opportunities, the number of new graduates will be an important homeostatic device, helping equilibrate the job market. If, contrarily, the young are only slightly influenced by economic incentives, equilibration will be more difficult; the major brunt of adjustment will then fall, even in the long run, on salaries and on employers, possibly leading to extended disquilibria over long periods of time. How responsive are the young to labor market incentives?

---

[1] National Science Board, *Scientific and Technical Manpower Projections*, NSB 74-286, (Washington, D.C., October 1974).

There is substantial and growing body of evidence that, contrary to traditional views of student decision making, young persons are highly sensitive in their educational and career decisions to the state of the labor market. For a wide variety of fields, ranging from law to physics to psychology to accounting, studies reveal a sizable positive link between the number of students pursuing the area and salaries or related indicators of economic opportunities. In physics, for example, in the flourishing job market of the decade that followed Sputnik, enrollments at both the undergraduate and graduate level increased greatly; by contrast, the deteriorating market in the late 1960s, despite a nearly twofold expansion in the size of the student body, junior- and senior-year majors declined from 14,900 (1961) to 11,400 (1971), while first-year graduate enrollments dropped by one-third.[2]

More importantly in terms of the market depression of the 1970s, "responsive supply behavior" appears to be the major cause of the dramatic fall in the fraction of young men choosing to attend college shown in Chapter 2. Formal statistical analysis[3] indicates that over 95% of the variation in the fraction of young men in college over the 1951–1974 period can be attributed to two simple measures of the economic incentive to enroll: the income of graduates relative to other workers and relative employment opportunities. As Figure 9 shows, the pattern of change in enrollments "predicted" by these variables does a good job of tracking the actual drop in the 1970s. Other factors that might be expected to influence enrollments—such as changes in the draft or the overall weakening of the economy in the mid-1970s—were important for only limited periods of time and appear to be dwarfed in importance by the continuous

[2] Evidence on supply responsiveness is given in R. Freeman, *The Labor Market for College-Trained Manpower* (Cambridge, Mass.: Harvard University Press, 1971); R. Freeman, "Labor Market Adjustments in Psychology" *American Psychologist* (May 1972), pp. 384–392; R. Freeman, "Legal Cobwebs: A Recursive Model of the Market for New Lawyers," *Review of Economics and Statistics* (May 1975), pp. 171–179; R. Freeman, "Supply and Salary Adjustments to the Changing Science Manpower Market: Physics, 1948–1973," *American Economic Review* (March 1975), Vol. 65, No. 1, pp. 27–39; R. Freeman, "A Cobweb Model of the Supply and Starting Salary of New Engineers," *Industrial Labor Relations Review* (January 1976). The data on physics are from R. Freeman, "Supply and Salary Adjustments to the Changing Science Manpower Market."

[3] The regression calculations are reported in R. Freeman "Overinvestment in College Training?" *Journal of Human Resources* (Summer 1975), Table 5.

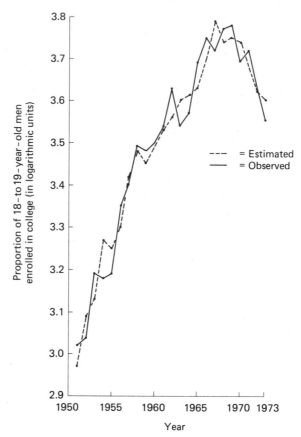

Figure 9. Proportion of 18- to 19-year-old men enrolled in college and proportion estimated from economic incentives, 1951–1973 (based on regression estimates in R. Freeman, "Overinvestment in College Training?" *Journal of Human Resources* (Summer 1975), Table 5).

decline of the job market. The reduction in numbers called and eventual elimination of the draft, for example, may have played some part in the drop in enrollments from 1969 to 1970 but cannot be invoked as a cause of subsequent changes. Similarly, the rising unemployment and inflation that cut into real family income in the mid-1970s does not explain the fall in enrollments at the outset of the decade. Only the change in market opportunities covers the entire period.

Surveys designed to elicit the importance attached by students to economic factors in education and career decisions support the "responsive supply" hypothesis. About two-thirds of male and one-half of female freshmen surveyed by the American Council of Education agreed, for example, that "the chief benefit of college is that it increases earning power" (see Table 4). Seventy-seven percent of men and 70% of women were going to college, in large part, "to get a better job" and 57% of the men and 42% of the women "to make more money"—all of which suggests that when earning power declines, so too will enrollments. With respect to career choice, nearly one-half of the men and over one-third of the women regarded "high anticipated earnings" as very important in their decisions, while 42% of the men and 52% of the women also thought that "job openings available" was very important. In addition, a relatively large percentage of students accorded considerable importance to the chance for steady progress and rapid advancement in their anticipated careers. These figures do not, however, mean that the labor market is the dominant factor in decisions, nor that it is critical to all persons. Because individuals have, as Adam Smith noted over 200 years ago, strong nonpecuniary preferences for specific kinds of work as well as having specialized abilities, the career decisions of many will not be affected by the market. Those with great love for certain jobs, for instance aspiring authors or priests, will choose that work at almost any "living" wage. Others with special abilities—athletes, singers, chess champions, movie starlets—will select a career on the basis of

Table 4. Percentage of Freshman Students Concerned with Economic Factors in Educational and Career Decisions

	Male	Female
Agree that "the chief benefit of college is that it increases earning power"	66	51
Factors reported as "very important" in going to college:		
To get a better job	77	70
To make more money	57	42
Factors regarded as "very important" in career choice:		
High anticipated earnings	48	35
Job openings available	42	52
Rapid advancement	40	30
Chance for steady progress	52	46

Source: American Council of Education The American Freshman: National Norms for Fall 1971, *Ace Research Reports,* Vol. 6, No. 6, 1971, pp. 27–28, 35–36, and (with University of California, Los Angeles): *The American Freshman: National Norms for Fall 1974,* p. 20, 32.

their particular abilities. Even such sharp changes in the market as the downturn of the 1970s will have little impact on the behavior of these types of people. At the same time, however, many individuals whose abilities and preferences make several options feasible will alter their plans when relative wages change, moving—all else the same—from careers with contracting markets to those with expanding markets. The responsiveness of supply to economic incentives depends not on the existence of a mythical species of *Homo economicus*, who, like Scrooge McDuck, views life strictly in terms of the almighty dollar, but rather on the apparently large number of "marginal decision makers" for whom the other advantages and disadvantages of various occupations balance out.

The major consequence of responsive supply behavior on the part of the young is that the fraction enrolled and the number of new graduates become critical adjustment mechanisms. With a relatively elastic supply of students to colleges and universities overall and to various careers, changes in salaries and in employment opportunities, like those experienced in the early 1970s, are translated into sizable changes in the number of new college graduates seeking work.

Long Working Life

The mundane fact that people work for 40 or so years means that the vast majority of college graduates invested in their education and chose their specialties many years ago, making the total supply of graduates relatively inelastic even when the supply of the young is highly adaptive to new circumstances. When, as in the 1970s, there are many more young persons in the cohorts entering the labor market than there are graduates in the retiring age brackets, total supply will grow even if the fraction of the young enrolled in college falls. As a consequence, the movement toward a long-run balance of supply and demand for graduates in the entire population will necessarily be slow, permitting disequilibrium to persist for many years. In markets with long-lived factors of production, supply—demand disequilibria are likely to be long lived also.

Two factors ameliorate the problem of adjusting the total supply of graduates to changed market conditions. First is the fact that younger and older graduates often perform different work tasks, the former doing work directly related to their training, the latter more general managerial work. Because of different activities, graduates of different ages may be only moderately substitutable for one another, leading to more or less separate labor markets. As a result, the market for new graduates could improve rapidly as the supply of the young declines at the same time that the total college-trained population grows. The "good news" is that the declining fraction of the young going to college may significantly alleviate the market for newly graduated workers in the next decade. The "bad news" is that persons in the large graduating classes of the late 1960s and early 1970s may suffer from a relative excess of supply over their entire lives, creating a significant intergenerational equity problem.

The second factor easing the supply adjustment problem is the possibility of occupational mobility and other forms of adaptive responses to market incentives on the part of experienced workers. Although because of their past commitments and training, the experienced react less to market ups and downs than do the young, they can still play a major role in the movement to equilibrium. Since there are many more experienced than new workers, even relatively small changes in the supply of the former can have a sizeable impact on the state of the market.[4] However, while the decisions of the experienced make the supply of college workers in different occupations more flexible, they have little impact on the total number of college workers in the entire economy, because decisions taken years ago to obtain education cannot be revoked today.

Alleviating factors notwithstanding, the long working life of college manpower raises the possibility that, despite supply responses to the depressed market of the 1970s, a relative surplus of college workers in the population as a whole will persist for many years to come.

---

[4] For example, if there are 10 times as many experienced workers as new entrants, a 10% drop in salaries that causes 1% of the experienced workers to leave the occupation will alter the total number by the same amount as will a 10% drop in salary that causes a 10% drop in the numbers of new entrants. Thus, even though new entrants evince 10 times as great a responsiveness as the experienced, the salary change causes a similar reduction in supply.

Demand and Employer Behavior

The dynamic "moving force" in the college job market is the demand for graduates, which is dependent on such basic economic forces as the structure of the economy, industrial activities and changes in technology, the possibility of substituting college graduates for other workers or for machines, and demographic changes. The structure of the economy is important because industries differ greatly in their relative employment of graduates, with, for example, 31% of workers in finance in 1970 having college degrees compared to 6% in the automobile industry. Whether industries that make intensive use of college manpower grow rapidly in the future as they did in the 1960s, when aerospace, the education sector, and related industries enjoyed a boom, or slowly as in the 1970s, will be a key determinant of market conditions. Industrial activities and technology are important because the relative employment of graduates within industries depends on what those industries do and how they do it. If resources are allocated to research and development or related activities that make extensive use of educated workers, demand for graduates will be high. Similarly, demand will also be high if, for whatever reason, new technologies are "biased" (at given factor prices) in favor of relatively educated manpower. Empirically, there has been considerable variation in expenditures for R&D, causing sizable shifts in the demand for college graduates, especially scientific and engineering personnel. On the other hand, there has been only modest change in the intraindustrial use of educated workers within periods of, say, a decade or so, and even over longer periods, intraindustrial changes in the employment of graduates appear to be dwarfed by shifts in the composition of industries.[5] Demography is important because the age structure and rate of growth of the

---

[5] Evidence that changes in distribution of workers are by industry, not in intraindustry coefficients, is given in R. Freeman "Manpower Requirements and the Skill Composition of the U.S. Work Force " (Paper delivered at National Science Foundation Conference on Manpower Forecasting, Hot Springs, Virginia, April 1974); S. Dresch, "Demography, Technology, and Higher Education: Toward a Formal Model of Educational Adaptation," *Journal of Political Economy* (March–April 1975), Vol. 83 finds that only 30% of the increased employment of college graduates from 1929 to 1969 was associated with increased employment of graduates within industries. While Dresch finds a greater role for intraindustry changes in the 1948–1969 period, the 1948 figures are "biased" by the World War II experience.

population are critical determinants of the size of the educational sector, which is the single largest industry employing graduates.

When, as in the 1970s, the relative wages of the college trained change, the possibilities of substituting better-educated for less-educated workers become critical in market adjustment. If substitutions are relatively easy to make, only modest declines in salaries will suffice to increase employment and equilibrate supply–demand imbalances. If substitutions are difficult, enormous changes in salaries may be required for a "surplus" of graduates to find jobs.

Empirical evidence on substitutability is mixed. In the late 1960s, several scholars who compared incomes and employment across countries found surprisingly large "elasticities of substitution," which suggests that only small declines in relative salaries are needed to increase greatly the employment of college workers. More recent work, including that of the Nobel Prize–winning Dutch economist Jan Tinbergen, indicate, however, that the possibilities of substitution are more limited and that significantly large changes in relative salaries are needed to have a major impact on employment. My work with time series finds sizable but by no means enormous long-run elasticities of demand for all graduates and smaller elasticities for such detailed specialists as engineers, R&D scientists, lawyers, physicists, and biologists.[6] Perhaps the 1970s experience in the job market most decisively supports the moderate substitution hypothesis. It would be difficult to explain the sharp decline in the relative earnings of graduates by the economic forces of supply and demand if college trained and other workers were such good substitutes that only minute adjustments in wages would be needed to equilibrate the surplus of new graduates that developed after 1969.

When employment of graduates in specific occupations is investigated, the possibility of increasing demand in response to lower

---

[6] See S. Bowles, *Planning Educational Systems for Economic Growth* (Cambridge, Mass.: Harvard University Press, 1969), Chapter 3; G. Psacharapoulous and K. Hinchcliffe, "Further Evidence on the Elasticity of Substitution," *Journal of Political Economy* (July–August 1972), Vol. 80, pp. 786–792; J. Tinbergen, "Substitution of Graduate by Other Labor," *Kyklos* (1974), Vol. 27, No. 2, pp. 217–226; P.R. Fallon and R. Layard, "Capital Skill Complementarity, Income Distribution and Capital Accounting," *Journal of Political Economy* (April 1975), Vol. 83, No. 2; R. Freeman, "Overinvestment in College Training?" pp. 287–310; R. Freeman, "Demand for R&D Scientists and Engineers," in *Engineers and Scientists in the Industrial Economy*, unpublished report to National Science Foundation (1971), and studies by Freeman cited in Footnote 2.

salaries appears even more difficult. In "good" college-level jobs, the percentage increase in employment caused by a percentage drop in salaries appears to be moderate, at best. Substitution possibilities are greatest in less desirable white-collar jobs, such as sales or clerical positions or lower-level management. The result is that, while lower earnings can resolve an unemployment problem, they do so by creating an underemployment problem that cannot be readily alleviated by cuts in salaries.

Cobweb Dynamics

Because 4 or more years are required to "produce" a college graduate, the college market tends to follow the classic *cobweb feedback system* that has long been associated with the markets for corn or hogs. Like these agricultural products, the supply of graduates is determined by market conditions several periods earlier, due to the fixed time delay in educational production, and is thus a lagging function of the state of the market. Such a structure generates oscillatory ups and downs, with shortages changing into surpluses every 4 or 5 years. The reason for this pattern can be readily

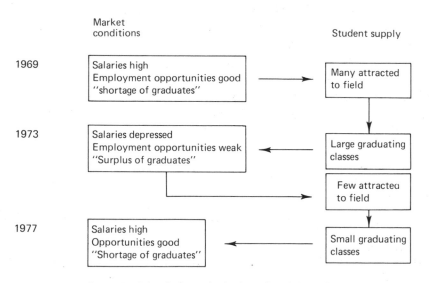

Figure 10. Cobweb dynamics in the college job market.

seen (Figure 10). If salaries and demand are strong in a specialty in, say, 1969, many students will be drawn into the field, becoming the new supply 4 or 5 years later. When they graduate in 1973, unless demand has increased commensurately, they will "oversupply" the market, depressing salaries and employment opportunities. With the decline in incentives in 1973, relatively fewer students will enroll in the field, causing a shortage in 1977, and so forth. Of course, other factors, notably shifts in demand, will also affect the market. What is important is that there is an underlying feedback structure tending to produce cyclical movements in the supply—demand balance. Econometric models based on the cobweb hypothesis have been quite effective in "explaining" the labor market experience of recipients of the Bachelor of Science (B.S.) in engineering, of graduates in accounting, and of Master of Business Administration (MBA) as well as law graduates, and those in other specialties in which there is a close one-to-one tie between education and occupation.[7] Cobweb dynamics help explain much of the recurrent shortages and surpluses of certain types of college-trained specialists in years past.

One other classic economic adjustment mechanism plays an important role in the market for graduates. This is the "accelerator" adjustment process, which is traditionally viewed as governing capital good production. In the case of the college trained, the fact that universities hire a relatively large number of graduates, particularly master's and doctoral degree recipients, means that demand depends in part on the number of students seeking academic careers. If many seek such careers, the demand for faculty and faculty salaries and employment opportunities will improve, leading to an increase in supply and further gains in demand. The situation tends toward instability, however, because once the number of students levels off, demand for new faculty will fall rapidly, causing a decline in the number of students considering academic careers, further reducing demand for faculty, and so forth. This feature of academia makes the market for university faculty and graduate studies exceptionally vulnerable to changes in the growth of enrollments. Academia stands

[7] The cobweb model of the job market is developed in Freeman, *The Labor Market for College-Trained Manpower.* The studies by Freeman cited in Footnote 2 apply it to different professions.

on a revolving ball—you have to run to stay in place, and when you stop, you fall.[8]

GOVERNMENT AND EDUCATED MANPOWER

To complete the story of the operation of the college job market, the role of federal, state, and local governments must be brought into the picture. Governmental policies have a sizable impact on both the supply and the demand sides of the market. The number of scholarships and fellowships, public subsidization and tuition policies, decisions to expand or contract educational systems, and moves to support students or provide grants to institutions have influenced and will continue to influence the supply of graduates—not only the quantity but also the composition in terms of the socioeconomic groups from which graduates are drawn and the specialties they choose. On the demand side, governments affect the market, directly as large employers of educated manpower and indirectly through their purchase of goods and services from the private sector. Some purchases, such as R&D, space programs, defense, health services, result in direct changes in demand. Other purchases have less immediate but still real impacts by the input—output linkages in the economy—the fact that industries purchase commodities from others, which employ graduates in turn and so forth. Analysis of federal, state, and local spending using the input—output table for the U.S. economy created by a Nobel Prize winner, economist W. Leontief, shows that dollars of public expenditure, especially at the federal level, generate more demand for college-trained workers than do dollars of private spending.[9]

In years past, the dependence of the college market on governmental activities has had a significant destabilizing effect on the

[8] More detailed analyses of the faculty are presented in A. Cartter, *Ph.D.'s and the Academic Labor Market* (New York: McGraw-Hill, 1976); R. Freeman "Demand for Labor in a Nonprofit Market: University Faculty," in *Labor in the Public and Nonprofit Sectors*, ed. D. Hammermesh (Princeton, N.J.: Princeton University Press, 1975), pp. 85–129.

[9] Evidence on the impact of defense spending is given in R. Dempsey and D. Schmude, "Occupational Impact of Defense Expenditures," *Monthly Labor Review* (December 1971), pp. 12–15.

economic status of graduates, because federal, and to a lesser extent state and local, policies have changed greatly within short periods of time, causing sudden turnarounds in demand. Federal R&D spending, for example, shot up in the years surrounding Sputnik, giving a sharp spur to the demand for graduate scientists and engineers, then fell (in real dollars) equally sharply in the late 1960s and 1970s, contributing to the market turnaround. Private R&D spending, by contrast, rose modestly through most of the entire period. Similar pronounced changes in spending are found in the health sector, in defense, and in other programs. One possible reason for governmental overreaction to problems is the "crisis mentality" of elected officials whose time horizon, given the periodicity of elections, is short. Another is that fewer institutions are involved in the decision-making process than in private markets involving many firms. In any case, governmental activities have exacerbated rather than ameliorated problems in the college market and will undoubtedly continue to play a major role in future developments, for better or worse.

THE OVERALL MARKET SYSTEM

The preceding analysis paints a distinctive picture of the functioning of the college job market, a market in which: young persons are exceptionally sensitive to economic opportunities; where the long working life of graduates makes overall supply adjustments sluggish; where demand changes substantially with changes in the structure of the economy, the demographic composition of the population, certain activities—like R&D—and governmental policies and expenditures; where employers substitute college graduates for less-educated workers in noncollege-level, white-collar jobs, in response to lower relative wages; where cobweb dynamics produce significant cyclical ups and downs; and where accelerator adjustments make one major employment area—the educational system—highly sensitive to changes in the rate of growth of enrollment. Given this model of the functioning of the college job market, what caused the depression of the 1970s? And what lies ahead?

WHY THE BOOMING SIXTIES BUST

The question of why the college manpower market deteriorated so suddenly at the outset of the 1970s can be turned around: Why was the market so strong in preceding decades, despite the continuous growth of supply?

Two factors appear to answer both of these questions and explain the state of the market over the entire post–World War II period. On the demand side, the relative position of the highly educated was maintained in the 1950s and 1960s by large increases in demand due to changes in the industrial mix of jobs, the growth of R&D, and the extraordinary expansion of the education sector. In the 1970s, all of these forces, which had provided a significant upward push to the market, weakened or actually declined relative to the overall state of the economy.

Table 5. Compound Annual Percentage Change in Employment in College-Manpower-Intensive and Other Industries in the Periods 1960–1969 and 1969–1974

Industries	1960–1969	1969–1974
College-manpower-intensive	4.4	2.8
Noneducational:	3.8	2.3
Professional services[a]	5.4	5.9
Federal public administration, except postal service	2.0	0.0
Finance, insurance, and realty	3.7	3.2
College-intensive manufacturing[b]	3.6	−1.2
Education	6.2	3.9
All other[c]	2.0	2.0
National total	2.8	2.2

Source: U.S. Department of Labor, *Employment and Earnings 1909–1972* Bulletin 1312-9, updated from *Employment and Earnings* (March 1975), Vol. 21, No. 9.

[a]Excludes educational services: includes SIC codes 80, 81, 84, 86 and 89. Employment in 1969 in 84 and 86 is for March from Bulletin 1312-9, p. 685. Employment in 1960 is the mean for 1959 and 1961, also from p. 685. Employment in 1974 in 84 and 86 estimated by multiplying their share of total service employment in 1971 using data on p. 685 by actual employment in 1974.

[b]Ordnance, chemicals, petroleum, professional instruments, aircraft, electrical machinery, and electronic computing machinery, with 1960 electronic computing machinery estimated.

[c]Agriculture included, based on data from U.S. Department of Commerce *Survey of Current Business* (July editions), with 1974 estimated.

The quantitative dimensions of the slackened demand are shown in Table 5 and Figure 11. Table 5 contrasts the growth of employment in industries that hire relatively large numbers of college graduates to the growth in those that employ relatively few. It covers both the booming sixties and the declining seventies. Among the industries with many graduates are: federal public administration, with one in six male graduates working for the national bureaucracy; professional services, ranging from law to welfare; finance, insurance, and realty; certain manufacturing industries, including ordnance, chemicals, petroleum, instruments, electronic computing, aircraft, electrical machinery; and, of course, education, which accounts for the employment of over one-half of female college graduates and one-tenth of male college graduates. Industries that hire very few college graduates include transportation, communication, agriculture, and the remaining areas of manufacturing.[10] The table reveals a marked slowdown in the rate of growth of college-manpower-intensive sectors relative to other sectors, between the 1960s and 1970s, During the 1960–1969 period, employment grew more than twice as rapidly in the college intensive industries as in other industries—a differential rate of 2.4% per annum. In the 1969–1974 period, the sectoral growth rates converged, as employment in college-intensive industries slowed relative to the previous decade—resulting in a differential of just 0.8%. The rate of change in employment in college-intensive manufacturing, in particular, which accounts for about one in nine male graduates, dropped from 3.6% per annum in the first period to −1.2% in the second period, while that in federal public administration fell from 2.0% to 0%. This shows that the market decline cannot—as some have asserted—be traced solely to changes in the size of the education sector and to demographic shifts in the number of persons of school age. The rate of growth of demand for college workers decelerated relative to that for the less educated in the 1970s as a result of a more general shift in the industrial composition of employment—a shift involving slower growth in those sectors of the economy where relatively large numbers of graduates have traditionally been employed.

[10] Data on the industrial employment of college graduates is presented in U.S. Bureau of the Census 1970 Census of Population, *Industrial Characteristics*, PC(2)-7B, Table 3; and 1960 Census of Population, *Industrial Characteristics*, PC(2)-7B, Table 21.

The changing pattern of demand is examined from a different perspective in Figure 11, which displays the proportion of GNP allocated to three college-manpower-intensive activities—R&D, defense, and education. After increasing rapidly from the early 1950s through the Sputnik era, the proportion of GNP spent on R&D

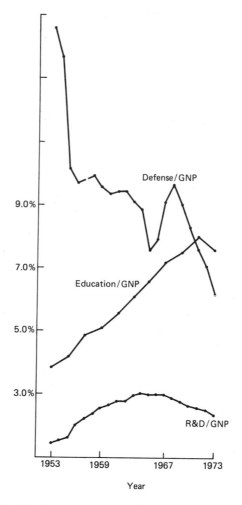

Figure 11. Share of GNP allocated to R&D, education and defense, 1953–1973 (From: U.S. Office of Education, *Digest of Educational Statistics 1974*, Table 172, p. 152; Ibid., Table 27, p. 26; Data for 1955 and 1960–1973 from U.S. Department of Commerce, *Statistical Abstract of the United States 1974*, Table 488, p. 306. Data for all other years calculated from *Statistical Abstract of the United States 1962*, Table 327, p. 248, and U.S. Department of Labor, *Manpower Report of the President* (1974), Table G—3, p. 376.)

began to fall in the late 1960s. Actual R&D spending dropped significantly in deflated dollars in the early 1970s. Similarly, defense spending, which had fluctuated around 9–10% in the 1950s and 1960s, fell to just 6% of GNP in the 1970s. The proportion of GNP devoted to education also rose rapidly in the 1960s and then fell, from 8.0% to 7.6%, between 1971 and 1973, a drop of similar magnitude to the fall in the R&D share of GNP.

On the supply side, there was surprisingly little net increase in the number of new college graduates seeking work during the period of rapid growth in demand. In the 1950s, the number of new college graduates fell somewhat, due to the diminished size of college-age cohorts—the result of falling birthrates some 20 years earlier. In the 1960s, when there were relatively many persons of college age, the enormous growth of graduate education delayed their entrance on the job market, so that the big increase in the supply of new college-trained workers did not occur until the end of the decade. Between 1958 and 1968, for example, despite a sizable increase in the number of male bachelor's graduates, the "net" number seeking work (defined as the number of graduates minus the number of first-year enrollees in graduate and professional schools), relative to the total male civilian work force, *was halved*. The 1960s were a period of declining relative supply of new college workers, not—as is often thought—a period of increasing supply. In the late 1960s and early 1970s, by contrast, the number of new college graduates entering the job market increased greatly, as graduate education became less attractive. Between 1969 and 1972, the *net* number of new college graduates seeking work relative to the total male work force increased threefold. Estimates by Allan Cartter of the ratio of students enrolling in professional and graduate schools for the first time (which differs from the number of first-year enrollees by excluding those who enrolled in previous years but had not completed their first year of study) to recent bachelor's graduates tells a similar though less drastic story. Cartter estimates that about 31% of college graduates went directly to graduate and professional schools in the late 1950s, 41% in the peak year of 1967, and 33% in 1973. On the basis of these figures, which suggest larger increases in the supply of graduates entering the market in the 1960s than the "net" estimates, the number of bachelor's degree recipients entering the job market per worker increased by 1.2% per annum from 1959 to 1967, compared to 7.6% per annum from 1967 to 1973.[11] However measured, it is apparent that the supply of new college graduates did not increase rapidly until the late 1960s and early 1970s, postponing the problem of adjusting to the large freshman classes of the 1960s.

The factors behind the increase in the number of young college graduates can be pursued further. As noted, demographic developments resulting from the post–World War II baby boom played a major role in increasing the number of college enrollments—and ultimately of degrees. Between 1950 and 1970 for example, the population aged 18 to 24 increased by over 9.5 million persons—in percentage terms, by a remarkable 65%. All else the same, this change would have substantially raised the ratio of new graduates to total employment and created problems in the market for new entrants. Since the proportion of the young choosing college is highly variable, however, due to *responsive supply behavior*, demographic changes do not necessarily translate into comparable changes in college enrollments or degrees. During the 1950s, enrollment rose by 1.3 million, despite the constant college-age population, as a result of an increase in the fraction of the young choosing college. During the 1960s, both the college-age population and the proportion of them choosing college grew, with a consequent doubling of enrollments and a gain of 4.3 million persons in college. The relative importance of these two factors in the 1950–1970 growth in the number attending college and in the supply of graduates is examined in Table 6, where changes in enrollments predicted by demographic changes are compared to actual changes. Lines 1 and 3 of the table give the actual changes, Lines 2 and 4 the changes predicted by the changing number of persons of the relevant age. The predicted values are obtained by multiplying the proportion in the age group enrolled or having a degree in 1950 (1960) by the change in population over the decade. Differences between these figures represent (*a*) the effect of supply behavior and (*b*) the interaction of changes in demography and the fraction choosing college. The data tell a clear story.

---

[11] The "net" data are from Freeman, "Overinvestment in College Education?" Table 6; and Cartter, *Ph.D.'s and the Academic Labor Market*. Cartter's figures are deflated by figures on the total labor force from the U.S. Department of Labor, *Manpower Report of the President* (1975), p. 203

Table 6. Demographic and Decision Factors in the Growth of College Enrollments and the College Work Force, Men and Women

	1950–1960 (in thousands)	1960–1970 (in thousands)
1. Actual change in enrollments	1296	4337
2. Change in enrollments predicted by growth of population of college age (assuming proportion enrolled fixed at initial year level)	2	1884
3. Actual change in 25- to 29-year-old college graduates in the labor force	281	862
4. Change predicted by growth of population aged 25 to 29 (assuming proportion with degrees fixed at initial year level)	−39	309

Source: U.S. Office of Education, *Digest of Educational Statistics, 1972*, Table 86, p. 74. U.S. Bureau of Census 1970 Census of Population, *Educational Attainment*, PC(2)-5B, Table 9, p. 74; 1960 Census of Population, *Educational Attainment*, PC(2)-5B, Table 4, p. 54, Table 5, p. 71; and 1950 Census of Population, *Education*, P-E No. 5B, Table 9, p. 74.

In the 1950s, when the number of persons of college age was relatively steady (Line 2) and the number of 25- to 29-year olds was declining (Line 4), essentially none of the growth in enrollments or degrees can be explained by demographic forces. In the 1960s, despite the large increase in the number of the young, only 30% to 40% of the *change* is attributable to demography. Responsive supply behavior—decision factors—are more important than population factors in explaining the growing number of new college graduates on the market.

A SUPPLY–DEMAND ANALYSIS OF THE BUST

The preceding discussion suggests that the collapse of the college job market in the 1970s can be attributed to changes in the supply of and demand for graduates, with supply increasing rapidly and growth of demand leveling off at the turn of the decade. Figure 12 shows the way in which the timing of the shifts in demand and supply interacted to bring about the striking deterioration in conditions in the early 1970s. It graphs an index of the ratio of demand

Figure 12. The deterioration of the demand–supply balance in the male college job market (from calculations in Freeman, "Overinvestment in College Training?" Table 6, Column 5, p. 306).

for college workers to the supply of new male bachelor's graduates. Demand is measured as a fixed-weight index of employment in industries, with the relative number of graduates used as a weight. [12] It captures the changes in demand that result from shifts in the industrial mix of jobs shown in Table 5. Supply is the estimated ratio of new bachelor's and higher-degree recipients seeking work to the male civilian labor force. Because of the distinctive features of supply and demand for female graduates, many of whom do not go on to seek employment, the figure deals solely with men, leaving developments in the female market for Chapter 7. The year 1960 is taken as the base, with an index of demand to supply of 1.00. What stands out is the sharp deterioration in the demand–new entrants balance begin-

---

[12] More precisely, let α_j be the ratio of college to all workers in industry j in a given base year. Then the index is calculated as $\sum_j \alpha_j N_{jt}/I$ where N_{jt} = employment in industry j in year t and I is the base year index. The indices are described more fully in Freeman, "Overinvestment in College Training?"; and Freeman, "Manpower Requirements and the Skill Composition of the U.S. Work Force."

ning in the late 1960s after more than a decade of rough stability. Between 1968 and 1972, the ratio of demand to supply of new graduates fell by 46%, due to the increase in supply and the slackened growth of demand. This change in the demand–supply balance in the college job market at the outset of the 1970s made the market ripe for a turnaround that would greatly depress salaries, job opportunities, and employment, particularly of young graduates—as in fact occurred.

The supply–demand explanation of the market downturn can be examined more rigorously by comparing the actual post–World War II changes in the relative salaries of graduates to those predicted by a supply–demand model focused on the shifts outlined above. The results of such an empirical investigation are summarized in Figure 13, which reveals a close link between predicted and actual

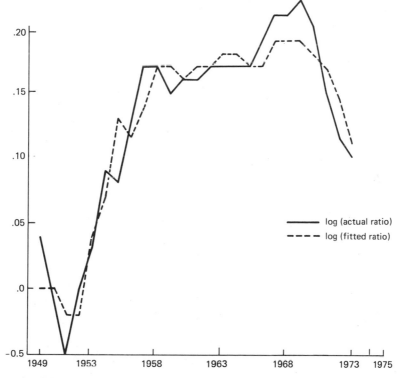

Figure 13. The ratio of college starting salaries to average annual earnings, actual and fitted, 1949–1973 per full-time employee in industry (based on computations in Freeman, "Overinvestment in College Training?").

ratios of college starting salaries to the average annual earnings of full-time workers. While the ratio of college *starting* salaries to annual earnings of *all* workers is by no means the best relative income comparison to make (since it will be affected by changes in age composition of the work force as well as in the position of graduates), the starting salary and annual earnings series are the only available data covering the entire postwar period. Surprising as it may seem, statistics on the starting pay of young high school graduates or of all high school and college graduates, which would provide better comparisons, have not been collected annually on a regular basis. As the evidence in Chapter 1 shows the basic pattern of decline in the 1970s is found in all comparisons; however, the contrast of starting pay to annual earnings probably does not overly distort reality. In any case, the figure shows that the explanation offered as to "why the sixties boom bust" does a good job of accounting for market developments, tracking the drop in relative salaries with reasonable accuracy. While this does not, of course, mean that the analysis will yield good forecasts, it does suggest the value of using it to evaluate future possibilities and to estimate, at least tentatively, the likely length of the depressed college job market.

Finally, it is of some importance to note that one alternative possible explanation of the market downturn—that it resulted from the overall economic recession of the 1970s—can be effectively ruled out. Under normal cyclic patterns, the position of college graduates, even starting workers, improves relative to that of the less educated in recessions and declines in booms. The blue-collar worker loses his job when unemployment rises, not the professional or college graduate—at least in past economic declines. More detailed analysis of the cyclic changes shows that, with the overall state of the economy fixed, the starting salaries of graduates fell relative to average earnings by 3.5% per year from 1970 to 1974 while the income of 25- to 34-year-old college graduates relative to 25- to 34-year-old high school graduates dropped by 3.6% per year.[13] While this does not of course "prove" that the depressed market of the 1970s represents a relatively long-term change in the market, it does support our overall interpretation of changes in terms of fundamental supply and de-

[13] See R. Freeman, "The Decline in the Economic Rewards to College Education," *Review of Economics and Statistics* (forthcoming), Table 5.

mand shifts rather than normal cyclic or temporary peculiar circumstances.

WHAT THE FUTURE MAY BRING

How long will the depression in the college job market last? Forecasts of the future economic situation of college graduates based on the model of the market given above suggest that, while the market is unlikely to return to the booming sixties, the relative economic status of graduates will level off in the near future and improve in the 1980s. On the basis of the type of analysis sketched out in this section, the economic standing of college graduates, barring unforeseen increases in demand, is expected to remain more or less at the depressed level of the mid-1970s until the end of the decade and then to improve moderately, at least for new bachelor's recipients, largely as a result of diminished growth in the number of graduates in response to the depressed market of the 1970s and to declines in the size of college-age cohorts. In the mid-1980s, the fall in the supply of new baccalaureates is expected to create a substantial boom in the market for new college-trained workers, which will level off in the 1990s. Unless there is a sharp increase in demand in the future, however, the boom will not restore the college income premium that existed among the young in the 1960s.

The future economic position of older graduates and of persons with master's and doctoral degrees in academic fields is less sanguine. First, it is unclear whether the improved job market for new graduates foreseen for the 1980s will "spill over" to the classes that obtained degrees in the early and mid-1970s and must compete with the most recent "vintages" of graduates in the 1980s. Lack of detailed studies of the substitutability of older and younger college workers makes it difficult to predict the result of such competition. Second, in the market as a whole, the relative number of college graduates will increase throughout the 1980s, as the number of new degree recipients will exceed the number of college workers retiring from the labor force, maintaining supply pressures for reductions in the economic position of graduates. Whereas young graduates will benefit from declining supplies, their older peers will not. There will be a very large number of college workers who were educated in the previous two decades.

Not until the 1990s is the total number of college-trained male workers relative to the male labor force expected to grow less rapidly, suggesting little improvement for older graduates until then.

As for master's and doctoral graduates seeking academic jobs, the main forces likely to improve the situation among new baccalaureates—declining numbers enrolled in college—will operate to reduce demand for teachers. While reductions in the supply of new Ph.D. and master's graduates should produce a more reasonable supply—demand balance than the catastrophe often given in forecasts that ignore individual responses to market reality, it is difficult to see how the relative economic position of these persons can fail to deteriorate through the rest of the 1970s and much of the 1980s. According to my analysis, the deterioration will come to an end in the late 1980s when college enrollments are likely to rise.

Particular fields and social groups are, it must be stressed, likely to experience quite different job markets in the future, as they have in the past. As will be shown in Chapters 4 through 7 of this book, some areas and groups have done well even in the 1970s and can be expected to do relatively better or worse than the average college graduate in the future, depending on conditions specific to them. Differences between college specialties will produce considerable divergencies in market conditions in the remainder of the 1970s and in the 1980s which are masked by forecasts for all graduates as a whole.

All of the forecasts are, moreover, best viewed as tentative and conditional estimates of likely future developments. They depend on various postulates about economic changes; they neglect many aspects of reality to focus on a few (important, in my analysis) behavioral and economic relations. At best they provide some notion of future possibilities and alert us to particular forces at work. *Caveat emptor.*

Forecasts for Bachelors Graduates

Figure 14 sets out formal forecasts of the relative salaries of male bachelor's graduates, of enrollments in college, and of the college graduate share of the male work force. The forecasts are obtained from the three-equation recursive adjustment model described in detail in Appendix B. In the forecasts it is assumed that

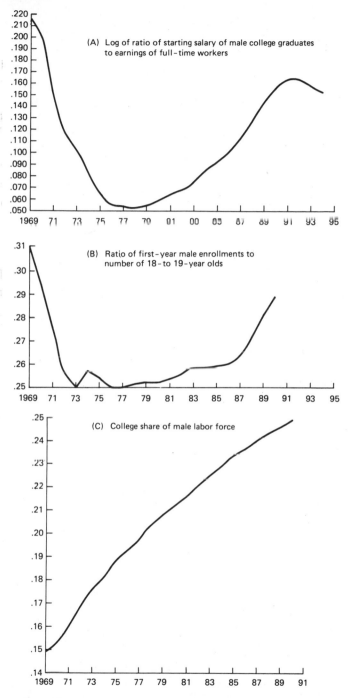

Figure 14. Forecasts of the state of the college job market, 1969–1990.

future economic growth proceeds at post–World War II rates, so that the real earnings of fully employed, year-round workers grows significantly in the future but that the relative demand for new college graduates increases less rapidly than in the past—at the reduced rate of the 1970s, about 0.5% per annum, compared to an overall postwar rate of 1.0% per annum.[14] There are several reasons for favoring the slower demand rate: the education sector is, for demographic reasons, likely to decline in the 1980s; manufacturing industries that employ many graduates cannot be expected to grow at the rates of the 1950s and 1960s; there does not appear to be a major governmental defense or R&D initiative on the horizon. In addition, the larger relative supply of older male college graduates than in the past, including graduates of the 1970s unable to obtain college-level jobs, and likely increase in female graduates seeking work in traditionally male occupations (see Chapter 7) will serve to depress the demand for new bachelors men. If, in fact, demand for graduates increases more rapidly, however, the basic pattern of the forecasts remains much the same: more rapid increases in demand impart a moderate upward trend to the forecasts, yielding a greater improvement in the market than depicted in the figure but one which varies over time in the same manner. Conversely, if the relative demand for graduates is depressed further in the late 1970s and in the 1980s, the upswing is dampened and delayed. Still, as the number of new graduates drops in the 1980s, the market improves.

The timing of the onset of the upswing is only approximate. The forecasts abstract, as long-run projections often do, from business-cycle developments in the economy at large, so that the 1980s improvement could be displaced 1 or 2 years by the timing of recessions or booms. Continued weakness in the job market for non-college workers through the late 1970s due to weak recovery from the mid-1970s recession would, for example, improve the position of college graduates relative to other workers (who tend to be more affected by economy-wide ups and downs) and raise college enrollments through the end of the decade. When the overall rate of

---

[14] These figures are based on the fixed-weight index of demand described in Footnote 12 and in greater detail in Appendix B. Note that the index measures demand for all male college graduates and thus is likely to overstate the net demand for new bachelors men when the supply of complementary graduates (women or recent baccalaureates lacking college level jobs) is larger than in the past.

unemployment begins to fall, however, the relative position of the college-trained would decline, leading to reductions in the proportion enrolled, a decline in the number of new graduates 4 to 5 years later, and an ensuing upswing along the lines sketched out above.

Panel A of Figure 14 displays the forecasted pattern of change in the ratio of the starting salaries of college men to average annual earnings. It shows a continued modest drop in the relative income of graduates until 1979–1980, when the premium for new male bac-calaureates begins a decadal increase, though one that does not restore the pre-1970s premium of over 20%. The improvement in the market is especially large at the end of the decade due to the sizeable fall in new bachelor's graduates in that period. Panel B gives the anticipated fraction of 18- to 19-year-old men enrolled as freshmen; because of the need to link initial enrollments to degrees, the numerator in Figure 14 is the number of first-year, degree-credit men, not—as in Figure 9—the number of 18- to 19-year olds in college. According to forecasts, the propensity to enroll bottoms out in the late 1970s and then increases through the 1980s. Relatively many young persons in the demographically small cohorts of the 1980s are expected to go on to college, providing a buffer to the demographic swings. Panel C provides estimates of the impact of the changing number of new bachelor's degree recipients and the retirement of older graduates at age 65 on the college share of the total work force. These estimates are obtained by assuming that all men aged 55 to 64 in 1974 will retire in the 1974–1984 decade, while those aged 45 to 54 will retire in the succeeding decade, and that all young men will enter the labor force.[15] What is important here is that the college

[15] More precisely, I used data from U.S. Bureau of the Census, "Educational Attainment," *Current Population Reports*, Series P-20, No. 272, Table 1, p. 15 to calculate the number of men 23- to 64-years old and proportion with 4 or more years of college in 1974. I subtracted the number of those 65-years old and over and added the number of those 22- to 24-years old to the reported numbers of those 25-years old and over. This yielded an estimate of 50,697,000 men 22- to 64-years old in 1974 and 9,251,000 college men. Comparable figures for earlier years were tabulated from relevant volumes of "Educational Attainment." To forecast future population, I subtracted away one-tenth the number of those 55- to 64-years old each year from 1975 to 1985 and one-tenth the number of those 45- to 64-years old, from 1985 to 1990 on the assumption that an even proportion of these age groups retired each year; then I added the number of persons turning 22-years old, using data from Series P-20 No. 272, and from U.S. Bureau of the Census 1970 Census of Population, *United States Summary*, Table 50, p. 265. The former volume reports numbers in 2-year groupings; they were divided in half to obtain the estimated number of those

share of the male work force continues to grow into the late 1980s, so that supply pressures for further deterioration in the economic position of graduates persist throughout the period. As a result, the economic position of older graduates, especially those who were in the large college cohorts of the 1970s, is unlikely to improve much in the next decade.

Alternative assumptions about the pattern of demand, retirement, cyclic conditions, and the like will yield—as noted earlier—somewhat different results, particularly with regard to the timing of changes. The general story, however, is clear: Barring marked changes in the demand for graduates, overeducation in the job market will be a problem for the next decade or so, though the extent of the problem will vary over time and among graduates. The decline of 1969 to 1975 will slacken in the late 1970s; the market for new graduates will improve in the 1980s, especially in the latter half of the decade, though not by enough to restore the economic rewards of college training of the booming 1960s. The position of older graduates may, however, deteriorate even in the 1980s. All told, the United States is moving from a world in which higher education is a highly profitable endeavor offering great payoffs even with sizeable increases in the supply of graduates to one in which higher education is a more marginal investment for individuals and society.

PROVISOS

Forecasts of the type given in this book must be treated cautiously, for several reasons. First, even within the confines of the analytic framework employed, various simplifications have been assayed, in part to focus on what appear to be the critical forces at work and in part because of problems with data availability. Second,

---

22-years old; the latter contain figures by single year of age. The future number of college graduates was obtained by first multiplying the number of those 22-years old in a year by the proportion expected to enroll 4 years earlier from the model in Appendix A. Since the regression equation relates enrollment to persons 18 and 19 years of age, I multiplied the proportion by two, on the crude assumption that the two age groups have about the same distribution and enrollment probabilities. Finally, I multiplied the figure by .575, the proportion of men 25-years old and over with some college training in 1974 who actually graduated, according to Series P-20, No. 272, Table 1, p. 15.

the track record of economists in forecasting even a few months into the future is notoriously poor, as the failure to predict the dimensions of the inflation and unemployment of the 1970s makes clear. With respect to college-trained workers, in 1949 Seymour Harris (then at Harvard) wrote a book predicting that the post–World War II period would be one of market glut. "A large proportion of the potential college students within the next 20 years are doomed to disappointment after graduating as the number of correlated openings (in professional jobs) will be substantially less than the numbers seeking them." Harris's expectations were falsified by the large increase in demand for graduates in the 1950s and 1960s, due, according to my analysis, to the shift in the composition of industrial employment, the spurt in R&D spending, and demographic changes that led to the expansion of the education sector.[16] Similarly, prior to the market turnaround in the 1970s, human capital economists were concerned with reasons for the stability in the ratios of the incomes of educated to less-educated workers and sought relatively long-term or permanent rather than temporary reasons for the pattern. Third, because government programs, particularly R&D and defense, tend to employ relatively many college graduates, significant changes in governmental policies could substantially alter the demand for graduates and thus the forecasted values even if the basic model is reasonably valid. A major increase in defense, R&D, or related college-manpower-intensive activities would greatly reduce the problem of "overeducation" in the job market and bring a much stronger upswing than I foresee in the 1980s.

Provisos and equivocation notwithstanding, the analysis in this book suggests that the college job market will remain in a relatively depressed state through the end of the 1970s, experience a moderate improvement in the following decade, but not return to the boom conditions of the late 1960s.

[16] Seymour Harris, *The Market for College Graduates* (Cambridge, Mass.: Harvard University Press, 1949). Harris also predicted that "it may frequently not pay to be educated" (p. 17), that "severe excesses of graduates would develop by 1968" (p. 19), and so forth. Clearly it is easy to be wrong in forecasting. On the other hand, however, Allan Cartter's 1964 analysis of the faculty job market has proved remarkably prescient. Not all economic forecasts look ridiculous 10 or 20 years later.

End of the Golden Age for Teachers and Researchers

O ne of the basic characteristics of the booming post–World War II market for college graduates was the ascendency of education and research-oriented occupations over business occupations and traditional independent professions. In the late 1950s and early 1960s the United States was intensely concerned with shortages of and needs for teachers and researchers, particularly in light of Soviet technological successes. There was a substantial boost in expenditures for space and military R&D. National investment in education at all levels increased greatly, with the result that the job market for elementary and high school teachers, Ph.D.'s, and research personnel boomed. Students were encouraged by high salaries and good job opportunities to enter the academic fields. The brightest sought academic degrees and careers. Relatively few expressed interest, and many disdain, for studies and work in the economic sphere, producing goods. To Galbraith, among others, it seemed as if the "scientific estate" was on the verge of achieving great power, which might be fruitfully used to institute Galbraithian socioeconomic changes.

The new depression in the college job market in the 1970s reversed this ordering. In the falling market, the economic situation of academic and research professions was exceptionally distressed, bringing to an end the "golden age" of rising salaries, job opportunities, and national concern. In business, law, medicine, and engineering, on the other hand, the downturn was sufficiently limited to restore their relative attractiveness. The "natural" decision for the top social science baccalaureates of the 1970s was to seek legal or business careers, not jobs as academic social scientists. The "natural" decision for science students was to apply for medical school, not for doctoral programs in the sciences.

In this chapter and the next one, this important reversal in the job market and its potential significance for the future are analyzed. The present chapter focuses on the end of the golden age for academic professions. Chapter 5 considers the changing fortunes of the business-oriented professions.

The transposed relative positions of the academic and business fields tell an important story about manpower adjustments to economic change, the operation of the free labor market as an allocative mechanism, and the dangers of extrapolating recent trends into the future. It shows that the college job market is a flexible and sensitive device for altering the flow of young persons to different fields, though one subject to cobweb lags and consequent supply–demand imbalances.

WHAT HAPPENED TO THE TEACHER SHORTAGE?

The turnaround in schoolteaching deserves particular attention because of the large number of college graduates involved; in 1970 there were over 2.75 million schoolteachers. Fifty percent of female and 9% of male college graduates worked as teachers.[1]

The great teacher shortage of the 1950s and early 1960s became the great surplus of the 1970s because families decided to have fewer children in the interim years, reducing the growth of demand, while supply grew rapidly in response to the previous shortages.

Figure 15 depicts the change in the number of children in school. It shows that after increasing rapidly from the early to the mid-1960s, enrollments began to drop at the outset of the 1970s, first at the elementary level, reducing the rate of growth and even-

[1] The number of teachers is reported in U.S. Bureau of the Census 1970 Census of Population, *Occupational Characteristics*, PC(2)-7A Table 1, p. 2; fraction of graduates working as teachers from Table 5, pp. 59–60, 73–74.

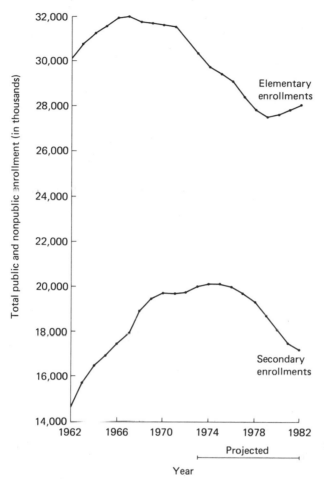

Figure 15. Enrollment in regular day schools (from U.S. Office of Education, *Projection of Educational Statistics, 1973*, Table 4, p. 33).

tually the numbers employed as elementary schoolteachers, and later at the secondary level. The demographic estimates show that at least through the early 1980s, school enrollments and, therefore, demand will continue to fall, promising a long, hard road for teaching. With the weakened demand, the percentage of GNP devoted to elementary and secondary education dropped from 8% in 1970 to 7.6% in 1972, after decades of substantial growth, and the number of teachers began to level off. Between the fall of 1973 and the fall of 1974, the total number of teachers was virtually unchanged; but the number in elementary schools fell by 0.8%.[2]

The conjunction of declining demand for and increasing supply of new teaching graduates brought about a rapid and disastrous shift in the market, from shortage to surplus. In 1967, nineteen states reported to the National Education Association (NEA) that they had a substantial shortage of applicants for teaching jobs, and 14 some shortage; none had an excess of applicants. Through 1969, the situation altered, with more and more states reporting excesses, and fewer shortages, until by 1973 no states reported general shortages, and 19 had substantial and 6 some excess of applicants—the virtual reverse image of the market 6 years earlier (see Table 7).

The number of teaching jobs unfilled in the summer preceding an academic year provides another indicator of supply and demand changes. Because schools contract for teachers in the spring, a large number of vacancies in July and August is indicative of a surplus of jobs, that is, a tight job market, while few vacancies reflect a shortage. Between 1964 and 1973, the number of unfilled positions reported to the NEA dropped by about 80% from nearly 8000 to less than 900.[3]

For young graduates, the change from shortage to surplus meant a fall in the number of new jobs available per education graduate. In a tight market, the number of persons newly hired as teachers is large relative to new education graduates, often exceeding unity (since schools hire many experienced personnel or persons not majoring in education). Contrarily, in a loose market, the number of newly hired teachers is below the number of new graduates. As the ratios in Figure 16 make clear, jobs per graduate declined rapidly in the late 1960s. Between 1969 and 1973, new jobs per person ready to teach dropped by 27% at the elementary level, to a level below unity. At the secondary school level, where more graduates traditionally seek employment elsewhere, the ratio dropped by 38%, until by 1973 there were twice as many graduates as newly hired teachers.

In the depressed teacher market of the 1970s, those who could not find a teaching job had to "make do" with other positions.

---

[2] U.S. Office of Education, *Digest of Education Statistics 1974*, Table 27, p. 26, for share of GNP; Table 11, p. 11, for numbers of teachers.

[3] *Teacher Supply and Demand in Public Schools, 1973* (Washington, D.C.: National Education Association).

Table 7. The Switch from Shortage to Surplus of Teachers, as Reported by State Departments of Education, 1967–1973

General condition of teacher supply and demand	Number of states reporting condition as of fall						
	1967	1968	1969	1970	1971	1972	1973
Substantial shortage of applicants	19	5	2	0	0	0	0
Some shortage of applicants	14	17	12	2	0	1	0
Shortage of applicants in some subject areas and excess in others	11	19	32	35	24	20	24
Sufficient applicants to fill positions	1	1	1	7	0	2	1
Some excess of applicants	0	0	2	1	11	9	6
Substantial excess of applicants	0	0	0	4	13	15	19

Source: Adapted from *Teacher Supply and Demand in Public Schools, 1973* (Washington, D.C.: National Education Association), Table 18, p. 34.

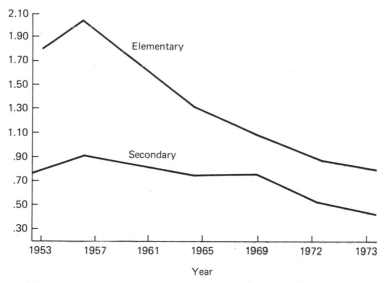

Figure 16. New teachers hired per 100 education graduates in selected states, 1953–1973 (from *Teacher Supply and Demand in Public Schools, 1973*, Table 13, p. 28).

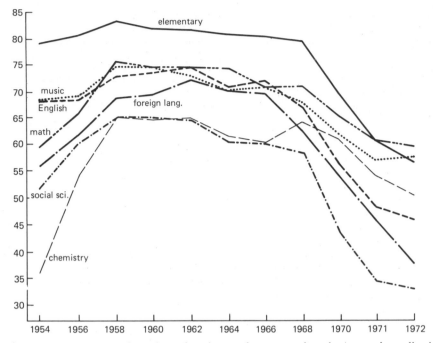

Figure 17. Percentages of teacher education graduates entering classrooms immediately following graduation, 1954–1972, by subject areas (from National Education Association, *Teacher Supply and Demand in Public Schools, 1973,* Table 8, p. 16).

Newspapers and magazines were replete with examples of the disappointment.[4]

> I have absolutely no prospects for a job. I'll keep searching for at least a year. If I can't find anything after that I'll have to sit down and reconsider. [an English education major from the University of Rhode Island]
> My mother always told me to go into education. I'm resentful, bitter, and bored about the wasted years in college. [an education major from the State University of New York at Stonybrook, who was unable to find a job 1 year after graduation]

The problem of finding a teaching job in the depressed market is illustrated in Figure 17, which depicts the percentage of education graduates obtaining jobs as classroom teachers upon graduation. The figure shows a precipitous drop in the probability of landing a teaching job in the early 1970s, following a gradual decline in the

[4] These stories are from *The New York Times*, 16 June 1974, p. 16.

early and mid-1960s. Between 1968 and 1972, the percentage of elementary education majors obtaining positions plummeted from 79% to 57%, while the proportion of secondary school education majors obtaining teaching jobs dropped below 50%. In some specialties, such as languages, English, and social studies, only one-third or so of graduates were able to obtain jobs; in others, the situation was less bleak but still much worse than in previous years.

For experienced teachers, the depressed market meant declines in salaries and possible layoffs with little chance of obtaining another teaching position. Salaries of teachers dropped in real terms by 2.5% from 1970–1971 to 1973–1974, after having risen in the preceding decade. Much to the chagrin of teachers' organizations, the NEA, and the American Federation of Teachers (AFT), the income of teachers, which had grown relative to that of other wage and salary workers during the golden age, declined relatively in the 1970s. In 1970–1971 teachers earned 27% more than the average full-time employee in the economy, up from a bare 3% advantage in 1949; by 1974, the relative advantage of teacher salaries had fallen to 12%. In 1969, year-round, full-time female teachers earned 45% more than the average full-time female worker; in 1973, 37% more. While not all of the relative gains of the 1950s and 1960s had eroded by the mid-1970s, the direction and magnitude of change promised a swift restoration of pre–golden age differentials.[5]

Layoffs became widespread in the mid-1970s, not only because of declining enrollments and demand but also as a result of fiscal problems in cities and states. In academic year 1974, Michigan reported that 6000 teachers had been laid off; in some cities, teachers struck to limit layoffs; Orange County, Florida, laid off 250 teachers, and so forth. The AFT monthly journal was replete with stories in early 1975 of potential and actual "pink slips" being given

[5]The average salary of a public teacher in 1970–1971 was $9269; in 1973–1974 it was $10,673. I deflated by the average Consumer Price Index (CPI) for 1970 and 1971, and for 1973 and 1974, respectively. Salaries from Office of Education, *Digest of Education Statistics 1974*, Table 56, p. 49. CPI from *Monthly Labor Review* (April 1975), p. 109. Relative earnings calculated by dividing by earnings of full-time workers, as reported in U.S. Department of Commerce, *National Income and Product Accounts of the U.S., 1929–1965*, Table 6.5, pp. 108–109 and in U.S. Department of Commerce, *Survey of Current Business* (July 1974). I averaged earnings for 2 calendar years to compare with teacher salaries given on an academic year basis. The figures for female workers are from U.S. Bureau of the Census, *Current Population Reports*, Series P-60, No. 75, Table 49, p. 112; and No. 97, Table 64, p. 139.

to teachers throughout the United States, reporting in April that 100,000 to 150,000 teachers faced layoffs in fall 1975.[6] While the union may have been exaggerating the situation for political purposes, the fact that the job market for teachers was approaching unprecedented imbalance is clear.

What about the Unions?

Teaching is the sole major profession that is heavily unionized and covered by collective negotiations. In 1974, the AFT had over 444,000 members, largely in big cities like New York, Detroit, and New Orleans; the NEA, once a relatively conservative professional society, represented some 1.7 million teachers in collective negotiations, and in many areas acted much like its rival, with strikes, demonstrations, and other militant activities.

Surprisingly, perhaps, the fact that teachers are organized apparently has little effect on their salaries. Numerous studies comparing union and nonunion teachers show the salaries of the former to be only modestly (about 5%) higher than those of the latter, other factors held fixed. By contrast, large industrial and construction unions appear to raise the wage of their members by 15% to 25%. Other aspects of the conditions of work, ranging from class size to authority relations, may of course be greatly affected by the teachers' union. Consistent with studies of the teachers' union, the rate of change of teachers' salaries in states with collective negotiations and in those without was roughly the same (37% versus 34%) during the period of market worsening.[7] The large supply of new graduates seeking work, and the availability of older experienced teachers relative to demand, favored school boards in negotiations, forcing

[6] American Federation of Teachers, *The American Teacher* (April 1975), p. 3. Throughout 1975 the AFT journal reported a bleak picture of the teacher job market. *Time* (5 July 1975), p. 28, describes the layoff of teachers.

[7] The studies of the impact of collective bargaining on teachers are summarized in D. Frey, "Wage Determinants in Public Schools and the Effects of Unionization," in *Labor in the Public and Nonprofit Sectors*, ed. D. Hammermesh (Princeton, N.J.: Princeton University Press, 1974). Most studies find an effect of 5% or less. The data for period when the market weakened refer to 1966–1971. They are from T. Brown, "Have Collective Negotiations Raised Teachers Salaries? A Comparison of Teachers' Salaries in States with and without Collective Bargaining Laws for Public School Personnel, 1961–1971," *Journal of Collective Negotiations in the Public Sector* (1975), Vol. 4, No. 1, pp. 53–65.

teachers' unions to accept overall increases below the rate of inflation. In New England in 1975, for example, teachers who had held
out for 9% to 10% increases in the late 1960s were realistically
agreeing to 3% to 4% increases, despite the higher rate of inflation.
"Teachers don't like that," the executive secretary of the Massachusetts Federation of Teachers was quoted as stating, "But they like
being laid off even worse." Not even the militant AFT could reverse
the impact of a major supply–demand imbalance on the marketplace.[8]

Some Consequences of the Teacher Surplus

The change in the teaching market, from shortage to surplus,
has meant continued increases in the teacher–pupil ratio and in the
academic qualifications of teachers, maintaining post–World War II
trends. In 1962 there were 28.5 pupils per teacher, in 1974 there
were 23.8, a decline due in part to the lower real cost of teachers and
the increase in their availability. Over the longer run the proportion
of elementary school teachers holding master's degrees rose from
13% (1955–1956) to 18% (1965–1966) to 25% (1972–1973), while
the fraction lacking bachelor's degrees fell from 22% to practically
zero.[9]

On the supply side, the number of young persons preparing to
teach began falling in response to the declining job market. As was
shown in Table 2, the proportion of first-year students looking for
teaching careers dropped from 11% to 4% among men and from 34%
to 12% among women. With graduates facing reduced chances for
jobs, some major universities began accepting fewer applicants in
teaching programs in the mid-1970s. The University of California at
Los Angeles cut its total of education students from 600 to 300. The
University of Washington's School of Education graduated 850 students in 1974 compared to 1300 four years earlier. Between 1972
and 1973 the number of new bachelor's and master's degree recipients prepared to teach declined by 30% in Minnesota, by 12% in

[8] *Time* (7 July 1975), p. 30.
[9] National Education Association, *Teacher Supply and Demand in Public Schools*,
1973.

Oregon, by 37% in Washington, and by 4.2% in the nation as a whole.[10]

As for the future, the market situation is likely to remain grim for at least a decade. Even with rapid declines in the number of education graduates, the continued fall in demand and the large supply of experienced teaching personnel can be expected to produce a weak job market. In the mid-1980s, when the demographic drop in the number of school-age children comes to an end, the market will rebound, the extent of the rebound dependent on the degree to which supply has diminished in the interim. If birthrates fall in the late 1970s and early 1980s, however, the depression in the teacher market can be expected to persist even longer. Paradoxically, the forces that reduce birthrates and "free" women from household chores will also reduce demand for them in what has traditionally been the most important occupation for college-trained women.

... AND THE NEED FOR COLLEGE FACULTY?

While demographic facts did not operate against higher education in the 1970s, the economic situation of college faculty underwent a slump similar to that for schoolteachers.

In the college and university market:[11]

• Expenditures for higher education, which had nearly tripled in the previous boom, leveled off in real terms in the early 1970s. As a share of GNP, higher education jumped from 0.9% in 1950 to 2.7% in 1970 and then stabilized.

[10] The figures for the University of California at Los Angeles and for the University of Washington are from *The New York Times* (16 June 1974), p. 16; those for the other states are from National Education Association, *Teacher Supply and Demand.*

[11] The data in this paragraph are from the following sources: share of GNP to higher education obtained by dividing current final income from U.S. Office of Education, *Digest of Educational Statistics, 1974* by GNP in the same volume, Tables 125, p. 110 and Table 27, p. 26; enrollment data from Table 87, p. 75; academic employment figures from Table 100, p. 85; professors' salaries from American Association of University Professors, *Annual Reports on the Status of the Professors*; (Summer 1974), Table 3, p. 174; (Summer 1970), Table 8, p. 126; and (Summer 1961). Calendar year annual earnings of full-time workers from U.S. Department of Commerce, *National Income Statistics Survey of Current Business* (July editions) averaged for comparability with academic year salaries of professors (for this reason the statistics differ moderately from those in R. Freeman, "Demand for Labor in a Nonprofit Market: University Faculty," in *Labor in the Public and Nonprofit Sectors*, ed. D. Hammermesh (Princeton, N.J.: Princeton University Press, 1975), pp. 85–129.

• The rate of growth of enrollments in colleges and universities decelerated from nearly 9% per annum in the booming 1960s to just 3% in the 1970s.

• Academic employment, which had doubled in the 1960s, grew slowly in the early 1970s, barely increasing from 1973 to 1974.

• The real salaries of professors dropped in the depressed market; the ratio of professors' salaries to average annual earnings, which had risen from 2.02 to 2.37 in the 1960s, falling to 2.18 by 1974.

The decline in the academic marketplace was especially severe, despite the continued growth of enrollments, because of the operation of the accelerator adjustment process described in Chapter 3. By this process, reductions in the growth of enrollments have *amplified* effects on demand for *new* faculty. With approximately 480,000 faculty in 1970 and an outflow due to retirement, mobility, and the like producing a replacement demand of perhaps 3% per year (approximately 15,000 positions), a deceleration in the growth of enrollment from 10% to 3% per year, as occurred between the 1960s and 1970s, would (with fixed faculty and student ratios) reduce demand for new faculty from 63,000 to just 29,000—a *70%* drop! Like highly leveraged stocks, academics experience far greater fluctuations in demand than does the "final product" that they produce.

The dwindling of demand in academia coupled with large supplies of doctoral degree recipients to produce the worst job market for Ph.D.'s in American academic history. As Table 8 shows, an extraordinary number of new doctorates in the mid-1970s—26% of the class of 1974—were in the undesirable position of seeking appointments but having "no specific prospects" upon receipt of their degree, according to the annual survey by the National Academy of Sciences—National Research Council. By contrast, 6 years earlier, only 6% had sought but not found specific employment upon graduation. In one of the hardest hit specialties, English, over one-third of Ph.D.'s had not found jobs at the time of the survey in 1974 compared to just 8% in 1959. The National Board of Graduate Education reported that in English:[12]

---

[12] D. Breneman, *Graduate School Adjustments to the "New Depression" in Higher Education* (Washington, D.C.: National Board of Graduate Education, Feb. 1975), Technical Report No. 3, pp. 61–62.

Table 8. Percentage of Ph.D.'s Seeking Appointments but Having No Specific Job Prospects upon Receipt of Degree, Selected Disciplines

Discipline	1968	1974
All	6	26
Economics	3	16
Engineering	7	26
English	4	36
Psychology	6	26
Biological Sciences	–	28
Physical Sciences	–	25
Chemistry	5	22

Source: Data for 1974 from National Research Council, *Summary Report of 1974 Doctorates*; data for "all" 1968 from H.S. Astin "Career Profiles of Women Doctorates," in *Academic Women on the Move*, A. Rossi and A. Calderwood (eds.), p. 158; other data for 1968 from D. Breneman, *Graduate School Adjustment to the 'New Depression' in Higher Education*, (1975), Technical Report No. 3, Table 30, p. 46, with electrical engineering used for *all* engineers.

• An English department at a well-rated public university with 40 candidates in the market had placed 12.

• A highly rated department at a private university had placed 7 out of 21 of its current graduates. The department was assisting over 60 individuals in job search, including former students who had not received tenure on the first job, and had placed only 15.

• A highly rated private department with 35 students seeking jobs had placed 13; of the 18 white males seeking positions, only 3 had been placed.

• A highly rated public department with 50 graduates on the market had placed only 11, and several of these were 1-year, terminal appointments.

Similarly, according to the Modern Language Association, no more than one-half of Ph.D.'s and master's degree graduates in that field have "any realistic present expectations of an academic job in 1974–1975."

The situation in most other disciplines was somewhat less disastrous, though still bad. In the physical sciences, an increasing number accepted postdoctoral fellowships, largely as a means of getting a job, albeit low paid. Academic institutions were able to obtain persons as "postdocs" rather than as assistant professors, saving upward of one-third of their salaries. In 1967, 23% of physics and astronomy students obtained postdoctoral positions, choosing them largely for educational and research purposes; in 1974, 34% had such positions, while an additional 13% sought them, impelled by the lack of academic jobs. In chemistry the situation was similar, with nearly one-half of the graduates of 1974 on the postdoctoral track.[13]

Because academics are greatly concerned with the academic quality of institutions and staff, the types of academic institutions at which Ph.D.'s find jobs and, conversely, the types of Ph.D. recipients hired by various institutions is an important component of adjustment in the faculty job market. Graduates desire jobs in prestigious high quality departments, universities want to employ Ph.D.'s from the top schools, and students prefer to study where quality is highest. Traditionally, the most able of the young faculty spend several years in the major research institutions, where they contribute to large research projects and "invest" in knowledge that benefits their future, then move on to teach in colleges and universities of lesser prestige. The depressed market distorted this pattern. Many of the best new Ph.D.'s ended up in the less highly rated schools, where they displaced Ph.D.'s from less prestigious institutions, who in turn dropped another rung in the academic hierarchy, displacing master's graduates and those with "all but the dissertation." Between 1967 and 1973, the proportion of new Ph.D.'s in colleges and universities rated I or II in the Cartter ranking was halved, while the proportion obtaining work in the four-year colleges grew from about one-third to over one-half. Among male Ph.D.'s, the proportion working in two-year colleges or in elementary and secondary schools shot up from 3.3% to 9.6%. As a result, faculty quality at the less highly rated schools improved, at the cost of lowering the prestige and value of academia to new Ph.D.'s.[14]

Institutional Rigidities

There are two important institutional features of academia that shape the operation of the job market and the adjustment to depressed conditions.

[13] Data from *Doctorate Recipients from United States Universities,* Summary Reports (Washington, D.C.: National Academy of Sciences) 1967, p. 6; 1974, p. 14.

[14] A. Cartter and W. Ruhter, *The Disappearance of Sex Discrimination in First Job Placement of New Ph.D.s* (University of California at Los Angeles, Higher Education Research Institute, 1975), Table 5, p. 12.

First is tenure, which guarantees lifetime employment, save in exceptional circumstances. Tenure is the chief institution whereby professors control the power to appoint new academicians and, claims of safeguarding academic freedom notwithstanding, is best thought of as a device to protect older faculty from competition by the young. It is essential to controlling jobs because, without tenure, faculty would have great difficulty in making appointments, with each new professor being viewed as a voter who would decide one's own future and as a potential replacement—a situation likely to produce extreme politicking, even beyond that currently practiced in academic appointments.

Tenure makes the age structure of faculty and the rate of expansion of academic employment critical features of the market. During periods of contraction, it becomes a serious fetter in the academic system, maintaining the position of older faculty regardless of competence and limiting the ability of universities to adjust offerings to changing student needs. In contracting markets, colleges and universities fire young faculty—some of whom are undoubtedly more qualified or in fields of great demand—to preserve tenure commitments. When contraction follows a rapid expansion like that of the 1960s, in which many less able Ph.D.'s were promoted, the problems of adjustment are exacerbated due to the relatively young age of the tenured and lack of replacement demand for retiring tenured faculty. The result is "a Balzacian society where if you want to be a professor, you wait until the man who is professor dies. Then the 15 of you who want the job compete in various ways. One of you gets it."[15]

The impact of the slumping faculty market on employment of young versus older personnel is examined in Figure 18. The figure shows that in the contraction of the 1969–1973 period the proportion of faculty who were 30-years old or less fell, while the proportion tenured rose. Among the faculty as a whole, 16% were below 30-years old in 1968–1969 compared to just 7% in 1972–1973. In the former year, 47% were tenured; in the latter, 65%. Among fields, the increase in the proportion tenured rose especially rapidly in engineering, mathematics, the physical sciences, the humanities, and

[15] D. P. Moynihan, "Peace—Some Thoughts on the 1960s and 1970s," *Public Interest*, 32 (Summer), pp. 3–12.

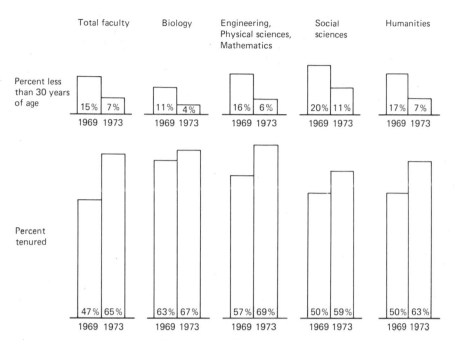

Figure 18. Aging of faculty, 1968–1969 to 1972–1973 (from A. Cartter, "The Changing Composition of College Faculties 1970 to 1990" [Paper delivered at MIT Symposium on Professional Labor Market Problems, May 1975], Tables 1 and 2).

The data used by Cartter are taken from American Council on Education surveys. Due to changes in methods of sampling, there is some bias in the data toward showing fewer persons under 30 in 1973 than in 1969. The bias results from using lists of faculty from 1972 for much of the 1973 survey. Despite this problem, however, it is generally agreed that the overall picture in the data is correct. See American Council on Education, "Teaching Faculty in Academia: 1972–3" *ACE Research Reports* (1973), Vol. 8, No. 2, pp. 3–4, 13.

least in the biological sciences. The aging of faculty and reduced opportunities for young scholars will be one of the major problems in higher education in the decades of the 1970s and 1980s. Already the fact that in many colleges the assistant professors are better trained and better teachers than many senior professors is producing serious grievances. How often it leads the tenured to think that they don't "deserve" to be where they are is another question.[16]

A second, less widely publicized feature of the academic market that also affects the adjustment process is the desire of institutions for an "equitable" salary structure—one that awards faculty of similar rank, experience, and scholarly prowess, but different spe-

[16] David Riesman has raised this issue with me (personal communication).

cialization—the same pay, regardless of market conditions.[17] As a compensation committee at Dartmouth College stated in 1973, "Since institutions constitute essential communities of scholars, there is a general feeling of what may be termed academic equity— that differences of compensation among faculty members of equal experience and standing within their own special fields should be as small as is consistent with maintenance of high quality faculty in each department." NEA surveys show that nearly all institutions have explicit faculty salary schedules, providing for minimum—maximum or average pay, based on merit, rank, and experience, and *applying equally across fields.*

In essence, universities affirm an intellectual value structure that accords little or no inherent superiority to knowledge in particular fields, regardless of market valuations. Faculty are judged by their intellectual quality and scholarly output, with differences in the market price of output (which is substantial between, say, economics and French literature) ignored as much as possible in determining wages. Underlying the rejection of market price is the realization that knowledge has distinctive characteristics that cannot be readily evaluated in a competitive market and the tendency for administrations and faculty committees to come from a wide range of disciplines, making unequal treatment of fields difficult. Only when faculties are divided by schools, as among law, business, medicine, and arts and sciences, is the pressure for wage equity across disciplines likely to be attenuated.

The desire for interfield equity exacts a price from the higher educational system. It requires reliance on expensive nonmonetary remuneration schemes, such as the provision of supporting facilities, altered hiring standards, and the like, to differentiate among fields in greater or lesser demand. It leads to surpluses of candidates in specialties in which nonacademic employment opportunities are slight and shortages in those with a strong nonacademic market. It greatly reduces the responsiveness of the market in alleviating supply—demand imbalances. This does not, of course, mean that colleges and universities should abandon the desire for equitable wages in troubled times, but rather, that they must weigh the equity goal against other goals in allocating resource funds.

[17] This analysis follows Freeman, "Demand for Labor: University Faculty."

Unionization of college faculty, which grew rapidly in the 1960s and early 1970s, is likely to strengthen tenure and "equitable" wage structures, further rigidifying the market. Since unions represent existing employees, they will seek to guard the position of current faculty at the expense of new job seekers. Part-time teachers, instructors, and other nontenured personnel are likely to suffer losses of jobs, as appointment and promotion policies become more formal. Faculty unionism is too new a phenomenon, however, to permit evaluation of its quantitative impact. If unionization in higher education has effects similar to those in the elementary and secondary teaching markets, it is unlikely to be a major determinant of the position of college faculty.

Affirmative Action

Few places of employment have been as dominated by white men in years past as academia. Outstanding black scholars like W.E.B. DuBois, Charles Johnson, and Horace Mann Bond (father of Georgia legislator Julian Bond) never obtained jobs at major research institutions. In 1945 less than 2% of black Ph.D.'s held academic jobs outside Southern Negro colleges. While about 20% of current faculties are women, female academicians have long been concentrated in lower-ranking jobs in the less prestigious colleges and universities.

A substantial effort to alter this traditional discriminatory pattern was instituted in the late 1960s. Students and various social groups pressed for black faculty appointments in primarily white institutions. In 1973, one-third of the faculty believed that preferential treatment should be given to minorities to break down all-white staffs. Perhaps more importantly, federal pressures for affirmative action [begun in 1968 under Revised Order No. 4 of Executive Order 11246 (1965)] required institutions with federal contracts to "develop and maintain a written affirmative action program," which is submitted to the Higher Education Division of the Office of Civil Rights of the Department of Health, Education, and Welfare (HEW) for approval. Failure to produce an acceptable plan carries the potential penalty that federal contracts will be blocked by HEW. By requiring detailed, written plans and numerical goals, federal policy produced a major change in university personnel policies, with the consequence of increasing demand for minority faculty, at the expense of white men.

The equal opportunity pressures appear to have been quite effective in improving the market position of black faculty. Between 1969 and 1973 the proportion of black college teachers employed in primarily white schools doubled; the academic salaries of blacks came to equal or, in some cases, exceed those of whites; in many universities the average black appointee had fewer publications than comparable whites (of the same age, field, etc.,) suggesting some alteration in hiring standards. It is no secret that college and university hiring decisions were "tilted" in favor of blacks in the 1970s, after decades of tilting against them. This does not, however, mean that overall academic quality was being diluted, for institutions may very well have been selecting black faculty with about the same qualifications as "marginal" whites who might otherwise have been hired.[18]

As for women, improvements in their position in academia appear to have occurred more slowly. In 1973 it was still true that female faculty had lower rank and salaries than their male peers, though the gap was diminishing. A 1975 study by the UCLA Higher Education Research Institute found that sex discrimination among new Ph.D.'s had disappeared in first job placements, with women Ph.D.'s getting jobs as good as those obtained by men.[19]

The market decline will create substantial problems for the future success of affirmative action. On the one hand, it will be difficult to meet affirmative action goals as the number of new hires is reduced. On the other, declining job opportunities should generate substantial counterpressures from young white men, who are bearing the full cost of past discrimination. Who gets the falling number of academic jobs will be one of the major problems in higher education in the 1970s and 1980s.

Adjusting to Decline in Academia

From one perspective, the decline in the academic job market in the early 1970s is fortuitous. It set in motion adjustments that might

[18] The data in this section are taken from R. Freeman, *Black Elite: The New Market for Highly Educated Black Americans* (New York: McGraw Hill, 1976), Chapter 8.

[19] Cartter and Ruhter, *First Job Placement of Ph.D.'s.*

not have begun until the 1980s, when it would have been too late to prevent the continued growth in the number of Ph.D.'s and the predicted demographic drop in the number of persons of college age from producing a market collapse that would have made the 1970s look like "the good old days." The earlier market drop promises to reduce Ph.D. production, prepare institutions for future changes, and smooth out the decline in academic demand. Enrollment in the 1980s will not fall as sharply as predicted, despite "bad demographics," because some of the decline will already have taken place in the 1970s and because the fraction enrolled will rise. By the end of the 1980s, academia should be on the path to a new, lower, "steady-state" plateau of operations.

Movement toward the new plateau will, however, be fraught with difficulties. Unless new personnel practices are adopted, the age distribution of faculty will be unevenly tilted toward older workers, and the field distribution of faculty distorted in the direction of the specialties of the old. The research skills and knowledge of the young who are forced out of academia will atrophy, so that much of an entire generation of scholars will be lost to the educational and research endeavor. Given institutional arrangements and pressures, the "natural" market adjustment process is unlikely to produce a socially "equitable" solution.

. . . AND THE SHORTAGE OF RESEARCH SCIENTISTS AND PH.D.'S?

Strange though it may seem to the doctorates of the 1970s, a decade earlier, *the* problem facing the nation was a lack of qualified research personnel. Professional societies issued solemn reports about the acute shortage of specialists in their discipline; congressional committees bemoaned the dearth of scientists; President Kennedy termed the shortage of Ph.D.'s "our most critical national problem." Many worried if a labor market based on individual career choice could compete with the Soviets' planned allocation of manpower in producing needed scientific specialists. Economic analysts debated the meaning of manpower shortages and devised ways to measure them. One leading theorist, Professor K. Arrow (to receive the Nobel prize in 1972) and a Stanford colleague argued that the United States faced a relatively permanent "dynamic shortage" due to the slow adjustment of salaries to continued increases in demand. Government specialists anticipated shortages into the 1980s.[20]

The sudden collapse of the science market in the late 1960s made a mockery of the forecasts, analyses, and national concern. Employment and salaries of researchers tumbled; the number of R&D workers dropped; real starting salaries declined—a stark transformation from the previous decade (see Table 9).

The predictions and fears of shortages were turned upside down for two reasons. On the supply side, the number of students choosing science soared far beyond expectations, with Ph.D.'s in the physical sciences and engineering doubling in the 1960s and graduate students nearly tripling. As early as 1966, the number of new doctoral graduates in the physical sciences, engineering, and mathematics surpassed the President's Science Advisory Committee's "national goal" by over 35%.[21] On the demand side, federal R&D spending operated as a major destabilizer, rising sharply relative to total GNP in the boom of the late 1950s and early 1960s, and dropping in the late 1960s and early 1970s to exacerbate the bust. Between 1955 and 1964 the federal R&D share of GNP doubled, then fell from its peak of 2.0% to just 1.2% by 1974. Indicative of the extreme instability of federal spending, the coefficient of variation (standard deviation divided by the mean) of the annual percentage change in federal R&D was nearly twice that for private R&D. Crisis reactions to Sputnik and related Soviet successes, followed by severe cuts in space and defense R&D made the federal government the "squeaking wheel" in the science market.

[20] See K. Arrow and W. Capron, "Dynamic Shortages and Price Rises: the Engineer and Scientist Case," *Quarterly Journal of Economics* (May 1959), Vol. 73, pp. 292–308. For forecasts of shortages, see National Science Foundation, *The Long Range Demand for Scientific and Technical Personnel* (NSF 61-65) Washington 1961 and *Scientists, Engineers, and Technicians in the 1960s* (NSF 63-34) Washington 1963. Also, National Industrial Conference Board, *The Technical Manpower Shortage: How Acute?* (New York, 1969). The quotation from President Kennedy is from his 15 January 1962 news conference.

[21] The committee's goal for 1966 was 4700 Ph.D.'s, compared to an actual production of 6400. See President's Science Advisory Committee, *Meeting Manpower Needs in Science and Technology* (Washington, D.C., 12 December 1962), Table 1, p. 7. Changes in Ph.D.'s from National Academy of Science-National Research Council, doctorals records file; number of graduate students in 1959–1960 from National Science Foundation, *Scientific Technical Manpower Resources*, NSF 64-28, Table U-9, p. 130 and Table U-7, p. 128, yielding 68,600. For fall 1970, there were 196,200 graduate students, according to U.S. Office of Education, *Digest of Educational Statistics 1973*, Table 93, p. 93.

Table 9. Boom and Bust in the Science Manpower Market, 1960–1974

Employment	Number of workers, salaries, and graduates			Compound annual percentage change	
	1960	1969–1970[a]	1974–1975[b]	1960–1969 1960–1970	1969–1974 1970–1975
Full-time equivalent R&D employment (in thousands)	292	387	363	3.0	−1.3
Aircraft	72	100	70	3.7	−7.1
Electrical equipment and communication	72	102	95	3.9	−1.4
Full-time equivalent R&D employment (per 1000 workers)	4.4	4.8	4.0	1.0	−3.6
Salaries (in 1967 constant dollars)					
Salaries of R&D doctoral workers	1156	1454	1342	2.5	−1.6
R&D salaries (as a percentage of the earnings of all full-time workers	259	268	247	0.0	−1.6
Graduates					
Ph.D.'s in physical sciences	2219	5622	4892	8.9	−2.7
Ph.D.'s in engineering	825	3432	3144	15.2	−1.7

[a]Degrees granted 1970 and R&D salaries in 1970.

[b]R&D salaries in 1975.

Source: National Science Foundation, *National Patterns of R&D Resources* (NSF 75-307), Table 2, p. 10. Total employment from U.S. Department of Labor, *Monthly Labor Review* (July 1975), Table 1, p. 71. Los Alamos Scientific Laboratory, Battelle Memorial Institute, *1970 National Survey of Compensation Paid Scientists and Engineers Engaged in Research*, p. D-28, with 1975 obtained from Battelle by personal communication. Salaries in 1960 estimated by changes in salaries from 1960 to 1970 for doctoral scientists in National Science Foundation, *American Science Manpower 1960*, NSF 62-43, Chart 6, p. 22 and *American Science Manpower 1970* NSF 71-45, p. 28. Deflators from U.S. Department of Labor, *Monthly Labor Review* (Sept. 1975), p. 97 with June 1975 used for 1975. Annual earnings per full-time employee from U.S. Department of Commerce, *Survey of Current Business* (July 1974), Vol. 54 No. 7, p. 37, with 1975 estimated by applying percentage change in average hourly earnings from *Monthly Labor Review* (Sept. 1975), p. 92 using June for 1975. 1960 from U.S. Department of Commerce, *The National Income and Product Accounts of the United States 1929–1965*, Table 6.5, p. 109. U.S. Department of Commerce, *Survey of Current Business* (July 1961 & 1970), August 1975. National Academy of Sciences, *Doctorate Recipients from United States Universities*, (Summary Report, 1974), p. 4. National Academy of Sciences, *Doctorate Production in United States Universities*, 1960–62, Table 3, p. 10.

In addition to contributing to market oscillations, federal spending had the unintentional but very real effect of altering the cost of R&D, and thus of private employment. The federal R&D buildup raised cost and reduced private R&D employment below what it would otherwise have been—by as much as one-third according to econometric estimates.[22] Despite hopes for the "spillover" of space and defense technology for civilian purposes, there appear to have been few indirect benefits of the R&D to the growth of productivity and GNP. In 1971, the number of R&D scientists and engineers employed for civilian purposes per 10,000 workers reached levels in Japan (39 per 10,000) and Switzerland (43 per 10,000) as high as or greater than that in the United States (37 per 10,000); the proportion of GNP spent on civilian research stood at 1.5% in the U.S. compared to 1.9% in West Germany, 1.8% in Switzerland and 1.6% in Japan. These developments contributed to the United States loss of its once dominant position as world technological leader.[23] By the same token, however, the space and military R&D cutback and shift in the federal R&D effort to nonmilitary activities will increase civilian R&D in the United States, which may augur well for future economic growth.

The Problem of Inelastic Demand

The process of adjusting to changes in demand for research personnel is rendered difficult by the highly specialized nature of

[22] The estimates are obtained from equations in R. Freeman, "Scientists and Engineers in the Industrial Economy," unpublished manuscript for National Science Foundation (1971), Table 7.4, Equation 3, p. 230. Between 1953 and 1964, federal R&D grew by 355% and by 173% when deflated by the cost of R&D per R&D scientist and engineer. This change would, by the estimated elasticity, have lowered private R&D employment by 34%. I have transformed percentage changes into log changes and then reversed the procedure in this calculation.

[23] The data for these comparisons are from O.E.C.D. Committee for Scientific and Technological Policy *Patterns of Resources Devoted to Research and Experimental Development in the O.E.C.D. Area 1963–1971*, Paris, May 1974. R&D science and engineering employment from Table 1, p. 2. Shares of GNP spent on R&D from Table 3, p. 14. To estimate the resources spent on civilian activities, I have multiplied the proportion funded by governments from Table 4, p. 20 by the proportion of government R&D devoted to defense and space from the Corrigendum to the O.E.C.D. document, p. 5. The resultant fraction gives the proportion of all R&D going for noncivilian activities. Data on numbers of workers taken from U.S. Department of Commerce, *Statistical Abstract 1973*, Table 1337, p. 315.

scientific and technical work, which makes research and development personnel poor substitutes for other workers. When demand increases, it is difficult to find substitute workers to perform needed research tasks; when demand decreases, it is difficult to find suitable other tasks for research and development specialists. As a result, demand for research and development scientists and engineers tends to be relatively inelastic, about one-fifth to one-half as responsive to changes in costs or salaries—by my estimates—as demand for college graduates in general.[24] Inelastic demand places a great burden on salary adjustments to equilibrate the market, creating volatile swings of the type experienced by farmers, whose products also often face inelastic demand: large profits one year, large losses the next. Market equilibrium in the short run is unlikely.

Famine and Feast: Physics versus Biology

The overall decline in the demand–supply balance for research workers did not affect all sciences equally. Physical science specialties, particularly physics, experienced an exceptional depression, while, by contrast, the biomedical sciences—which had been bypassed in the space and military R&D boom—fared reasonably well through the mid-1970s. The differences between the two are striking. Between 1964 and 1973, the ratio of salaries of physicists, traditionally the highest-paid scientists, to biologists dropped from 1.21 to 1.06 and to just 1.03   among new Ph.D.'s.[25] Federal support for physical science research fell in the period, while that for biomedical research rose. The employment of life scientists at doctorate-awarding institutions increased twice as fast as the employment of physical scientists.

These very different market developments caused substantially different flows of students into the fields. Physics attracted a large and increasing number in the late 1950s and early 1960s, when it had a strong market, and a smaller, decreasing number in the late 1960s

[24] I am comparing an estimate from Freeman, "Scientists and Engineers" of −.40 to −.50 with an estimate of −1.0 to −2.6 in R. Freeman, "Overinvestment," p. 309. Because one set of estimates are based on the salary equations and the other on employment equations, the comparison is crude and provides an order of magnitude estimate only.

[25] 1964 salaries from National Science Foundation, *American Science Manpower 1964* (NSF 66-29), Table A-12, p. 113; 1973 salaries from National Academy of Sciences, *Doctoral Scientists and Engineers in the U.S. 1973 Profile*, Table 8, p. 19.

and early 1970s (Figure 19). The proportion of male graduate students in physics, for example, increased from 3% (1955) to 4.14% (1961), then dropped to a mere 1.73% in 1972. First-year graduate enrollments, an especially sensitive indicator of the adjustment margin in supply, fell by one-third from 1961 to 1971 in physics and dropped even when compared to a decreasing number of bachelor's graduates. In the life sciences, on the other hand, supply grew relatively moderately in the late 1950s and early 1960s but rapidly in the early 1970s. The life sciences share of enrollments in doctoral

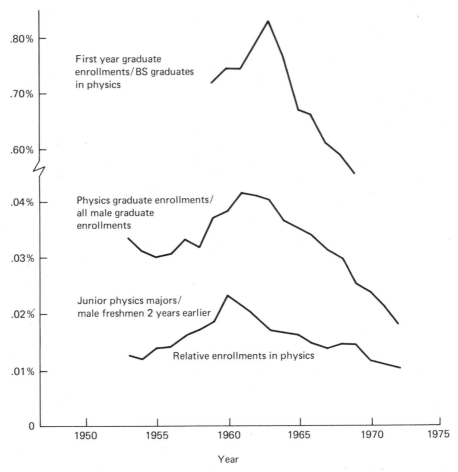

Figure 19. The response of physics enrollments to the depressed market (from R. Freeman "Supply and Salary Adjustments to the Changing Science Manpower Market: Physics 1948–1973," *American Economic Review* (March 1975) Vol. 65, No. 1, pp. 27–39).

science programs increased from 7% (1965) to 23% (1974); the number of first-year enrollments rose by over 80%. In 1965, there were roughly as many graduate students in physics as in the biological sciences; by 1974 there were nearly three biology students per physics graduate student.[26]

These differences highlight an important feature of high-level job markets, the wide diversity of market fluctuations experienced among fields due to the very specific nature of occupational skills and of different supply and demand conditions. One profession can be facing a famine in job opportunities; another field, a feast—because of differential market developments.

THE DECLINING ECONOMIC VALUE OF DOCTORAL AND MASTER'S DEGREES

The falling market for college faculty, schoolteachers, and researchers severely reduced the economic value of higher academic degrees. In engineering, the largest single Ph.D. specialty, there was a precipitous fall in the ratio of starting salaries of doctoral and master's graduates to the starting salaries of bachelor's graduates (see Figure 20). In 1965, beginning doctoral graduates in electrical engineering earned 82%, and beginning master's graduates 22%, more than beginning bachelor's graduates. Ten years later, these differentials had narrowed to 42% and 8%, respectively. The real dollar differential between the starting pay of Ph.D. or M.S. as compared with B.S. engineers, scientists, and mathematicians also fell sharply, reducing the absolute rewards to obtaining postgraduate training. In 1965, the Ph.D. chemist earned $428 (in 1967 dollars) more on his first job than the B.S. chemist; in 1975, just $343 more.

Declines in starting salary differentials of this magnitude can be expected to reduce significantly the rate of return to investing in

[26] The data for physics are from R. Freeman, "Supply and Salary Adjustments to the Changing Science Manpower Market: Physics, 1948–1973," *American Economic Review* (March 1975), 65, pp. 27–39. The data for biology and the comparative figures for physics are from National Science Foundation, *Graduate Student Support and Manpower Resources in Graduate Science Education*, Fall 1965–Fall 1966 (June 1968), p. 88. I have deducted agriculture from the life science totals. The data relate to full-time students. 1974 data from National Science Foundation, *Graduate Enrollment up in Biological Sciences* (Fall 1974), NSF 74-321, with corrections supplied by NSF.

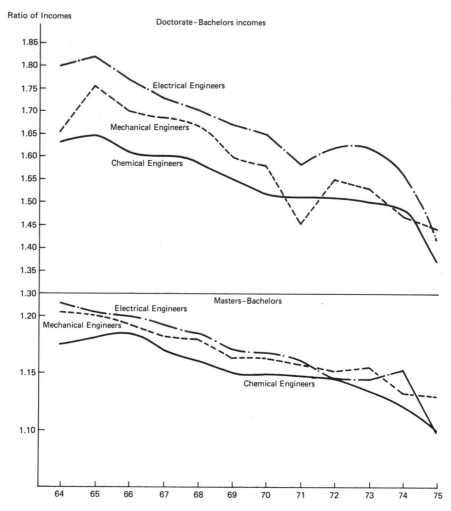

Figure 20. The falling income advantage of doctoral graduates in engineering, 1963–1975 (from College Placement Council, *Salary Surveys*, 1964–1975).

doctoral or master's degrees. If, for example, it is assumed as a first approximation that income differentials over the working life compress to the same extent as the starting salaries, the return in electrical engineering would have dropped by as much as 5.5 percentage points at the doctoral and 7 points at the master's level.[27]   In other areas the drop appears to be more moderate.

[27] I have made the crude calculations on the hypothesis that part-time earnings and the cost of schooling balance out and that individuals forgo 5 years of income at the Ph.D.

In reaction to the falling value of a higher degree and the lack of good job opportunities, the supply of doctoral students and graduates began to dry up in the early 1970s. Especially large declines were recorded in the physical sciences; the number of doctoral degrees dipped by 15% from 1971 to 1974, as many students "in the pipeline" abandoned doctorate plans in response to the worsened job market; first-year enrollments fell by about 15% from 1969 to 1973, guaranteeing a decline in all levels of degrees through the end of the 1970s decade. Overall, after growing at more than 9% per annum in the 1960s, total graduate enrollments increased by just 2.5% from 1970 to 1973, despite the greater number of potential graduate students. Cartter estimates that in 1968 about one in three bachelor's graduates went on to graduate school; in 1973, about one in four. The number of all Ph.D.'s granted to men dropped by 4% between 1972 and 1974, though the number awarded to women increased by 21%, possibly as a result of improved opportunities due to affirmative action.[28]

In some hard-hit academic fields, however, such as arts and humanities, the change in enrollments was relatively small when measured against the worsened job market. In English and literature, philosophy and history, first-year graduate enrollments appear to

---

and 2 years at the master's level. Then, if individuals obtained their starting salary differential over the life cycle, the rate of return formula would simplify to $Y/Y_0 = (1+r)^t$ where Y = salaries of Ph.D.'s (master's), Y_0 the salaries of bachelor's, t = period of training (2 or 5) and r the return. We obtain r by solving to get log $(1+r) = (1/t)$ log Y/y_0 and taking antilogarithms. The rates for electrical engineering obtained in this fashion are: at the Ph.D. level in 1964, 12.5% and in 1975, 7.0%; at the master's level in 1964, 10.9% and in 1975, 3.9%. See M. Friedman and S. Kuznets, *Income from Independent Professional Practices* (New York: National Bureau of Economic Research, 1954), p. 142, for the simplified present value formulae.

[28] Data on degrees from National Academy of Sciences, *Doctorate Recipients from United States Universities*, Summary Reports: 1971, 1972, 1974. Physical science enrollments are for doctoral-granting institutions only. Data for 1969 from National Science Foundation, *Graduate Student Support and Manpower Resources in Graduate Science Education* (Fall 1969), (NSF 70-40), Table C-6, p. 44. Data for 1972 from *Graduate Student Support and Manpower Resources in Graduate Science Education* (Fall 1972), (NSF 73-315), Table C-4B, p. 104. Data for 1972 to 1973, National Science Foundation, *Science Research Studies Highlights* (30 July 1974), NSF 74-308, Chart 1. First-year enrollments were roughly unchanged. Total graduate enrollments for 1959 to 1969 estimated from Office of Education, *Digest of Educational Statistics 1972*, Table 88, p. 75; for 1970 to 1973, estimated from the number of first-year students going on to graduate work estimated from A. Cartter, *The Academic Job Market* (New York: McGraw-Hill, 1976), Table V-7.

have grown modestly in the early 1970s. It may be that students in these areas, many of whom are women, are less responsive to job market forces than the science and technology students or that many seek master's degrees or doctorates as the best way to obtain secondary school teaching jobs. Alternatively, some may be pursuing these fields for nonvocational reasons.

In other fields where the job market did not collapse, such as life sciences (as noted earlier), psychology, and geo-sciences, enrollments grew unabated in the early 1970s. The danger in these specialties is that the rapid increases in enrollments will create a serious supply–demand imbalance in the late 1970s and early 1980s. As the job market for bachelor's graduates deteriorated in the mid-1970s, moreover, there was even an upturn in overall graduate science enrollment, according to the National Science Foundation, which reported rises from 1973 to 1974 for the first time since 1969.[29]

SCENARIO FOR THE FUTURE

The adjustment process just described will lead to a distinct set of future manpower problems for holders of doctorates, researchers, faculty, and related specialists. First, there will be a significant relative decline in the number of Ph.D.'s, substantially easing the surplus in the future. While the expected decline in demand for faculty in the 1980s is an almost certain guarantee that the reduction in supply will not lead to cobweb shortages in most fields, in specialties like chemistry, physics, or engineering where, many holders of doctorates work outside academia, such shortages are possible. As Table 10 shows, the supply response in physics will cut in half the number of Ph.D.'s by 1985—to levels far below those forecast by various governmental and other experts. Such a decline will, at least, restore a reasonable supply–demand balance at the end of the decade and could create a shortage in physics. On the other hand, in fields like biology and psychology, where enrollments continued to increase in the early 1970s, it is reasonably likely that surpluses will develop in the future. If, furthermore, the downward trend in gradu-

---

[29] From "Graduate Science Enrollment in 1974 Shows First Increase Since 1969 " (Washington, D.C.: National Science Foundation, 1975), NSF 75–328.

Table 10. Forecasted Supply of New Ph.D.'s in Physics, 1970–1980

		Trend forecasts without supply response		
	Supply Response Model	Office of Education	·Cartter	NAS–NRC
1969–1970^a	1500	1500	1500	1500
1974–1975^b	1189	2153	1853	2153
1979–1980	786	2492	2654	3350

^{a}The various projections use different base year numbers of Ph.D.'s due to differences in the source of data. National Academy of Science–National Research Council (NAS–NRC) data differ somewhat from those of the Office of Education. I have set the base year number as 1500 and made projections on the basis of implicit percentage increases in the actual forecasts.

^{b}The number of degrees in 1974 was 1277, that is, 23% lower than the 1657 in 1969–1970, according to the National Academy of Sciences, yielding about 1155 Ph.D.'s in that year, about "on target" for the supply model.

Source: R. B. Freeman, "Supply and Salary Adjustments to the Changing Science Manpower Market: Physics 1948–1973," *American Economic Review*, (March 1975), Vol. 65, pp. 27–39. National Academy of Sciences–National Research Council *Doctorate Recipients from United States Universities*, Summary Report, 1970, 1974.

ate enrollments which began in 1970 in the sciences and the slow-down in enrollments elsewhere is ameliorated or reversed, the depressed state of the doctoral and master's market will continue for some time to come. In 1975 the National Academy of Science began a major manpower study with the hope of developing a policy to avoid such future problems in the biomedical areas.

Second, there will be a considerable aging of faculty and researchers, which may create serious problems in the rate of scientific progress and flexibility of academia. To the extent that science is a "young man's game," the nation may get less and less output from older and older researchers.

Third, the income of Ph.D.'s and academic faculty will be considerably lower relative to that of other workers than has been the case in the recent past. A decline in relative (though not real) income on the order of 20% beyond that experienced in the early and mid-1970s is quite possible. The potential ways in which this decline is distributed—who experiences the largest relative loss of income and in what form—are important issues that policy can affect.

Fourth, there will be—even with all of the postulated adjustments—a likely "maldistribution" of doctoral specialists, with some of those trained for academic research or teaching obligated to seek industrial or other nonacademic employment. This could create problems in graduate education unless programs are adjusted for the training of industrial, rather than academic, specialists.

Fifth, with supplies declining, any new R&D, or related Ph.D.-intensive, initiative—as in the energy area—will run into possible shortages, which, because of the period of production, will not be lessened until the mid-1980s.

The Market for Business Sector Specialists and Independent Practitioners

Not all college-level occupations were as hard hit by the new depression of the 1970s as the academic professions. Differences in past patterns of growth, in the nature of demand, and in conditions of entry created divergent and changing markets for various specialties. In business-oriented fields, where the supply increases of the 1960s were moderate and demand little affected by educational, defense and R&D spending, the market decline was relatively moderate. Cobweb fluctuations of the type described in Chapter 3, indigenous to each occupation, often had greater impact on the market than the overall relative surplus of graduates. In medical specialties, growing demand due to Medicare and Medicaid combined with slowly growing supply to maintain the high income of doctors. This chapter examines the experience of several important business-oriented professions and medicine, explains why some occupations fared well and others poorly in the depressed job market, and analyses those factors that appear most important to their future economic situation.

THE CLASSIC COBWEB CYCLE: ENGINEERS

Engineering, which is the major profession for men in the U.S., has long been plagued by recurrent "shortages" and "surpluses." In the late 1940s—early 1950s, the problem was one of post—World War II shortages; in the mid-1950s, of surpluses; in the years following Sputnik, of shortages; in the late 1960s, of surpluses, particularly of aeronautical engineers laid off from space and military programs. By the early 1970s, manpower shortages were once again the center of discussion. The *Wall Street Journal* warned the nation of "The New Shortage of Engineers," while the head of manpower analysis for the Engineering Manpower Commission reported, "Surprise. There's a Shortage of Engineers Ahead."[1]

The ups and downs of engineering are not the result of random economic developments or of the general business cycle or of peculiar circumstances but rather represent the classic case of cobweb fluctuations produced by the internal dynamics of the job market. Engineering has all of the requisite labor market characteristics needed to generate recurrent shortage—surplus cycles along the lines described in Figure 10. On the supply side, engineering is a technical area chosen by students almost entirely for vocational purposes. Over two-thirds of engineering baccalaureate graduates, for example, compared to barely one-half of all male graduates, report selecting their college field to obtain the best vocational training. Virtually all college-trained engineers major in the field. In addition, engineering students tend to be highly sensitive to salary and employment opportunities and well informed about market developments. The Engineering Manpower Commission continually surveys and analyzes the state of the market, providing reasonably up-to-date and widely publicized information. Many engineering schools post job offers to alert students to changes in opportunities, and keep careful records about placement. All of which tends to make the supply of students, in terms of enrollment and graduation, highly responsive to the job market. Once students choose the field, moreover, there is a long and relatively inflexible training period of 4 to 5 years—which is what renders the cobweb analysis applicable. Most engineering graduates

---

[1] J. Alden, "Surprise: There's a Shortage of Engineers Ahead," *New Engineer* [Oct. 1972]. *Wall Street Journal* 18 November 1972, p. 1.

seek jobs as engineers upon completion of training, with 80% or more generally ending up as engineers. On the demand side, employers hire engineering graduates for the specific skills they possess. There are no good substitutes for engineers as there are, say, for English majors, who can generally be replaced by other liberal arts graduates. Salaries and employment opportunities are thus highly dependent on the number of specifically engineering graduates.

As a result of these characteristics, engineering tends to undergo shortage–surplus oscillations every 4 to 5 years, oscillations that produce corresponding swings in the number of students and the salaries in the field.

Figure 21 shows the extent of the swings over the post–World War II period. The line giving actual first-year enrollments reveals the extreme changes in the attractiveness of engineering to students, with the number enrolling going from 50,000 (1952) to 78,000 (1957) to 64,000 (1964) to 80,000 (1965), and finally dropping to about 50,000 in 1973. As a proportion of male freshmen, engineering enrollments varied in a similar manner, rising from 14% in 1950 to 23% in 1957 and then dropping to an unprecedented low of 9% in 1973. The "fitted" line gives the enrollments predicted by a simple cobweb analysis, according to which enrollments grow when demand (measured by R&D spending and output in the durable goods industries that hire many engineers) increases and fall when income opportunities in other occupations are strong or when many bachelor's engineers graduate and flood the market. While actual and predicted values are not perfectly aligned, the cobweb analysis clearly does a good job of tracking ups and downs. In the statistical computations, about 95% of the variation in first-year enrollments is explained by cobweb dynamics. It is estimated that when the number of new B.S. engineers grows by 10%, enrollments fall by 5% in the short run and by somewhat less than 10% in the long run, generating further cyclical ups and downs. Because of the lag structure of adjustment, the oscillations tend to be dampened over time unless shocked by exogenous disturbances.[2]

Other economic measures of the state of the engineering market also fluctuate every 4 to 5 years in the cobweb pattern. I have found

[2] The regressions are given in R. Freeman, "A Cobweb Model of the Supply and Starting Salary of New Engineers," *Industrial Labor Relations Review* (January 1976), Table 4.

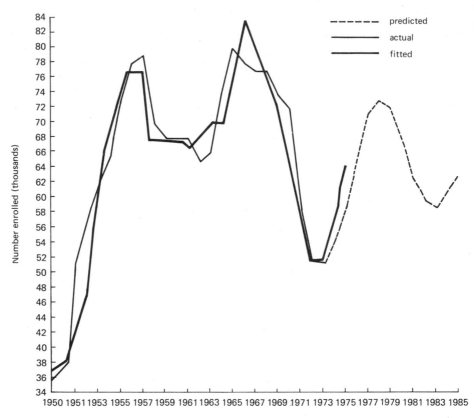

Figure 21. Actual, fitted, and predicted B.S., first-year engineering enrollments, 1950–1985. (From R. Freeman "A Cobweb Model of the Supply and Starting Salary of New Engineers, *Industrial Labor Relations Review* (Jan, 1976), Table V, Figure 2. Also Center for Policy Alternatives, American Society for Engineering Education *Future Directions for Engineering Education* (Washington, 1975), p. 27. Predicted values assume that alternative salaries increased one-half their previous trend rate.)

cycles in the starting salaries of engineers to be of similar length to those in enrollments and graduations. Using the relatively sophisticated technique of spectral analysis, two Israeli scholars have found a comparable 4-to 5-year cycle in engineering job placements by the U.S. Employment Service. Indices of want-ads for engineers also reveal distinct cyclical ups and downs. The evidence of cobweb oscillations is nowhere as compelling as in engineering.[3]

[3] My work is reported in Freeman, "A Cobweb Model." The spectral analysis is reported in Y. Comay and A. Melnick, "A Note on Cyclical Changes in the Excess Demand for Engineers," unpublished paper, Technion, Israel, 1975. Want-ads are reported monthly by Deutsch, Shea, and Evans, Inc., *Engineer/Scientist Demand Index*, New York.

The dominant role of indigenous ups and downs in engineering makes the market for engineers diverge greatly from that for all graduates. At the outset of the 1970s, engineering was at the trough of a cobweb cycle—an especially severe and long trough due to the late 1960s' decline in NASA and related engineering-intensive expenditures, which cut off a potential upswing. From 1969 to 1972, the market for engineering became progressively worse: white-collar employment in engineering-intensive industries fell sharply, by as much as 33% in aircraft and missiles and 12% in electrical machinery; unemployment of engineers rose from 0.8% to 2.9%; salaries of starting engineers increased less than one-half as fast as those of other workers; and, on the supply side, in response to the job market, engineering enrollments plumeted by a remarkable 27%, to reach the unprecedented low shown in Figure 22.[4]

The decline in the economic state of the engineering profession began to bottom out in the mid-1970s, as a cobweb upturn commenced, even though the overall college job market grew increasingly bad. Engineering starting salaries rose reasonably rapidly from 1972 to 1975—by 17% for mechanical engineers, 21% for metallurgical engineers, and 19% for chemical engineers—more or less in line with other wages and salaries. Employment of engineers grew by 5.6%, while total male employment in the economy was increasing more slowly. Unemployment dropped to one-half of its 1972 level by 1974.[5] The improved situation in engineering and the depressed market elsewhere produced a sharp change in enrollments. As can be seen, first-year enrollments leveled off in 1973 and jumped sharply, by 10,000, in 1974. This increase is roughly in line with forecasts made in 1973 at MIT's Center for Policy Alternatives, using the cobweb model. The MIT forecasts, given in the dotted line in Figure 21 were based on developments through 1972 and certain "reasonable" postulates about changes in the factors that affect engineers. In particular, R&D was expected to increase at the same trend rate as GNP, preserving the R&D share of national product; durable produc-

[4] These data are from Freeman, "A Cobweb Model."

[5] The starting salary data are from College Placement Council, *Salary Survey* 1972 and 1975 final reports. Employment statistics are from Bureau of Labor Statistics, *Educational Attainment of Workers*, Special Labor Force Report No. 175, Table I, p. A-17 and 148, Table I, p. A-15. Unemployment is given in National Science Foundation, *Science Resources Studies Highlights* (19 May 1975), NSF 75-309, Table 1; levels differ from those in Freeman, "A Cobweb Model" because of differences in surveys.

tion was expected to continue to grow at its trend rate; while incomes in alternative activities were expected to increase at only one-half their past rate, because of the overall depression in the college market. As can be seen, the forecasts correctly caught the 1973–1974 turning point, which is the best test of the value of the model for projecting the future. When everything grows or everything declines, it is easy to forecast—just assume more of the same. When the directions of change alter, the problem is more difficult. Most economic models fail to pick up such turning-point changes.

As for the decades of the 1970s and 1980s, engineering enrollments are expected to peak at between 71,000 and 73,000 in 1978, then drop and flatten out between 1982 and 1987, rising again thereafter. Because R&D, durable goods output, and professional salaries will undoubtedly change differently from the assumed simple trend, these forecasts will probably be at least somewhat inaccurate. What is important is that the internal dynamics of engineering supply and demand will continue to generate very different market developments than those in the overall college job market.

Do All Engineers Fare the Same?

What about engineers trained in the top schools? How have they fared in the changing market?

Surprisingly, perhaps, evidence from the placement office of MIT—perhaps the nation's foremost engineering school—shows that MIT graduates have quite similar experiences to other engineers. Indeed, to the chagrin of school officials, the typical starting MIT graduate tends to earn only about 5% to 10% more than graduates from less-renowned schools and faces the usual ups and downs in the market. Between 1960 and 1969, for example, when average starting salaries for mechanical engineers rose by 57.1% in current dollars, those for MIT graduates rose by much the same rate, 58.6%; from 1969 to 1974, when the average rose by just 22%, those of MIT graduates rose by 20%, and so forth.[6] Where MIT, and, it may be surmised, graduates from other top schools, get ahead of their peers is in attainment of managerial jobs later in life. In engineering, it is

---

[6] MIT data supplied by Placement Office, with data for 1974 from *Report of the Career Planning and Placement Office*, 1973–74, Table III, p. 12.

common for the most able to switch into higher-paying management jobs in mid-career. MIT graduates have a higher probability of attaining management jobs than other engineers and thus tend to have an increased salary advantage later in life. It's difficult, however, to attribute this to MIT education.

More important than the school in determining labor market success is the precise area of engineering in which the individual specializes. The relative position of the major engineering curricula in the job market has changed greatly in recent years. In the early 1960s, aeronautical engineering stood near the top in salaries and job opportunities, metallurgical engineering near the bottom. In 1975, as a result of changes in the demand for and supply of these specialists, metallurgical engineering was one of the highest-paying specialities, aeronautical engineering the lowest.

WHY DOCTORS EARN SO MUCH

In 1971, self-employed physicians had median earnings of $42,700, according to the American Medical Association (AMA); obstetrician-gynecologists earned $50,000; even the declining number of general practitioners had incomes over $37,000, far outstripping all other professionals, including those with 3 to 5 years of postgraduate training such as LL.B.'s or Ph.D.'s. Internal Revenue statistics show that the average net income of doctors working as sole practitioners or partners exceeded that of lawyers by 70% in 1970. Census of Population statistics for 1969 show doctors having earnings more than twice those of average male graduates and 83% above those of Ph.D. scientists reporting in the National Scientific Register. More than 25% of M.D.'s in 1969 had incomes above $50,000; young M.D.'s serving as residents or interns at hospitals, whose salaries had once been below the scholarship income of graduate students in the sciences, earned $11,000 to $12,000. In 1966, the rate of return for investing in 4 years of medical school, 1 year as an intern and 1 year as a resident, exceeded 18%![7]

[7] The 1971 data are from U.S. Bureau of the Census, *Statistical Abstract 1974*, Table 112, p. 75. I report 1971, rather than 1972, data because the latter include those over 65. The IRS data from P. Pashigan, "The Earnings and Number of Lawyers, Physicists, and Dentists from 1910 to 1970—A Historical Review," University of Chicago, Mimeo (18 June 1975), Table 4, p. 15. The census data are given in U.S. Bureau of the Census, 1970 Census

Doctors did not always earn such a large premium compared to other highly trained workers. In 1929, they averaged $5224 per year, somewhat less than lawyers ($5534) and 70% more than college teachers. In 1933, doctors, who were hard hit by the depression, earned three-fourths as much as lawyers and "only" 40% more than college faculty.[8]

The medical profession attained the incomparable income levels of the post–World War II period through its trade union powers. The AMA is perhaps the strongest trade union in the United States. It has virtually complete control over the supply of doctors, and actively uses this control to restrict supply and raise doctors' incomes. The source of AMA power lies in the fact that practicing physicians must be licensed and that licenses are given only to graduates from schools in the United States that are approved by the AMA's Council on Medical Education and Hospitals. When doctors' incomes fell during the Depression, the AMA sought to reduce admissions. Indicative of the AMA attitude is the 1934 statement by the association's president, calling for the closing of medical schools: "A fine piece of educational work could well be done if we were to use only half of the 70-odd medical schools in the U.S." In 1934 and 1935, the Council on Medical Education warned medical schools against the admission of larger classes, noting that "seven schools have definitely stated that their enrollment will be decreased and others have indicated adherence to the Council's principles." These pressures were effective in reducing acceptances in medical school in ensuing years, much to the joy of the AMA-dominated Federation of State Medical Boards. "Careful estimates made during the past year indicate that

---

of Population, *Earnings by Occupation and Education*, PC(2)-8B, Table 1. The doctor figures are for 25- to 64-year-old physicians. I report figures for full-time, year-round workers. Also U.S. Bureau of the Census, 1970 Census of Population *Occupations of Persons with High Earnings*, OPC(2)-7F, Table 7, p. 50. The scientist figures are medians from National Science Foundation, *American Science Manpower 1950*, NSF 71-45, p. 28. I have multiplied the medians by the ratio of mean to median incomes for life and physical scientists in *Earnings by Occupation and Education*, p. 13. Rate of return is from F. Sloan, "Economic Models of Physician Supply," Ph.D. dissertation, Harvard University, 1968, p. 164. Similar estimates are given in R. Fein and G. I. Weber, *Financing Medical Education* (New York: McGraw-Hill, 1971), Table C-3, pp. 252–253.

[8] In 1933, doctors earned $2948 compared to $3868 for lawyers. Doctor and lawyer figures from U.S. Bureau of the Census, *Survey of Current Business*, May 1934. Faculty incomes from G. Stigler, *Employment and Compensation in Education* (New York: National Bureau of Economic Research Occasional in Paper 33, 1950).

500 fewer students registered in acceptable medical schools in
1935 . . . if this condition should prevail for 20 years, it would mean
approximately 10,000 fewer graduates entering the practice of medicine. The implication of this on the welfare of the future practitioner
is evident."[9]

Restrictionist policies cut the number of medical school acceptances from 7578 in 1933 to 6211 in 1939 and kept the number
below the 1933 "peak" for some 20 years. In 1926, 64% of applicants to medical school were accepted; in 1952, 52%; in 1973 just
35%. While there was a moderate increase in the number of M.D.s
conferred (and in approved medical schools) through 1960, and a
more rapid increase thereafter, medical schools are the only major
segment of higher education that did not expand rapidly in the
post–World War II years. In 1950, 5.2% of postbaccalaureate degrees
were awarded in medicine; in 1972, 2.9%. In 1950 doctors, dentists,
and related practitioneers constituted 3.9% of the professional work
force; in 1974, 2.8%.[10] Medical incomes were raised and maintained
by the AMA's control over supply.

The economic position of doctors was enhanced even further in
the 1960s and 1970s by federal subsidization of medical services
under Medicare and Medicaid. Because the increased demand brought
about by federal spending had relatively little impact on the output
of doctors from American medical schools, the price of doctors'
services and their incomes increased greatly. From 1959 to 1969,
physicians fees grew at twice the rate of the consumer price index.

[9] Analysis of the medical profession's use of its control over supply is given in the
classic work by M. Friedman and S. Kuznets, *Income from Independent Professional
Practices*. Also E. Rayack, *Professional Power and American Medicare* (Cleveland: World
Publishing, 1967). The quotation from the AMA president is from Rayack, p. 75.
The quotation from the Council on Medical Education is from Friedman and Kuznets, p.
13. The quotation from the Federation of State Medical Boards is from Rayack, p. 78.

[10] Data for degrees in 1950 are from U.S. Bureau of the Census, *Statistical Abstract
1950*, Table 149. I include law, optometry, dentistry, and medicine with master's and
Ph.D.'s as post-baccalaureate degrees. Data on degrees in 1972 from U.S. Office of Education, Xeroxed forms, with M.D.s from AMA, "Medical Education," *JAMA* (Supplement,
January 1975), Vol. 231; Table 9, p. 8. Data on the fraction of professionals who were
doctors in 1974 from U.S. Department of Labor, *Employment and Earnings* (June 1975),
Vol. 21, No. 12, Table 1, p. 7. For the fraction who were doctors in 1950, U.S. Bureau of
the Census 1950 Census of Population, *Occupational Characteristics*, P-E No. 1B, Table A,
p. 1B-10. Osteopaths were included in the 1974 data and are added to the number of M.D.s,
for comparability with the 1950 data.

Median net earnings of physicians rose by 80%. By contrast, the average hourly earnings of production workers grew by just 50%.[11]

Are Medical Incomes Really That High? Is There a Shortage?

Because doctors undertake considerable postbaccalaureate training and work an extraordinary number of hours (50.8 per week on average in 1970), it can be argued that the income comparisons tell a misleading story. If the earnings of doctors are put on an hourly basis, their advantage over, say, average college men falls sharply from the greater than two to one ratio reported earlier to about one and three-fourths to one. On an hourly pay basis, the advantage to doctors and the return to medical training is not that high.[12] Does this mean that doctors' incomes are really "about right" and that there is no "shortage" of medical personnel?

This "defense" of the high income of doctors is specious for several reasons. First, the fact that M.D.s *choose* to work more hours than other professionals means that the return from a 40-hour week understates the pecuniary value of the degree. Most people would also work more than 40 hours given the hourly fee and activities of doctors.

More importantly, however one estimates a rate of return to medical education, it is clear that the value of the training is sufficiently high to motivate thousands more *able* students to apply to medical schools than are accepted. In 1973, for example, there were over 40,000 applications and just 14,000 acceptances. Most students applied to seven or eight medical schools, in the hope of finding one

---

[11] Physicians fees from U.S. Department of Labor, *Handbook of Labor Statistics, 1974*, Table 126, p. 317. Consumer prices from *ibid.*, Table 120, p. 301. Median net earnings, U.S. Bureau of the Census, *Statistical Abstract 1974*, Table 112, p. 75. Average hourly earnings, *Handbook of Labor Statistics*, Table 96, p. 241.

[12] Hours of work for male doctors and male professionals are given in U.S. Bureau of the Census, *Occupational Characteristics*, PC(2)-7A, Table 45, p. 747. Doctors work 20% more hours per week than other professionals. They earn 2.10 times as much as bachelor's graduates, according to U.S. Bureau of the Census, *Earnings by Occupation and Education*, PC(2)-8B, Table 1. Dividing, they earn 1.75 times as much on an hourly basis. If the net earnings of doctors were zero for the 4 years of medical school, 1 year as an intern, and 1 year as a resident, and if the 2.10 ratio persisted over the life cycle, the return would be 13.2%. The 1.75 ratio implies a return of 9.8%. Sloan's 18% (see Footnote 8) would, by this argument, drop to 13–14%.

that would accept them. The economic rewards to becoming a doctor are so great that some medical schools receive enough applications from Ph.D.'s and other highly qualified personnel to fill their classes. When the University of Chicago had an accelerated three-year program of medical studies for Ph.D.'s, for example, there was a sufficient number of applicants to fill the entire entering M.D. class. No other occupation rejects so many able candidates. The "excess supply" of applicants is large enough by itself to imply that, from the point of view of individuals choosing a career, incomes are abnormally high and the number of M.D.s in short supply.[13]

As the economic standing of most other professionals has deteriorated in the depressed college market, moreover, the return to medical training has gotten even more out of line than in the past, with substantial consequences on the career decisions of the young. In the depressed 1970s, while graduate enrollments leveled off in most fields, medical school applications more than doubled. During the late 1950s, by contrast, when the job market for teachers and researchers was strong, medical school applications actually fell— though never approaching the number of places available. In 1949, there were 24,434 persons who applied; in 1961, just 14,381—compared to the 40,000 plus in 1973.[14]

While the number of places in medical school is fixed by restrictionist AMA policy, the quality of students is not. When the job market for doctors is strong relative to that for, say, scientists, the number of applicants tends to increase, permitting schools to be more selective in their acceptance policies. Conversely, when the medical market is relatively weak, acceptance standards are lowered.

In the 1950s and early 1960s, 10% to 15% of accepted students reported A averages in undergraduate studies; in 1973, as the number applying rose, so too did the proportion with A's, reaching 36%. Other measures of academic qualifications, such as scores on the Medical College Aptitude Test (MCAT), also went up for those accepted. According to econometric studies, both the fraction with

[13] The application and occupational data are from AMA, "Medical Education," *JAMA* (Supplement, January 1975), Vol. 231, Table 8, p. 17. The University of Chicago information by personal communication from the Dean of Students in the Biological Sciences.

[14] Data for 1949 are from R. Fein and G. Weber, *Financing Medical Education* (New York: McGraw Hill, 1971), Table 14, p. 80; data for 1961 and 1973 are from AMA, "Medical Education," Table 8, p. 17.

A's and the number of applicants appear to be largely determined by the state of the medical job market compared to that for biological scientists. A rise in doctors' incomes increases, and a rise in the incomes and stipends of biological scientists decreases the quantity and quality of medical applicants.[15]

With the supply of U.S.-trained M.D.s limited, the country has come to rely increasingly on importing foreign doctors, especially after the 1965 amendments to the Immigration and Naturalization Act. These amendments removed restrictions on Asian and other non-European persons seeking to enter the United States, but required that entrants have appropriate skills, thus making occupation the main selection criteria. As Figure 22 shows, there has been an extraordinary increase in the number of M.D.s from foreign schools in the United States. By 1974, forty-five percent of persons passing the medical examinations and 22% of practicing physicians were foreign trained. There is an on-going debate within the medical profession about the professional quality of these persons. Without them, however, the doctor shortage would be enormous and the costs of medical services greatly raised.

Whether the high private returns, excess of applicants to medical school, increasing academic qualifications, and substantial imports mean that there is a societal shortage of doctors is not obvious. Medical education is heavily subsidized. So too is the purchase of services. Medical insurance distorts the decision to seek hospital care; since individuals do not pay the full cost, there is an inducement for greater purchases. Doctors may recommend treatment that could be avoided. In the United States payment of fees for operations induces surgeons to advise patients to be operated on. In Britain, where most doctors are paid salaries, one-half as many operations are done, at no apparent loss to the health of the British people.[16] If all of these factors

---

[15] The fraction with A averages are given in AMA, "Medical Education," Figure 2, p. 20. Analysis of the impact of the job market on this fraction is reported in Sloan, Economic Models of Physician Supply."

[16] J. P. Bunker, "Surgical Manpower: A Comparison of Operations and Surgeons in the United States and in England and Wales," *The New England Journal of Medicine* (Jan., 1970), Vol. 282, No. 3, pp. 135–149. Dr. Bunker reports 7400 operations per 100,000 of population in the U.S. compared to 3770 per 100,000 in England and Wales (p. 136). He writes, "fee-for-service invariably results in the provision of more services than provided by capitation or salaried plans . . . fee-for-service encourages unnecessary operations [p. 137]." When the United Mine Workers Medical Care Program took part of the decision to operate

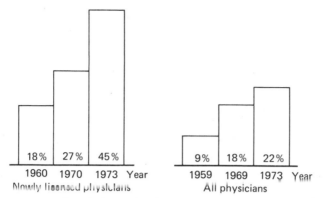

Figure 22. Percentage of newly licensed and practicing physicians who were foreign medical graduates, 1959–1973 (Data on newly licensed physicians from U.S. Bureau of the Census, *Statistical Abstract of the United States 1974* [Washington, D.C.: U.S. Government Printing Office, 1974], Table 115, p. 76. Data for 1959 and 1969 from Charles T. Stewart, Jr. and Corazon M. Siddayao, *Increasing the Supply of Medical Personnel: Needs and Alternatives* [Washington, D.C.: American Enterprise Institute for Public Policy Research, 1973], p. 30. 1973 total supply estimated by adding new licentiates from "Medical Licensure 1973," *Journal of the American Medical Association* (22 July 1974), Table 6, pp. 448, to the total stock of physicians in 1972 reported in Thomas D. Dublin, "Foreign Physicians: Their Impact on U.S. Health Care," *Science* (2 August 1974), p. 409, and subtracting deaths and emigration estimated on p. 448 in the *JAMA*. Supply of FMGs estimated by adding FMG licentiates as reported in Table 7, p. 449 of the *JAMA* to the stock of FMGs in 1972 as given by Dublin, and subtracting estimated emigration. From these numbers the percentage of FMGs in 1973 was calculated.)

are taken into account, the United States may have roughly the "right" number of doctors, but be pricing their training and services incorrectly. What is clear is that, with current methods of financing medical education and care, there is a shortage of places in medical schools and of doctors in the job market.

LEGAL COBWEBS

"Respect for the legal profession . . . will be raised when the lawyer occupies his proper place at the top of the economic structure."[17] Although law is often viewed as a profession with similar

---

out of the hands of the surgeon performing the operation, by requiring consultancy, "The number of operations fell by as much as 75% for hysterectomies, 60% for appendectomies, and 35% for hemorrhoidectomies [pp. 139–140]."

[17] Illinois Bar Association, 1963, as quoted in Mark J. Green, "The High Cost of Lawyers," *The New York Times Magazine* (10 August 1975), p. 9.

characteristics to medicine, it has in fact very different job market features. Unlike doctors, lawyers are no longer primarily independent practitioners. According to the Martindale–Hubbell Directory, only 37% worked for themselves in 1970 compared to 61% in 1948. Many lawyers work for private industries or for the government, and many are in large law firms or partnerships. Unlike medicine, legal services are not heavily subsidized by the government. Legal services for the poor was a major issue in the 1960s, when the Johnson administration set up a Federal Legal Service Program to help poor persons obtain legal aid, but the budget was never large and the program was limited by President Nixon. The Legal Services Corporation, the successive agency set up in 1975, was funded at $17.5 million—less than 0.4% of the dollars spent on Medicare and Medicaid.[18]

Most importantly, lawyers *do not control entry* into the profession. There are numerous law schools in the country, many of them lacking the approval of the American Bar Association, and they expand when additional students seek entry. To take the bar exam, one does not have to have been trained at an approved school. Efforts to close "low quality" night and other law schools have failed to pass state legislatures—some say because many of the legislators themselves prepared for the bar in those institutions. Schools face, of course, capacity constraints and turn away students; but conditions of entry are easier than in medicine.

Because the supply of lawyers is not limited by the American Bar Association, student career decisions are the essential determinant of the number of new entrants. Contrary to Justice Frankfurter, who believed that "on the whole they come by default," most law students appear to be highly economically motivated and responsive to economic opportunities in the profession. A National Opinion Research Center (1965) study found that over 50% of persons intending to go to law school placed great value on "making a lot of money."[19] Over three-fourths of LL.B. recipients tend to work as

---

[18] See American Bar Foundation, *The 1971 Lawyer Statistical Report*, Table 5, p. 10. The data on legal services are from Office of the President, *U.S. Budget for Fiscal Year 1976*, p. 303. The data for Medicare and Medicaid are from Office of the President, *Special Analyses Budget of the U.S. Government Fiscal Year 1976*, Table U-20, p. 183 and Table U-22, p. 184, where $17.2 billion are reported as being spent for these services.

[19] The Frankfurter quotation is given in S. Warkov and J. Zelan, *Lawyers in the Making* (Chicago: Aldine, 1965), p. 82. The percentage who want to make a lot of money is from *ibid.*, p. 11. I averaged the figures from Columns 11 and 21.

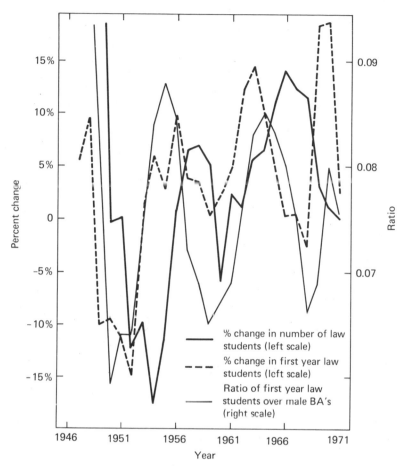

Figure 23. Supply of new lawyers, 1947–1971 (from R. Freeman, "Legal Cobwebs: A Recursive Model of the Market for New Lawyers," *Review of Economics and Statistics* (May 1975).

lawyers upon graduation and an additional 13% in closely related occupations, such as insurance or accounting.[20] With these supply conditions and the difficulty of substituting nonlegal personnel for lawyers, the supply of LL.B.s, like that of engineers, could be expected to undergo cobweb ups and downs in the job market.

As Figure 23 illustrates, changes in the number of first-year law students have, in fact, fluctuated every 3 to 4 years, in the cobweb

[20] National Science Foundation, *Two Years after the College Degree*, NSF 63-26, Table 69, p. 96.

manner. Enrollments (and salaries) grew slowly in the early 1950s, rapidly in the early 1960s, and so forth. In 1961, the National Opinion Research Center worried that "young lawyers are in such short supply." In 1975, *Newsweek* reported a great "surfeit of lawyers," with the attendant job market problems.[21]

Econometric estimates indicate that about 90% of the variation in supply of new lawyers and in legal salaries can be explained by the cobweb model.[22] According to the calculations, a 10% change in legal salaries, with other wage and salaries fixed, raises the number of first-year law students by about 10% in a year and 30% to 40% over the long run. Similarly, increases in the number of law school graduates are found to reduce the salaries paid to attorneys and consequently the number of first-year enrollees. Roughly a 10% increase in LL.B.s reduces enrollment by 4% within a year and by 8% in the long run.

Toward the end of the 1960s, the market for young lawyers underwent a significant economic boom. Expenditures on legal services increased from \$3.9 billion to \$9.3 billion in the period 1965 to 1973. The number of federal court cases increased by 73%; the fraction of national income spent on the legal industry rose from 0.7% to 0.9%. The increase in demand, coupled with the relatively slow growth in supply, produced a major boom in the market for young lawyers in the late 1960s.[23]

The boom was sparked by the remarkable decision of major Wall Street firms to raise the starting pay of new LL.B.s by 58% in a single year. What happened is this: Traditionally the Wall Street firms had hired a large number of top graduates, those on the law review of the most prestigious schools. Young lawyers chose the large firms for the training they provided, in much the same way as young Ph.D.'s obtained postdoctoral degrees or instructorships or assistant professorships at major research institutions. These lawyers worked

[21] Warkov and Zelan, *Lawyers in the Making*, p. xv; *Newsweek* (9 Dec 1974), p. 74.

[22] The estimates given in this section are from R. Freeman, "Legal Cobwebs: A Recursive Model of the Market for New Lawyers," *Review of Economics and Statistics*, (May 1975).

[23] Expenditures in legal services and national income are from U.S. Department of Commerce, *Survey of Current Business* (July 1966 and 1974); court cases are from U.S. Bureau of the Census, *Statistical Abstract 1973*, Tables 260, 261, p. 160. In 1960, there were 91,320 cases in U.S. Courts of Appeal and District Courts; in 1972 there were 157,751.

as associates for 8 to 10 years and then, on an up-or-out system, were either promoted to partners or helped into other good law jobs. Firms refer to those who leave as "graduates" and, when recruiting LL.B.s, stress the training and future positions they will obtain. Between 1950 and 1956 nearly one-half of the five top men in each Harvard law school class went to work for New York firms. By this system, the firms got the best of the law graduates and then chose from among that group the type of legal talent that can command $100 or so per hour in fees. In the 1960s, however, opportunities for legal work and training in the federal government in Washington, a new desire to help underprivileged persons or to work on "socially beneficial" activities, and the growth of demand outside New York made it more and more difficult to attract top students to the big Wall Street firms. Fearful of losing out in the competition for the best young lawyers, one of the leading firms, Cravath, Swain & Moore, which has been described as "well-known, influential, and large . . . a model for other law offices," raised starting rates in 1968 from $9500 offered the previous year to $15,000—an increase of $5500, which exceeded the total income of over one-third of male workers. Other Wall Street firms followed. The increase made the front page of the *New York Times* and attracted considerable national attention. It spearheaded a marked improvement in the economic position of new attorneys throughout the country, although of course the $5500 gain was exceptional. According to the annual Cantor survey of law salaries, large firms in the United States raised their salaries in 1968 by 28%. The University of Minnesota Law School Placement Office reported an increase of 33% for their graduates between 1967 and 1969, even though about two-thirds of the graduates work in Minnesota. Nationwide, Bureau of Labor Statistics data reveal an annual gain of 10% per annum for beginning young attorneys, compared to a 2% gain for male professionals as a whole. By 1974 the median annual income of attorneys in law firms stood at $40,000, according to the Cantor survey.[24]

[24] The story of the Cravath Swain, and Moore salary change is found in *The New York Times* (23 March 1968); The Cantor salary figures are from *The New York Times* (23 March 1968); the University of Minnesota data are from the *Minnesota Law School News*, Vol. 29, No. 2, p. 10. Bureau of Labor Statistics data are from U.S. Bureau of Labor Statistics, *Handbook of Labor Statistics 1974*, p. 254. (They relate to "class II" lawyers.) The 1974 Cantor survey figure is given in Green, "The High Cost of Lawyers," p. 9. The description of Cravath, Swain, and Moore is from E.O. Smigel, *The Wall Street Lawyer*, (Gary, Ind.: Indiana University Press, 1969), p. 113.

One apparent effect of the higher Wall Street salaries was a substantial movement of young lawyers back into private law offices. At Harvard, the percentage working for such firms rose from a low of 44% in 1967 to 62% in 1975. As early as 1970, the director of placement at Harvard reported that students no longer differed greatly in their career plans from students in past years. Students were much more serious about interviewing with the big firms. The much-heralded "new breed of lawyers" from the elite schools, interested in careers in poverty and public interest, had essentially died out by the early 1970s—in part as a result of the increase in salaries.[25]

The improving economic situation of lawyers and the deteriorating position of other college graduate workers led to an exceptional growth in the number applying to and entering law school. Between 1969 and 1971, first-year enrollments in law school increased by 44% (from 26,000 to 37,000), far exceeding the growth of male B.A.s (27%) or graduate students as a whole (15%). Prospective applicants to law school, consisting of persons taking the Legal Scholastic Achievement Test (LSAT), increased by an astounding 116% in the 3-year span. What makes this development remarkable is that law was a slowly growing field of study in the early postwar years and has expanded relatively modestly over the long run. In the 1950s and 1960s, for example, master's and doctoral graduates quadrupled while the number of LL.Bs (or LL.D.s) grew by just 25% (1950–1970). Lawyers constituted 0.37% of the labor force in 1900, 0.31% in 1950, and 0.37% in 1970; as a fraction of the professional labor force, law declined from 6.5% in 1910 to 3.6% in 1950 to 2.5% in 1970.[26]

In 1974 and 1975, the large entering classes of 1971 and 1972 graduated and sought jobs as lawyers, with the expected "cobweb" depressant effect on the labor market. Many LL.B.s in the class of 1975 reported problems in obtaining jobs as lawyers. Those that did received lower real salaries than comparable starting lawyers several years earlier.

As for the future, the economic situation of law graduates is likely to remain depressed through the end of the decade, as the large

[25] The Harvard data were calculated from final statistics on the activities of the graduating classes of 1975 and 1967.

[26] These data are from Freeman, "Legal Cobwebs," p. 171.

first-year classes of 1972, 1973, and 1974 flood the market. The normal cobweb upswing is, moreover, likely to be at least partially attenuated by the depressed market for liberal arts and social science graduates, many of whom are likely to seek legal careers. Even so, the market will improve toward the end of the decade, as the large increases in new graduates diminish and ultimately decline.

BUSINESS GRADUATES

Despite the suspicion that academicians and intellectuals have traditionally harbored against business education in colleges and universities (Thorstein Veblen referred to it as "an endeavor to substitute the pursuit of gain and expenditure in place of the pursuit of knowledge as the focus of . . . modern intellectual life "),[27] business administration and related curricula have come to be a major area of study. In the 1970s, the economic standing of college graduates in managerial jobs or with specialized business training, notably accountants and MBA (Masters of Business Administration) graduates, was only modestly depressed by the declining college job market. Business specialists were less affected by the overall relative surplus than most other college workers for several reasons: They are employed throughout the economy, making their economic position relatively immune to such sectoral shifts as those against education or R&D; they compete with high school graduates in many managerial markets, where their training offers an advantage; and their supply grew only moderately in the 1960s, as students were attracted to the booming research and teacher markets rather than to business administration. In addition, like engineering, business administration tends to undergo cobweb ups and downs, and was in the midst of a cyclical upswing at the time that the overall college market fell.

As a result of these forces, there was a marked improvement in the economic position of managerial specialists relative to other college graduates. Between 1969 and 1974, the annual earnings of male managers rose from $200 below to about $1000 above that of professionals; the number of college graduates working as managers increased by 57% compared to a 41% increase in the number em-

[27] T. Veblen, *The Higher Learning in America,* American Century Series (New York: Hill and Way, 1957), p. 175.

ployed as professionals; among beginning bachelor's graduates, the differential in the starting pay between accounting, business, and commerce graduates in production management or sales on the one hand and liberal arts or science graduates on the other increased markedly. In 1968, accountants earned 11% more than liberal arts graduates and 6% less than mathematics graduates; in 1975, their salary was 28% higher than the salary of liberal arts graduates, according to the Endicott Survey, and 8% higher than that of their mathematics counterparts. Similarly, the advantage for production managers and sales and marketing personnel grew, though that for general business trainees did not. At the graduate level, the story is similar, with MBA graduates and master's in accounting graduates far outpacing other personnel with master's degrees.[28]

Corporate recruiters clearly favored business graduates, especially those with technical specialization, over other college-trained young persons, with more serious adverse consequences for the latter than in the past because of the relative surplus of college personnel. The comments of company officials made this clear:

> As long as students with business and technical degrees are available, we will hire very few liberal arts graduates.
> Specialization seems to be the trend in business and the most competitive graduates will be those who have majored in the specific areas that the market requires.

Whereas a decade ago companies had eagerly sought college graduates in most fields, with the depressed job market, some took the view that they would hire only business and technical majors. "If a liberal arts graduate, by his own choice, decided not to prepare himself for business, why should a company hire him."[29]

---

[28] Earnings data from U.S. Bureau of the Census, *Current Population Reports*, Series P-60. No. 75, Table 49, p. 110; No. 99, Table 7, p. 10. The data are median earnings. Employment data are from U.S. Bureau of Labor Statistics, *Educational Attainment of Workers*, (March 1974) Special Labor Force Report 175, p. A-17 and *Educational Attainment of Workers*, (March 1969), Special Labor Force Report 125, p. A-28. The starting salary data are from F. Endicott, *Trends in Employment of College and University Graduates in Business and Industry* (Evanston, Ill.: Northwestern University, 1968), p. 5 and 1975, p. 4.

[29] The recruiter quotations are from Endicott, *Trends in Employment*, 1974, p. 8.

The Supply Response

Just as in engineering and medicine, the improved market for business graduates relative to liberal arts and other college specialties induced more students into these fields. Since most business students tend to be highly oriented to economic forces, with less than 9%—according to a Bureau of Social Science Research study—choosing the field for academic reasons, a significant supply response might be expected. In fact, the fraction of bachelor's degrees in business and commerce rose from 19.3% to 22.1% among men and from 2.4% to 3.0% among women between 1966 and 1972. The proportion in accounting also increased. By 1972, there were 22,307 men and 2494 women earning degrees with specialization in accounting compared to 14,203 and 898 six years earlier. In the mid-1970s, business administration was by far the largest single major for male students, with twice as many graduates as the second largest, engineering.[30] Antibusiness sentiment on campuses, which had reached a crescendo in the late 1960s—when the essence of business, economic production, as well as its excesses were attacked—receded rapidly.

Business students have traditionally come from families of lower socioeconomic status than other students, and they rank near the bottom of college students in intelligence tests. The field is more likely to be chosen at the undergraduate level by "first generation" college students than by those from families having a longer tradition of college going.[31] This suggests that the field plays an important role in upward social mobility through college training and thus that the more favorable market for business majors than other graduates may help maintain enrollments of persons from lower status backgrounds in the era of overeducation.

[30] Degree data for 1966 are from U.S. Bureau of the Census, *Statistical Abstract 1967*, Table 199, p. 135. Data from 1972 from xeroxed sheets provided by U.S. Office of Education. I divided the number of bachelors in the fields by the number of bachelors degrees granted, *not* by the number of bachelor's and first professional degrees. Total bachelors degrees for 1966 from U.S. Office of Education, *Earned Degrees Conferred 1965–1966*, OE-54013-66, Table 2, p. 4. The Bureau of Social Science Research data are in National Science Foundation, *Two Years after the College Degree*, NSF 63-26, p. 228. The largest percentage citing academic reasons is 8.2% of those working as salesmen.

[31] See E. Cheit, *The Useful Arts and the Liberal Tradition* (New York: McGraw-Hill, 1974), p. 98.

The Boom in MBAs

Students graduating with MBAs obtained exceptionally rapid increases in starting salaries in the period of overall market depression. From 1968 to 1975, the College Placement Council showed MBA starting pay up by 5.25% annually, compared to 3.5% for social science and humanities graduates and 2.5% for beginning B.S. chemists. Master's degree engineers also did not fare as well as MBAs, though bachelor's engineers did only slightly worse. The starting rates for Harvard Business School MBA graduates rose even more rapidly, by 6% per annum over the period.[32]

In contrast to the situation of other postgraduate fields, moreover, the premium of an MBA over a bachelor's degree grew rather than decreased (Figure 24) and the real (1967) dollar differential in monthly pay between the levels of training nearly doubled, from $158 to $302. As a result, while the rate of return to other master's degrees was falling, that for MBAs appears to have risen. Among master's graduates specializing in accounting, salaries rose to exceed those of master's in engineering. In some critical areas, such as corporate finance, companies reported that "all recruiting is at the MBA level."

The economic rewards from business involve more than high and increasing initial salaries. The MBA, and related business specialties, offers substantially greater opportunities than other careers to "strike it rich," especially over a lifetime. In 1969, college-trained men working as managers were nearly twice as likely to earn more than $50,000 than other graduates, exclusive of doctors. Even in initial jobs, there is much greater variation in business opportunities than in those for most other college graduates. In 1975, beginning MBA graduates with nontechnical undergraduate preparation averaged about as much as master's graduates in engineering; the probability that an MBA graduate would earn either more or less than average, however, far exceeded that of engineers: One-sixth of

---

[32] College Placement Council, *Salary Survey, 1968, 1975.* The Harvard data are from Harvard University Graduate School of Business Administration, *Placement Report on the MBA Class of 1974,* Table 4, p. 7. The years are from 1968 to 1974.

Figure 24. The rising salary advantage of the MBA (calculated from College Placement Council, *Salary Surveys, 1961–1975*, Bethlehem, P.A. Data refer to males only, with 1973–1974 and 1974–1975 adjusted to reflect addition of females to published data. MBA salaries relate to graduates with nontechnical bachelor's degree.)

starting MBA graduates, had incomes in excess of $1300 per month, and one in twenty had incomes below $1050 per month, while *no* engineers reported salaries in excess of $1300 or less than $1050. [33]

The impact of the comparative improvement in the market for MBA graduates on the supply of young persons obtaining the degree is examined in Figure 25. This figure records the ratio of MBA degrees to all master's degrees and the ratio predicted by the economic incentive to get the degree as reflected in MBA salaries

---

[33] Probabilities on earning $50,000+ calculated from U.S. Bureau of the Census, 1970 Census of Population, *Occupations of Persons with High Earnings*, PC(2)-7F, Table 7, p. 50: for managers, 6.6%; for other graduates, save doctors, 3.6%. Figures for starting MBAs in 1975 from Endicott, *Trends in Employment*, 1975.

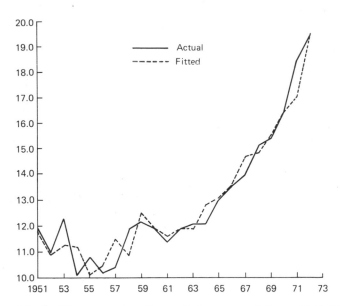

Figure 25. The MBA proportion of master's degrees awarded men, 1951–1972.

compared to the salaries of professionals.[34] What stands out in the figure is the sharp actual (and predicted) increase in MBA graduates in the late 1960s and early 1970s. Between 1966 and 1972 the business administration share of master's degrees awarded to men jumped by nearly 50%, from 13.6% to 19.6%, after growing relatively moderately over the previous decade. The business administration share of female master's degrees increased even more rapidly, though from an extremely low base. With the decline in the college job market in 1974, the upward trend in enrollment into graduate business schools accelerated. Thousands of young persons, including new LL.B. and Ph.D. recipients, as well as bachelor's graduates, applied to the major business schools. A *Business Week* survey showed applications in 1975 up by an average of 24% from 1974 and 69% from 1972. Women applicants to business schools increased

[34] The fitted values are from regression equation

$$MBA = 1.48 + .96\ MBSAL - 1.21\ PROF + .70\ MBA\ (-1)$$
$$\quad\quad\quad\quad (.31) \quad\quad\quad\quad (.51) \quad\quad\quad (.12)$$

$$R^2 = .915\ SEE = .057$$

where numbers in parenthesis below the lines refer to standard errors. *SEE* = standard error of estimate; *d.w.* = Durbin-Watson statistic; variables defined in log units: *MBA* = number of *MBA* degrees given males divided by total male master's plus law degrees; *MBSAL* = salaries

particularly rapidly in 1975, by 58% at Columbia, 31% at Harvard, and 25% at Dartmouth.[35]

Future Developments and Implications

The booming market for MBA graduates, accountants, and other business specialists, will not be maintained throughout the decade. Like law and engineering, the business specialties are subject to cobweb ups and downs, as can be seen in the fluctuations in the MBA share of graduates in Figure 25. The sizeable business school enrollments of the early 1970s are likely to produce a cobweb decline toward the end of the decade. By the mid-1970s, in fact, the rate of advance in the relative position of business graduates was already beginning to level off. Because the demand for business occupations will increase more rapidly than it will for academic occupations, however, the proportion of bachelor's and master's enrollees in the field will probably drop only slightly when the market for BBA and MBA graduates weakens. The effects of the depressed market for researchers and teachers will be diffused to the business fields by increasing the supply in those areas, maintaining their historically large share of degrees through the turn of the decade. When the job market for new college graduates improves in

---

of Harvard Business School graduates; $PROF$ = median income of male professional, technical, and kindred workers; MBA (-1) = lagged MBA share of master's degrees; The Harvard salary series is used as the only readily available set of figures providing an *indicator* of market conditions.

I have made several other calculations with different measures of alternative salaries and relating MBA degrees to master's plus law degrees and obtained results similar to those in the regression above. The sources of the data are: MBA, M.A. figures from the U.S. Office of Education, *Earned Degrees Conferred,* (various editions). Because of a sharp "increase" in MBAs in 1966 due to reclassification of first professional degrees requiring 5 or more years, I have adjusted degrees for 1949–1965 upward by the 1965 ratio of reported master's and first-professional degrees in business and commerce to master's degrees as given in U.S. Office of Education, *Digest of Educational Statistics* (1967), Table 110, p. 87. PROF, medians as given in U.S. Bureau of the Census, "Consumer Income," *Current Population Reports,* Series P-20, various editions. MBSAL, 1949–1963 in W. Lewellen, *Executive Compensation in Large Industrial Corporations* (New York: Columbia University Press, 1968), Table 14, p. 179, giving mean figures. Harvard Placement Office data, 1964–1972, are medians after 1963. I have adjusted them to means by splicing in the overlap year.

[35] As reported in Scientific Manpower Commission, *Manpower Comments,* Vol. 12, No. 5, June, 1975, p. 5.

the 1980s, however, the number choosing business majors is likely to increase less rapidly than the number choosing other areas.

If this analysis is correct, the 1970s will be a period of reallocation of college-trained majors from academic to business fields, with potentially significant implications for the composition of national leadership. As more and better students select business and independent professional fields at the expense of academics, Galbraith's "scientific–educational estate" will continue to lose influence and power in the society. The consequences of a college graduate population heavily weighted with nonacademic specialists could be substantial for various socioeconomic and cultural developments. A detailed study of the relation between field of study, behavior, and decision making is needed, however, to make more than speculative guesses as to its impact.

The "New Labor Market" for Black Graduates

Despite the popular connection of discrimination with poverty, labor market differentials by race traditionally have been greatest at the top of the economic ladder. College-trained black men, in particular, have long suffered from low incomes and poor job opportunities. In 1959 the income of white male college graduates exceeded that of nonwhite graduates by 81% while white grade school graduates had an advantage of 46%. Young (24- to 34-year-old) nonwhite men earned $4760 per annum, compared to $7146 for young white degree recipients. With rare exceptions, black graduates were excluded from high-level jobs in major corporations and were concentrated in low-paying professions. Virtually no major corporation visited the predominantly black colleges in the South. Nearly one-half of black male seniors planned on teaching careers compared to one-seventh of white male seniors. Partly as a result of these conditions, proportionately fewer blacks than whites attended college.[1]

A major effort began in the 1960s to reduce job market discrimination. Title VII of the Civil Rights Act of 1964 made it "an unlawful practice for employers to fail or refuse to hire or to

---

[1] These data are reported in R. Freeman, *Black Elite: The New Market for Highly Educated Black Americans* (New York: McGraw-Hill, 1976), Chap. 1. Also in R. Freeman, "The Implications of the Changing Labor Market for Minorities," in *Higher Education and the Labor Market*, ed. M. Gordon (New York: McGraw Hill, 1974), pp. 82–110.

discharge or otherwise discriminate against any individual with respect to his compensation, terms, conditions or privileges of employment, because of such individual's race, color, religion, sex or national origin." Executive Order 11246 outlawed discrimination by federal contractors and required "affirmative action to ensure that applicants are employed, and that employees are treated during employment, without regard to their race, creed, color, or national origin." Sixteen states enacted state fair employment practice laws. Court interpretations of federal and state laws tended to favor active intervention in the employment process. Voluntary private efforts to aid minority workers were undertaken by business, with the Plan for Progress program especially oriented toward those in high-level occupations. The NAACP and other civil rights groups shifted their focus from school and public facility integration to employment issues.[2]

What impact did these developments have on the economic status of black college workers? Did the market for their services improve noticeably? How did black youngsters and experienced college personnel react to the new opportunities? What happened to black graduates when the college job market collapsed in the early 1970s?

This chapter is concerned with these important questions about the changing market for black college men and women. It finds a remarkable transformation in traditional patterns of discrimination against highly educated blacks in the 1960s and early 1970s. According to the empirical evidence:

1. Discrimination against black graduates declined drastically, with black female graduates attaining rough economic equality with white female graduates by the mid-1960s and young black male graduates attaining equality in the late 1960s. However, while older black men made economic advances relative to comparable whites, they continued to trail their white peers—the legacy of past discrimination.

2. Black youngsters and qualified personnel responded with extraordinary speed to the changed market situation, with the young enrolling in colleges and altering occupational plans rapidly in ac-

---

[2] A detailed description of the governmental effort is given in Freeman, *Black Elite*, Chaps. 5, 6, and 8.

cordance with new economic opportunities. Perhaps because of generally low family incomes, black youngsters appear more attuned to monetary incentives than whites.

3. The economic gains of educated blacks were not reversed by the falling college job market. To the contrary, black college workers either maintained past or enjoyed continued advancement relative to whites in the depressed 1970s.

THE DECLINE IN DISCRIMINATORY DIFFERENCES

The evidence supporting the proposition that the economic status of college-educated black workers improved greatly in the 1960s and early 1970s, *eliminating the historic disadvantage of educated black women and of young black male graduates* and reducing the disadvantages of older black male graduates is compelling.

To begin, the income of black college women increased to the extent that by the outset of the 1970s they were earning more, over the year, than their white peers. According to the Census of Population, in 1969 black women with 4 years of college averaged $6545 in the job market, compared to $6220 for comparable white women, giving blacks a 5% premium. By 1973, the black income advantage among women with 4 or more years of college stood at 15%—a remarkable change from the historic pattern of discrimination against blacks. Two factors explain the premium: the fact that black female college workers are more likely to be employed full-time, year-round than their white peers and the likelihood that they are especially committed to the job market and hence accumulate more years of experience and seniority than do white women. When the incomes of full-time, year-round black and white college women workers are compared for 1969, black graduates turn out to have earned 95% as much as whites. Assuming a similar pattern in 1973, the 15% black premium would be a more modest 5%. In any case, by the early 1970s, black college-trained women were not suffering from discrimination in income opportunities because of race; the problems they faced were those of college women in general.[3]

[3] U.S. Bureau of Census, 1970 Census of Population, *Earnings by Education and Occupation*, PC(2)-8B, Table 8, p. 310, Table 7, p. 342; U.S. Bureau of the Census, "Consumer Income," *Current Population Reports*, Series P-60, No. 97, Table 58, p. 129.

That young black college men also attained economic parity
with their white peers, after decades of economic disadvantage, is
documented in Table 11. This table compares the starting salary of
starting black college graduates in 1968–1970 to that of comparable
white graduates. The data were obtained from the placement offices
of black colleges and the annual national salary survey by the College
Placement Council (CPC). Despite the fact that the figures are drawn
from diverse sources, the general pattern is clear. Young black men
with college degrees had roughly the same starting salary as white
male graduates. Even in such out-of-the-way places as Alabama
Agricultural and Mechanical College (in Normal, Alabama), "Salary
offers . . . compared favorably with the national averages as reported
by the CPC survey." Additional evidence from the U.S. Census of
Population confirms the picture of rough equality in starting pay for

Table 11. Comparable Starting Salaries of Black College and All Male Graduates, by Field
and College, 1968–1970

	Average salary of black graduates	Comparable average national salary	Ratio
Howard (1968–1969), bachelor's degrees in:			
Civil engineering,	$800	$797	1.00
Electrical engineering	805	826	.98
Mechanical engineering	810	820	.99
Accounting	758	761	1.00
Other business fields	666	687	.97
Mathematics, chemistry and physics	706	784	.90
Other liberal arts	644	667	.97
North Carolina A&T (1969–1970), bachelor's degree in:			
Engineering	800	873	.92
Texas Southern (1969–1970), bachelor's degrees in:			
Industrial engineering,	833	849	.98
Business	816	836	.98
Liberal arts	615	682	.98
Texas Southern Graduate, 1969–1970			
Law (J.D.)	1050	988	1.06
Business (MBA)	1097	1026	1.07

Source: Data on black salaries, from college placement at various schools; data on
national salaries, from the College Placement Council,*Salary Survey 1969–1970.* Bethlehem,
Pa.

1969. The census data reveal that black male graduates aged 22 to 24 had a 5% advantage in median and a 1% advantage in mean incomes over comparable whites. Census data on the median earnings of full-time, year-round 18- to 24-year-olds shows that blacks with 4 years of college had 90% of the earnings of comparable whites; those in professional jobs had a .5% advantage; those with 5 or more years of college and professional jobs a 2.4% advantage. Overall, black male graduates aged 22 to 24 had 5% higher income than whites in terms of median and 1% higher income in terms of means, in 1969. More recent evidence, for 1973, from the smaller current population reports sample, shows black male graduate workers in the 25 to 29 age group earning $11,169, compared to $10,242 for comparable whites.[4] In short, black college men beginning their careers did about as well, possibly a bit better, than starting white college men—a far cry from the discriminatory past.

Placement officials at black colleges tell a similar story about the market. In 1970, 19 of 21 directors at major black colleges reported that salaries of graduates from their schools were "equal to national average" while the remaining two reported earnings "above national average." Despite the collapse of the college job market in the 1970s, the situation in 1975 appears to have been the same, with recent black graduates suffering no more than whites in the depressed market.

Changes in the recruiting practices of major corporations in the 1960s provide more dramatic evidence of the transformation of the market for black college graduates. Table 12 shows the number of companies recruiting and hiring at the predominantly black colleges of the South in 1960, 1965, and 1970. The increase in recruiting activity between 1965 and 1970 is very striking. From essentially zero in 1960 and about 30 recruiters per campus in 1965, the number of recruiters rose to more than 300 per campus in 1970. Between 1970 and 1975 the number of recruiters visiting black colleges did, however, fall as the college job market worsened. A sample of 10 schools surveyed by mail in 1975 reported a drop in the

[4] Census data from U.S. Bureau of the Census, 1970 Census of Population: *Educational Attainment* P(2)-5B, Table 7, pp. 150, 152; *Earnings by Occupation and Education* PC(2)-8B, Table 5, p. 224. *Current Population Survey* data from March 1974 survey tape. The tape provides income figures for 1973.

Table 12. Recruitment Visits of Corporations to Predominantly Black Colleges and Universities

| | Number of corporations interviewing job candidates | | |
	1960	1965	1970
Atlanta University	0	160	510
Howard University	—	100	619
Clark College	0	40	350
Alabama A. & M. College	0	0	100
Alabama State College	0	7	30
Hampton Institute	20	247	573
Jackson State College	—	—	280
Johnson C. Smith University	0	25	175
Morehouse College	—	—	300
Miles College	0	12	54
Norfolk State Campus of Virginia State College	5	100	250
North Carolina Ag. and Tech. State University	6	80	517
Prairie View A. & M. College	—	—	350
Southern University and A & M College	0	25	600
Southern University at New Orleans	0	5	75
Texas Southern University	0	69	175
Tuskegee Institute	50	85	404
Virginia State College, Petersburg	0	25	325
Winston-Salem State College	—	—	25
Virginia Union University	5	25	150
Xavier University	0	44	185
Average per school	4	50	297

Source: R. Freeman, *Black Elite: The New Market for Highly Educated Americans* (New York: McGraw-Hill, 1976).

average number of recruiters from 309 per school in 1970 to 240 in 1975.[5] This decline of 22% matched that for MIT over the period 1970–1974 shown earlier in Figure 8, which suggests that recruiting fell off at the black colleges at about the same pace as elsewhere. From these data and the records of those hired by national corporations, it becomes clear that for the first time the national professional–managerial job market was open to blacks.

The economic position of all black male graduates also improved, though not by enough to obtain equality in income or employment possibilities with whites. This is because the labor

---

[5] These results are given by Albert Maule in a paper, "Effect of the Recession on Graduates of Black Colleges," for Economics 1650, Harvard University, 1975.

market is not a structureless bourse in which persons of different ages are interchangeable units of labor. Just as young college graduates were more (negatively) affected by the market downturn than experienced personnel, young black men were more (positively) affected by the decline in market discrimination than their elders. Older black college men lacked the relevant training or managerial experience to take advantage of new opportunities and advanced only moderately in the new job market. One unfortunate consequence of this is that, even though income discrimination has been eliminated for new entrants, the legacy of past discrimination is likely to maintain a sizeable black–white gap among college men as a whole for many years to come.

Although older college-trained black men did not reach parity with whites, they did, it is important to stress, make sizable gains in income and job status. From 1959 to 1969, the rate of increase in the income of black college graduates 25 years of age and older exceeded that for white graduates by 1.9% per year. From 1969 to 1973, the rate of black gains exceeded those of whites by more than 2.4% per annum.

As the market declined in the mid-1970s, however, the economic position of black graduates appeared to weaken: the ratio of the average weekly earnings of all black male graduates to all white male graduates dropped slightly from 1973 (79%) to 1975 (77%) while relative annual earnings also fell, at least from 1973 to 1974. On the other hand, black graduates appear to have continued to improve their occupational position: between 1970 and 1974, the proportion of blacks in such important professions as accounting, engineering, personnel labor relations, and computer specialties rose fairly sizeably. For example, the proportion of accountants who were nonwhite rose from 3.8 to 5.6%; the proportion of engineers from 3.0 to 4.6%, and so forth.[6]

The economic gains of college-trained black men reversed two traditional patterns of economic discrimination that had, rightfully, received considerable attention. First is the shocking fact that, as late as 1959, nonwhite college men earned markedly less than white high school men—nearly 20% less, according to

[6] Figures on employment refer to both men and women. They are from U.S. Bureau of Census, 1970 Census of Population, *Occupational Characteristics* PC(2)–7A, Table 2, p. 12 and U.S. Department of Labor *Employment and Earnings* Vol. 21, No. 12, June 1975, p. 7.

the 1960 Census of Population! Even young (25- to 34-year old) nonwhite college men trailed similarly aged, white, male high school graduates by about 20%. In 1973, by contrast, all black college men averaged 5% higher incomes than white high school men while black graduates aged 25–29, who were in especially great demand in the market, had 15% higher incomes than white high school graduates in the same age bracket.[7] Second, for decades, discriminatory differentials between black and white men had increased with education, so that the more schooling a black had, the greater would be the gap between his income and that of a comparable white, measured as a percentage differential or in absolute figures. Largely because of this, the rate of return for black investments in college was below that for white investments, which, according to the analysis of Chapter 3, could be expected to deter black youngsters from going on in their schooling. The improved income of young and older black male graduates reversed the traditional difference in rates of return. As Table 13 shows, the economic position of black college workers relative to that of high school workers improved sufficiently in the 1960s and 1970s, when that of white collegians fell, to give blacks a *higher rate of return for investment in college than whites.* The table compares estimated returns for black and white men in 1959, before the new market for black graduates developed, and in 1973, under two assumptions about the future income of graduates in the 1970s. Under Assumption A, black (and white) graduate incomes are expected to increase as they age according to the 1973 cross-section profiles of college and high school graduates (with an additional 1.5% increase in incomes due to overall economic growth). This implies that the gains of black graduates will dissipate rapidly in the future, with their incomes approaching those of older black college men while the losses suffered by young whites in the depressed market will be

[7] The 1960 Census showed all nonwhite college graduates with median incomes of $4447 and those aged 25–29 with medians of $3839 compared to medians of $5441 and $4745 for all and 25- to 29-year-old high school graduates. U.S. Bureau of the Census, 1960 Census of Population, *Educational Attainment*, P(2)-5B, pp. 88–89. In 1973 black graduates earned $12,035 compared to $11,452 for white high school graduates, according to U.S. Bureau of Census, Current Population Reports, Series P-60, No. 97, p. 125. The income of 25- to 29-year-old black graduates was $11,167 compared to $9702 for white high school graduates as tabulated from the underlying computer tapes for the Series P-60 reports.

Table 13. The Increased Private Rate of Return to Black Male Investments in College, 1959–1973

	Black males	All males
1959	6.0	10.1
1973A	11.0	10.0
1973B	13.0 +	7.5

Source: 1959 from G. Hanoch, "An Economic Analysis of Earnings and Schooling," *Journal of Human Resources* (Summer 1967); 1973 from R. Freeman, *Black Elite*, Table 31, with 1973A calculated by assuming future incomes follow 1973 cross-section profile, with 1.5% additional increase per year due to overall economic growth and 1973B calculated by applying *actual* 1963 to 1973 cohort income gains to the income of 25- to 29-year olds. See Appendix A.

recouped. I view this assumption as a highly conservative one that gives an exceptionally *low* return to blacks and high return to whites. Even so, the A estimates indicate that the return to black male investments in college will exceed the return to white investments. Under Assumption B, the future incomes of blacks (and whites) are expected to increase at the actual rates obtained by white cohorts over the 10 years from 1963 to 1973. While this may be, as argued in Chapter 1, a reasonable assumption with which to calculate white lifetime incomes, it is probably overly optimistic for blacks. It assumes that blacks will maintain *all* of the gains in starting salaries over their working life. With Postulate B, blacks have an estimated return that is far above that for whites. The basic reason is that the incomes of young black college men have approached that of their white peers while young black high school graduates continue to have much lower incomes than young white high school men. While the difference in rates of return is undoubtedly exaggerated under Assumption B, even pessimistic Assumption A shows that in the mid-1970s the economic incentive to enroll in college was greater for black than for white men, apparently for the first time in American history.[8]

In some occupations, the increase in demand for black college workers was sufficient to give older as well as young black graduates

[8] For more details of the higher return to black graduates, see Freeman, *Black Elite*, Chapter 3. See also the preliminary results in Freeman, "Implications for the Changing Labor Market for Minorities," (Forthcoming).

approximately the same income as their white peers. Black college faculty, for example, appear to have earned about as much as or somewhat more than white college faculty with similar qualifications in 1973; black Ph.D.'s, most of whom worked in academia, earned more, according to one survey, than other Ph.D.'s. In virtually every profession detailed in the Census of Population, the ratio of black to white male incomes increased in the 1959–1969 decade, often at rates that, if continued, promised attainment of parity by the end of the decade.[9]

The most important change in employment opportunities occurred in the "traditionally closed" field of management, from which blacks had historically been excluded by national corporations. Since management is the highest paying broad occupation in the United States and plays a critical role in the operation of the U.S. economy, the sudden opening of corporate management to blacks in the late 1960s and early 1970s was a key element in the improved status of college men. As Figure 26 shows, the proportion of black male graduates obtaining jobs as managers roughly tripled in the decade following the 1964 Civil Rights Act, while the fraction of white graduates was roughly stable in the late 1960s and early 1970s, after rising from 1959 to 1964. The gap in the proportion of black and white graduates in management, while not eliminated, was greatly reduced by 1972. A similar pattern is found in salaries, with full-time, year-round black managers obtaining a remarkable 74% increase in income from 1969 to 1973, presumably due to their movement into high-paying corporations, while the income of white managers increased by just 31%.[10]

In sum, despite the depressed market for college workers, black graduates did relatively well in the early 1970s, generally continuing the advance in the market that began after the initiation of equal employment activity in the mid-1960s. Although the gains may have been marred by "tokenism"—the desire of companies to meet affirmative action goals by employing black graduates solely in "community relations" positions—there is no denying the extraordinary

[9] This is documented in Freeman, *Black Elite*, Chaps. 1 and 8.
[10] U.S. Bureau of the Census, "Consumer Income," *Current Population Reports*, Series P-60, No. 75, Table 50, p. 113; No. 97, Table 65, p. 140.

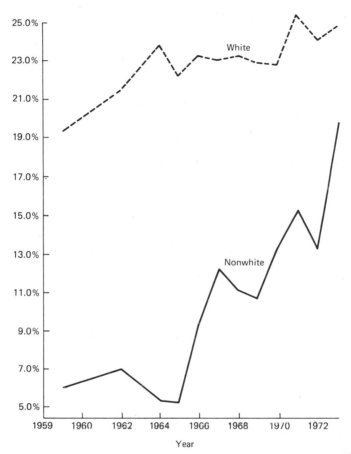

Figure 26. The fraction of nonwhite and white college graduates employed as managers, 1959–1973 (from Bureau of Labor Statistics, *Educational Attainment of Workers*, Special Labor Force Reports, various years).

improvement in the economic status of black graduates, after decades of severe discrimination in high-level job markets.

RESPONSES TO NEW OPPORTUNITIES

In 1969, at the height of student disorders, when black students were demanding separate black studies programs and majors, Sir Arthur Lewis called for an alternative strategy. "The road to the top

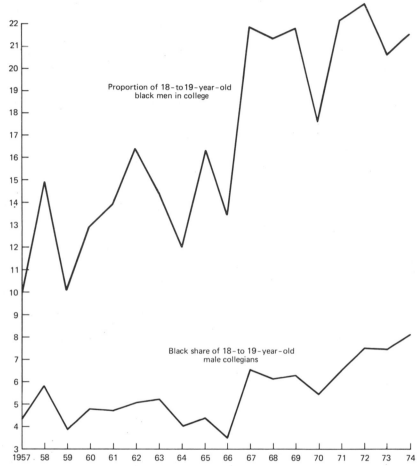

Figure 27. Proportion of young black men enrolled in college and black share of young college men, 1957–1974 (from U.S. Bureau of the Census, *Current Population Reports*, "School Enrollments," Series P-20, various editions, 1957–1974). Statistics prior to 1964 are estimated from census statistics on nonwhites, using the black proportion of nonwhite, 18- to 19-year-old men in college and of nonwhite, 18- to 19-year olds from Series P-20, No. 148, p. 11, 12.

is through higher education—not black studies," he wrote in the *New York Times*. "Let the clever young black go to a university to study engineering, medicine, chemistry, economics, law, agriculture"— vocational fields that prepare students for high-paying jobs in industry.[11]   Separatist   rhetoric   notwithstanding,   black   youngsters

[11] *The New York Times Magazine*, 11 May 1969.

responded to the new economic opportunities in the manner recommended by Sir Lewis. They enrolled in colleges and universities in increasing numbers and chose business and technical rather than black studies majors.

The quantitative dimensions of the movement of young black men into college is depicted in Figure 27, which records the proportion of 18- to 19-year-old black men enrolled in college and the black share of young male collegians in post–World War II years. Beginning in the mid-1960s, there was a significant increase in the fraction of young black men in college, an increase that was maintained in the 1970s, despite the overall fall in male enrollments due to the market decline. From 1960 to 1974 the number of young black men in college quadrupled, raising the black share of 18- to 19-year-old male college students from 5% to 8%. That this movement was, in fact, an adaptation to new market opportunities is indicated in the close link between the timing of enrollment increase and the improvement in opportunities, both of which were late 1960s and early 1970s developments. Regression analysis of the proportion of young black men in college shows that 82%–85% of the variation in enrollment from 1959 to 1972 can be attributed to the change in labor market opportunities.[12]

Among women, a similar though less pronounced pattern of increased college enrollments by blacks is found. Between 1960 and 1974 the proportion of 18- to 19-year-old black women enrolled in college increased by 95%, compared to a 32% increase for white women. As white female enrollments did not fall relative to the student-age population in the early 1970s, however, the extent of black female gain vis-à-vis whites was more moderate than that of black males.[13]

The increase in black student enrollments was concentrated in predominantly white colleges and universities. In 1964 just 114,000 black students were enrolled in schools outside the predominantly black institutions of the South, less than one-half of the total

[12] Freeman, *Black Elite*, Table 32.

[13] U.S. Bureau of the Census, "School Enrollment," *Current Population Reports*, Series P-20, No. 110, Table 5, p. 12; No. 148, Table 5, pp. 11–12; No. 278, pp. 5–6. The 1960 black figures are estimates obtained by multiplying the black share of college enrollees and population in 1964, from Series P-20, No. 148, the first report giving Negro data separately. See Freeman, *Black Elite*, Table 21 for exact figures.

number enrolled; by 1970 nearly three-fourths of black collegians were in national, largely white, institutions, ranging from the major mid-Western public colleges and universities to elite Eastern schools. At MIT, the black share of enrollments jumped from less than 1% in the early 1960s to 6% by 1973; at Yale, to 7%; at Brown to 11%, and so forth—indicative of a major change in the recruitment and admission policies of these and other Northern schools, which, after decades of neglect, began seeking out able black youngsters. Ninety-two percent of the 1960–1970 growth of black college enrollments occurred in predominantly white institutions and only 8% of the increase in the traditional black colleges of the South.[14]

In a striking example of supply responsiveness to labor market incentives, black college students moved rapidly into the newly economically attractive fields, shunning the traditional ones of teaching, the ministry, segregated professional services, and also nonvocational black studies. Figure 28 compares the actual and intended occupations and fields of study of black collegians from the graduating classes of the early 1960s to that of the class, 1978, which entered college in 1974.[15] What stands out in the figure is the remarkable jump in the proportion of black men planning on business careers. In the class of 1961 (for which data on occupational plans are available) just 7.3% of black college students chose business careers, compared to over three times as many white students. In the class of 1978, 22.0% of black students intended to become businessmen—36% more, proportionately, than among their white peers. Similarly, whereas in the graduating class of 1962 (for which data on fields of study are available) just over 5% of blacks at predominantly Negro colleges, where most blacks were enrolled, graduated in business; in the class graduating in 1978, nearly 25% anticipated studying business, while the white proportion declined modestly.

In engineering, also, the fraction of black majors in the field rose steadily from the classes of 1961 and 1962 to that of 1978, though not sufficiently to equal the white fraction. In the class of

---

[14] Data on specific colleges from personal interviews. Enrollment of black students in primarily white colleges given in U.S. Bureau of the Census, "The Social and Economic Status of the Black Population in the U.S.," *Current Population Reports*, Series P-23, No. 38 (1970), Table 69, p. 83.

[15] While the data in Figure 28 relate to blacks in primarily black colleges, evidence in Freeman, *Black Elite*, Chap. 3, shows that career choice of black students in other colleges follows a similar distribution.

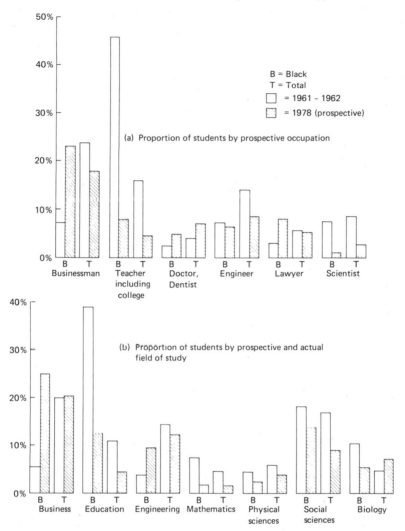

Figure 28. Occupations and fields of study of male black college graduates or students, actual and intended, 1961–1962 and 1978 (data for 1961 from J. Fichter, *Young Negro Talent: Survey of the Expectations of Negro Americans Who Graduated from College in 1961* (National Opinion Research Center, processed 1964), Table 54, p. 51, and J. Fichter, *Negro Women Bachelors* (National Opinion Research Center, processed 1965), Table 54, p. 73. I have subtracted the females from the total figures to obtain the estimates for males; data for 1961 prospective occupation from U.S. Department of Labor, *Manpower Report of the President,* 1965, Table H-9, p. 266; data for field of study of blacks from U.S. Office of Education, *Earned Degrees Conferred, 1965;* data for 1978 fields of total men, from American Council on Education (with U.C.L.A.) *The American Freshmen: National Norms for 1974,* pp. 20–21). Note: Career plans for 1961; degrees for 1962 Data are for students in primarily black colleges.

1978, 8.8% of black male students were prospective engineers, compared to 3.9% in 1962. Even in the predominantly black colleges, where the absence of strong engineering programs contributed to the lack of black engineers, the proportion increased toward that for whites. A third traditionally closed area with a major influx of black graduates is law. In the early 1960s, 3% of black graduates were working as lawyers, compared to nearly twice as many whites. In the class of 1978 more black than white male students planned on legal careers.

Counterpoised to the swing into business, engineering, and law is a precipitious decline in the number of blacks intending to teach. Between 1962 and 1978 actual (expected) degrees in education fell from 39% to 10% of all black male degrees. The expected number of teachers plummeted from 46% of the class of 1961 to 11% of the class of 1978.

There can be little doubt that these remarkable shifts in career patterns reflect economically rational responses on the part of young persons who are highly sensitive to income and employment opportunities. Surveys of students show that, to an even greater extent than white students, young blacks place great weight on economic factors in their educational and career decisions. For example, 75% of black (66% of white) freshmen view the major benefit of college to be monetary, 53% (48%) regard "high anticipated earnings" as very important in career choice. Similarly, a larger proportion of black than white students are concerned with being "very well off financially."[16] Multiple regression analysis of black career decisions in the post–World War II period support the survey implications: Most of the changes in the occupational distribution of blacks and of blacks relative to whites appear to be a result of economic supply behavior.[17] This sensitivity to economic factors may be attributable to the low family income and socioeconomic background of most

[16] "The Black Student in American Colleges," *ACE Research Reports* (1969), Vol. 4, No. 2, p. 31; and American Council on Education (with the University of California, Los Angeles), *The American Freshmen: National Norms for Fall 1974*, p. 32. The data in the later relate to students at black colleges only.

[17] See, Freeman, *Black Elite*, Chap. 3. See also R. Freeman, "Changes in the Labor Market for Black America, 1948–1972," *Brookings Papers on Economic Activity* (Summer 1973).

young blacks, for whom college remains a major avenue for mobility into the middle class, even in the depressed market of the 1970s.

GRADUATE TRAINING AND CAREER OPPORTUNITIES

In the highly specialized market for workers with postbaccalaureate training, where blacks had historically been exceptionally underrepresented, especially large gains were scored in the post-1964 period.

Many major universities made increased black (and other minority) representation in graduate student bodies institutional goals, assigning the task of minority recruitment to particular administrators, initiating special fellowship programs for minority students, waiving application fees, and actively seeking qualified applicants in various ways (for instance, by writing to all those scoring well on the Graduate Record Exam). Preferential treatment in admissions became sufficiently widespread that *Graduate and Professional School Opportunities for Minorities*, published by Educational Testing Service, recommended that minority students "identify your minority group" in applications when the law prohibits schools from requesting ethnic and religious information. To increase minority representation in business schools, several universities banded together in consortia that provide financial aid and engage in recruiting activities (e.g., Council for Opportunity in Graduate Management Education, Accelerated Business Leadership Education, Consortium for Graduate Study in Management). Law and medical schools also undertook joint action to increase the number of minority students in their fields. Perhaps the most striking indication of the changed environment is the statement by the School of Medicine of the University of Mississippi that "for equal abilities, we would give preference to a minority student" in awarding fellowships—surely a far cry from past policies.[18]

[18] Various programs to aid black students are described briefly in Freeman, *Black Elite*, Chap. 2. Educational Testing Service, *Graduate and Professional School Opportunities for Minorities* (Princeton, 1975), p. 189, contains the quotation from the University of Mississippi.

Job opportunities and incomes for black workers with master's, doctoral, law, and other advanced degrees also improved markedly. In higher education, primarily white colleges and universities that had rarely if ever hired black faculty suddenly began seeking black doctorates and master's graduates. In 1969, just 29% of black college teachers were employed outside the predominantly black institutions of the South; in 1973, the proportion was 49%. Black faculty salaries, particularly for academic "stars," that is, those with many publications—the usual indicator of academic prowess—jumped substantially, until by 1973 a black scholar with five or more scholarly articles earned about $2000 more than a comparable white. At given institutions, different standards appear to have been employed in black and white appointments, for blacks tended in 1973 to have fewer publications than whites, other factors held fixed.[19] Mommsen's survey of black Ph.D.'s in 1970 revealed a general black income advantage, ranging from $92 in the physical sciences to $2603 in the social sciences and over $4000 in education and the humanities.[20] As early as 1969, Census of Population data show young black engineers with 5 or more years of college earning slightly more than young white engineers, while highly educated young blacks in other professions earned slightly less than their white peers.[21] As the data in Table 11 suggest, moreover, there is evidence that new black MBA and law graduates were doing at least as well as their white peers.

Overall, the income of black men with graduate training increased much more rapidly than that of whites. From 1959 to 1969, census figures reveal a 117% increase in the income of black men

[19] These data were calculated from the American Council on Education computer tape for its 1972–1973 and 1968–1969 faculty surveys. See American Council on Education, "College and University Faculty, A Statistical Description," *ACE Reports* (1970), Vol. 5, No. 5, and "Teaching Faculty in Academia 1972–73," *ACE Reports* (1973), Vol. 8, No. 2. The calculations are described in detail in Freeman, *Black Elite*, Chap. 8.

[20] K.G. Mommsen, "Black Doctorates in American Higher Education: The Case for Institutional Racism" (Paper presented at Southwestern Sociological Association at San Antonio, Texas, 1973); K.G. Mommsen, "Black Ph.D.'s in the Academic Marketplace: Supply, Demand, and Price" (Paper presented at the Sixty-eighth Annual Meeting of the American Sociological Association, 1973).

[21] U.S. Bureau of the Census, 1970 Census of Population, *Earnings by Occupation and Education*, PC(2)-8B, Table 2, p. 129, gives the earnings of blacks aged 25–34 with 5 years or more of college as $13,133, compared to $12,946 for white engineers in Table 1, p. 6.

aged 25 to 29 with 5 or more years of college, compared to a 70% increase for comparable white men. Over the same period, the income of 30- to 34-year-old black workers with graduate training increased by 86%, that of similar whites by 69%.[22]

The major consequence of these income changes was that the economic return to black male investments in graduate education exceeded those of whites at the outset of the 1970s, producing markedly different patterns of black and white graduate enrollments in the late 1960s and early 1970s. Between 1969 and 1973, the number of black men enrolled for 5 or more years of college tripled, while the number of whites so enrolled increased by just 9%. As a fraction of the relevant population—college graduates less than 35 years of age—black enrollments quadrupled, according to current population survey data—a far different trend than that for all men, whose relative enrollment fell by 18%, leading to the striking fact that in 1973 proportionately more black than white college men may have been enrolled for graduate studies. Because of the small sample on which they are based, the current population data must, however, be treated as rough estimates, providing orders of magnitude only. Even given the possibility of error, however, the pattern of change is clear.[23]

Turning to specific graduate and professional programs, by 1973, 5.1% of students in law school, 7.1% of students in medical school, 4.4% of students in Ph.D. programs were black—figures still below the black share of the population but far above those in the recent past. At one elite school, Harvard, black enrollments in law and medicine accounted for 10% and 13% of first-year students in 1973. However, blacks accounted for just 3.5% of Harvard MBA students and at most 2.2% of all MBA students in the country. In

[22] U.S. Bureau of the Census, 1960 Census of Population, *Educational Attainment*, PC(2)-5B, Table 6, pp. 88–89 reports median incomes of $3483 and $5167 for nonwhite men aged 25–29 and 30–34 with 5 or more years of college and medians of $5060 and $7250 for all men. U.S. Bureau of the Census, 1970 Census of Population, *Educational Attainment*, PC(2)-5B, Table 7, pp. 150–152 reports incomes in 1969. I have averaged the median figures for men with 5 and 6 or more years of college to obtain $7371 and $9618 for black men aged 25–29 and 30–34 and $8611 and $12,243 for white men.

[23] Enrollments for 5 or more years from U.S. Bureau of the Census, "School Enrollment," *Current Population Reports*, Series P-20, No. 206, Table 4, pp. 16–18; No. 278, Table 3, pp. 22–24. Comparable data on men with degrees from Series P-20: No. 194, Table 1, pp. 10–12; No. 274, Table 1, pp. 24–25.

arts and sciences, intensive recruitment efforts notwithstanding, Harvard was able to obtain justly new black students in the Graduate School of Arts and Sciences in 1973—a fact partly attributable to the attractiveness of law, medicine, and business administration to top black students.[24]

Despite the dramatic improvement in the economic status of black college workers and those with graduate training, and the consequent increase in enrollments, blacks remained significantly underrepresented in the overall college work force in the 1970s. In 1974, when 9.5% of the population over 25 years of age was black, blacks constituted just 4.6% of those with college degrees. Because of the long working life of the average person, even if the black share of enrollments and new graduates continues to rise, the black—white gap in college attainment in the current work force guarantees continued underrepresentation through the year 2000.[25]

OTHER MARKET PROBLEMS

Attainment of approximate black—white economic parity among women and young men and significant improvement in the relative position of older black college men does not mean that all problems of market discrimination have been eliminated for the "black elite." There are several important areas of current or future potential difficulty. First, to the extent that recently hired black graduates and managers are restricted to jobs relating to the black community in national corporations, the statistical gains overstate the true advance in reducing discrimination and increasing opportunities. Second, parity in starting jobs does not guarantee parity in promotions in the future. Market discrimination could simply have a more delayed reaction on the economic status of black graduates

[24] Data from Freeman, *Black Elite*, Table 26.
[25] Data from U.S. Bureau of the Census, "Educational Attainment," *Current Population Reports*, Series P-20, No. 279, pp. 15—17.

than in the past. Third, if governmental pressures for affirmative action weaken, so too will demand for black college personnel. Fourth, to the extent that poor family background, low scores on standardized tests, and related disadvantages that have long plagued blacks are indicators of white-collar job skill, black graduates may, discrimination aside, not perform as well on average as whites in the newly opened positions and consequently may suffer in a market with "surplus" graduates.

These possibilities notwithstanding, the fact remains that there was a remarkable transformation in the college job market for black Americans in the late 1960s—an improvement that was maintained in the 1970s, despite the overall deterioration of the demand–supply balance. Given over 100 years of little or no black economic advance relative to whites, this transformation represents one of the most striking socioeconomic developments in American history.

Does the College *Man* Still Have the Advantage?

Did college-trained women also make significant progress in the job market relative to white men in the late 1960s and 1970s? What was the impact of equal employment opportunity, the women's movement, and declining birthrates on the career path of female graduates? Does the college man still have the advantage?

Large as were the gaps in the income and occupational position of black and white college-trained men, those between men and women have traditionally been greater. As late as 1969, women with 4 years of college, working full-time, year-round, had annual earnings that were more than $1000 below those of male high school dropouts and barely half those of comparable male graduates. The vast majority of women held teaching jobs, usually in elementary schools. Many of those in other occupations reported explicit job discrimination. In the leading vocational interest test, girls were not scored on some traditionally "male" occupations, such as accounting or public administration. Estimates of the rate of return to female investments in college invariably showed women getting a lower return than men in the job market. Consequently, fewer women than men went on to obtain academic degrees. In 1960, just 35% of bachelor's, 32% of

159

master's, and 10% of doctoral degrees were awarded women.[1] Statistics from the Census of Population show a sharp fall between 1930 and 1960 in the fraction of professional workers who were women, indicative of a deterioration in the position of highly trained women in the job market, relative to men.[2]

Some of the male–female differences in the job market are presumably the result of discrimination by employers and fellow workers. Most female professionals report encountering discrimination in their careers. In separate studies, 65% of female lawyers, 41% of female psychologists, and 66% of female anthropologists claimed, for example, that their careers were adversely affected by sex discrimination. Among doctoral graduates, one in three expressed similar beliefs, according to Helen Astin's 1969 study. The explicit behavior and attitudes of employers also reveals the pressure of sex discrimination in the job market. In the early 1960s, asked whether or not, "employers stated a policy to you of discrimination against the hiring of women as lawyers," 86% of female lawyers reported such employer statements. "Significant" or "extensive" discrimination against female LL.B.s was also reported in 1967 by upwards of 90% of law school placement offices. As late as 1970, academic employers who were presented with comparable descriptions of male and female applicants gave less desirable employment offers to the female applicants.[3]

[1] The income figures are from U.S. Bureau of the Census, *Current Population Reports*, Series P–60, No. 75, Table 47, pp. 101, 105. The degree data are from U.S. Bureau of the Census, *Statistical Abstract 1961*, Table 177, p. 137.

[2] In 1960, 38.1% of professionals were women; in 1930, 44.4%. While the fraction of professionals who were women fell, the fraction of all workers who were women rose from 22.1% to 32.7%. See R. Blitz, "Women in the Professions 1870–1970," *Monthly Labor Review* (May 1974), pp. 34–39; D. Knudsen, "The Declining Status of Women: Popular Myths and the Failure of Functionalist Thought," *Social Forces* (December 1969), Vol. 48, No. 2, pp. 183–93.

[3] The data on lawyers are from J.J. White, "Women in the Law" *Michigan Law Review* (1967), Vol. 65, No. 6, pp. 1084–1095, reprinted in A. Theodore, *Professional Women* (Cambridge, Mass.: Schenckman, 1975), pp. 647–659; those for psychologists and anthropologists are given in L. Morlock, "Discipline Variation in the Status of Academic Women," in *Academic Women on the Move*, ed. A. Rossi and A. Calderwood (New York: Russell Sage Foundation, 1973), Table 13.29, p. 293. The preference for male applicants is reported in Morlock, p. 293. Reports of discrimination against women lawyers are from White, pp. 648–649. Data for doctoral graduates from H. Astin, *The Women Doctorate in America* (New York: Russell Sage Foundation, 1969).

The attitudes of faculty and fellow students in graduate and professional education have also operated to the detriment of college women. One-fourth of male faculty and one-fourth of male graduate students, and about 10% of female faculty and 15% of female graduate students agreed in 1969 that "female graduates are not as dedicated as males" to their studies.[4] While attitudes of this type partly reflect reality rather than prejudice—women have, after all, had higher dropout rates than men in years past—they may also be partially self-fulfilling, creating an environment that fails to take female students seriously.

Other more complex factors, however, also underlie the labor market problems of college-trained women. Perhaps the most important is the fact that, unlike men, most women workers hold another job—as producers of services and goods in the home—which draws time and effort away from the labor market and leads to disjointed career paths, as can be readily seen in census statistics. During the childbearing age bracket of 25 to 44, the participation of college women in the work force drops sharply. In 1970 only 42% of college-trained women 25- to 44-years old were working, compared to 82% of those in the next youngest and 60% of those in the next oldest age bracket. Among married women with children under 6 years, only 30% worked in 1970 compared to 53% of their peers without children. Even fully employed Ph.D.'s devote considerable time and effort to home activities, upwards of 19 hours per week in 1969.[5]

The loss of experience and the atrophy of skills during a critical part of the work life has deleterious consequences for women in their careers, reducing promotions and potential gains in income. During the 1960s, the income of college men aged 25 to 34 in 1960 and 35 to 44 in 1970 increased by 116%, as they advanced in their jobs. By contrast the income of college women in the same age group increased less rapidly (by 72%), presumably due to their obtaining less

[4] S.D. Feldman, *Escape from the Doll's House* (New York: McGraw-Hill, 1973), Table 38, p. 104. I have grouped Feldman's data to obtain the figures in the text.
[5] The labor force statistics in this paragraph for all college women relate to those with 4 years of college. They are from the U.S. Bureau of the Census, 1970 Census of Population, *Educational Attainment*, PC(21-5B, Table 6, pp. 125–127. The data for Ph.D.'s are from Astin, p. 95.

experience and investing less in job skills. As a consequence, the female age—earning profile is much flatter than that of men, producing greater sex differentials with age. Discrimination aside, the dual career of married women is a serious fetter on their progress in the job market.[6]

The negative effects of family responsibilities on female but not on male careers is recognized by women professionals. One-third of female psychologists in one study viewed the marriage institution as a professional liability compared to just 5% of male psychologists. Conversely, 75% of the male but just 28% of the female psychologists regarded marriage as a professional asset. One in four women working part-time said that marriage was the chief factor in abandoning their full-time careers.[7]

Indicative of the difficulty of combining household and labor market work, a large proportion of women with graduate training choose to remain single. In the 1930s, 80% of female Ph.D.'s (in all fields) were unmarried; in the 1960s the proportion was 55%. Only one-half of female faculty in 1969 were currently married, compared to 87% of male faculty. The story is similar for female doctors (39% unmarried or not living with husbands), physicists (46%), microbiologists (44%), and psychologists (57%).[8]

On the other hand, the majority of college-trained women, with less career orientation, have historically looked upon household activities as their major function and employment as a secondary issue. In a 1968 national study, for example, 50% of college women stated that they expected their life-long satisfaction would come from marriage and family, compared to 18% who cited careers as the major source of satisfaction. Two-thirds of the students in the class of 1964 in one women's college said they wanted to be housewives

---

[6] The 1960 data are from the U.S. Bureau of the Census, 1960 Census of Population, *Educational Attainment*, PC(2)-5B, Table 7, p. 112, and Table 6, p. 88. To obtain incomes for 25- to 34-year-old women, I averaged the figures for women aged 25 to 29 and 30 to 34. The 1970 data are from U.S. Bureau of the Census, 1970 Census of Population, *Educational Attainment*, PC(2)-5B, Table 8, p. 183, and Table 7, p. 150.

[7] J. Bernard, *Academic Women* (University Park, Pa.: Pennsylvania State University Press, 1964), p. 217.

[8] The data for faculty, physicists, microbiologists, and psychologists are from Morlock, "Discipline Variation," Table 13.7, p. 264; the data for doctors and Ph.D.'s are from Astin, *The Women Doctorate*, p. 27. The figure for the 1920s is given in Feldman, *Escape*, p. 5.

with one or more children, rather than married career women. Most married female professionals and graduate students, moreover, have viewed their careers as subordinate to their families and to the careers of their husbands. In a 1969 Carnegie Commission survey of graduate students, nearly half (46%) of the women, compared to less than a third (32%) of the men, agreed strongly that "career will take second place to family obligations." More female than male students (35% versus 25%) believed that "emotional strain" would or might force them out of graduate school and more female than male students (16% versus 11%) gave pressure from spouses as a deterrent to completing studies.[9]

In a social system where, as sociologist Alice Rossi puts it, "What a man 'does' defines his status but whom she marries defines a woman," the problem of combining or choosing between household and marriage versus work activities is by no means easy.[10]

CAUSES AND EFFECTS OF INCOME INEQUALITY

Why do women college graduates earn less than men? What is the impact of earnings inequality on the work commitment of college women?

Economic analyses usually decompose the male–female income differential into two parts: that associated with differences in attributes, especially years of work experience, which results at least in part from the dual role of women in the home and at the place of work; and that between persons having similar job market attributes or productivity, such as training, experience, and the like, which can only be explained by discrimination.

Through the early 1970s studies found that, no matter how many labor market attributes were held fixed, women invariably earned less than men, which implies the presence of substantial

[9] The data from the women's college is given in K. Cross, *Beyond the Open Door* (San Francisco, Calif: Jossey-Bass, 1971), p. 147. The Carnegie survey data are contained in American Council on Education, "The American Graduate Student: A Normative Description," *ACE Research Reports* (1971), Vol. 6, No. 5, pp. 41, 68. I grouped the fraction answering yes and maybe to obtain the figures on emotional strain.
[10] A. Rossi, "Women in Science: Why So Few" in A. Theodore, *Professional Women*, p. 616.

"pure" sex discrimination in employment. On the basis of less work experience and other factors, women might be expected to earn about 20% less than men, on average, compared to the 40% gap found across broad groups. Even within narrowly defined professions, where differentials are smaller, "correcting" for differences in male and female work attributes generally leaves a substantial discrimination "residual." Among academic faculty, for example, $1410 of a $2450 male–female income difference in 1969 was attributed to differences between men and women in 32 salary determinants, such as articles published or years on the job. Thus 41% of the difference was attributable to discrimination.[11]

Disparity between male and female earnings, whatever its cause, contributes to the differential allocation of time to the job market by the two sexes. As long as male earnings exceed those of women, economic considerations dictate (all else the same) a division of labor in the family in which men devote most effort to employment and women specialize in household "production." It does not pay to have the person with the higher wage devote an equal amount of time to the household. This incentive structure is compounded by the progressive tax system, which taxes female earnings at the marginal family rate, so that in a family where the man earns, say, $20,000, the take-home pay of a woman earning $10,000 may be no more than $6000, from which—if there are young children—child care must be deducted. In addition, higher male earnings also make it economically rational for wives to be geographically mobile, often at the expense of their own careers, when their husbands get better jobs, and not conversely. There is no inherent sexism in these types of decisions—they can be viewed as normal economic responses to differential opportunities to improve the economic position of the family.

The behavioral response to differences in income means, however, that even if all of the female–male income differential were allocated to differences in attributes, discrimination would not be eliminated as a potential cause of inequalities. The difference in time

[11] In 1973, women earned roughly 60% as much as men. Most studies show that, with experience, occupation, and related factors fixed, they would earn 80%. See for example, Council of Economic Advisors, *Economic Report of the President* (1973), Chap. 4, pp. 103–106. For academic women see H. Astin and A. Bayer, "Sex Discrimination in Academia," reprinted in *Academic Women*, ed. Rossi and Calderwood, Table 15.7, p. 353.

worked, career commitment, and investment in skills on the job could themselves be at least partly induced by discrimination in the labor market. Explaining the low incomes of female graduates would require another stage of analysis.

FORCES OF CHANGE

The traditional position of college-trained and other women in the job market came under attack in the late 1960s by four inter-related forces.

First, a series of federal laws and executive orders made discrimination on the basis of sex, as well as of race, illegal. The Equal Pay Act of 1963 was adopted by Congress to require similar pay for similar work within an establishment. In 1972, the Act was extended from largely low-paying blue-collar activities to executive, mana-gerial, administrative, sales, and professional workers. At the behest of Howard Smith, the representative from Virginia, who hoped that inclusion of discrimination on the basis of sex would increase opposi-tion to Title VII of the 1964 Civil Rights Act or make it a "joke," sex discrimination was outlawed in that key piece of legislation. While initially the Equal Employment Opportunity Commission de-voted most of its effort to minorities, treating the problems of women as secondary, by 1972 over one-fifth of cases concerned discrimination against women. In 1968, President Johnson issued Executive Order 11375, which required affirmative action in female as well as minority employment by federal contractors and the federal bureaucracy. Guidelines for affirmative action progress for women were issued by the Office of Federal Contract Compliance (OFCC) in January 1969. In perhaps the most important court case dealing with discrimination against women, AT & T was ordered in 1968 to pay $15 million in reparations to women who had faced job discrimination in the past. Congressman Smith's joke was having substantial consequences on the job market.[12]

---

[12] Federal activities to end discrimination against women are described in J. Freeman, "Women on the Move: Roots of Revolt," in *Academic Women*, pp. 1–36, ed. Rossi and Calderwood; also in B. Sander, "A Little Help from Our Government: WEAL and Contract Compliance," in *ibid.*, Chap. 19, pp. 439–462; and in Carnegie Commission on Higher Education, *Opportunities for Women in Higher Education* (1973), Chap. 8. The A.T.&T. figure is taken from P. Wallace (ed), *Equal Employment Opportunity in the A.T.&T. Case* (Cambridge, Mass: MIT Press 1976) p. 1.

Second, for the first time since the suffragettes of the 1920s, American women initiated a serious woman's movement. Unlike the civil rights movement, which of necessity had to deal first with voting rights and education, woman's liberation concentrated from the beginning on job market issues and the dual role of women in the family and employment sectors. College women played a major role in the movement, and their problems were given special attention. The National Organization of Women (NOW) filed complaints in June 1970 with the OFCC against 1300 companies on charges of sex discrimination, after having pressed for Executive Order 11375. The Women's Equity Action League instituted class action suit against *all* colleges and universities in the same year, galvanizing the Office of Civil Rights of HEW to begin major investigations of the academic sector. By 1971 many more charges had been filed with HEW concerning sex discrimination than concerning minority discrimination.[13]

Within professions, the woman's movement spawned numerous caucuses and groups seeking to improve the position of females. From 1968 to 1974 at least 90 such organizations were formed, in areas ranging from vocational guidance and secondary and elementary school teaching to modern languages, public administration, engineering, and economics. The American Association of University Professors' Committee on the Status of Women, which had been founded in 1919, was reactivated in 1970 after years of dormancy. These groups provided detailed studies of the position and problems of female professionals and pressures for change. The Committee on the Status of Women in Economics reported in 1973, for example, that only 14 of the tenured faculty of 43 leading departments were women and pressed for change in this situation. Many of the organizations publish rosters of women in their fields as an aid in job placement and recruitment. The Committee on Women in Statistics publishes a list of more than 1000 women trained in statistics, computer science, and related areas. The American Association for the Advancement of Science has available a roster of rosters. One

---

[13] The activities of women's groups are described by Freeman and Sanders, in *Academic Women*, ed. Rossi and Calderwood. The importance of college-educated women in the movement is reported in J. Mitchell, *Women's Estate* (New York: Pantheon, 1971).

consequence of these efforts was to make employers aware of and sensitive to the position of women professionals.[14]

Third, less dramatically but possibly most importantly, there was a sharp drop in the birthrate in the late 1960s and early 1970s, which meant that young college women had less family responsibilities than their peers in the past. In 1974, college-trained women aged 25–34 reported 1158 children ever born per 1000 compared to about 1800 children ever born per 1000 women in that age group in 1967. Since a cause of women leaving the work force is the presence of children under 6 years, the declining production of children operated to increase commitment to work. Among college (and other) married mothers with children under 6, moreover, the rate of participation in the work force rose. The change in fertility rates cannot be invoked, however, as a "cause" of the greater work commitment on the part of women. The decision to have children and the decision to devote full-time to work are to be viewed as part of the same phenomenon.[15]

Fourth, possibly in response to woman's liberation or related socioeconomic incentives, traditional attitudes toward the role of women appear to have undergone significant change both among

[14] K. Klotzburger's "Political Action by Academic Women," in *Academic Women*, ed. Rossi and Calderwood, Chap. 13, provides the best summary of the diverse caucuses and activities. She reports "at least fifty" from 1968 to 1971 (p. 360). The American Association of University Women's *Women's Caucuses and Committees in Professional Associations* reports 90 groups by 1974. The statistical roster and roster of rosters are reported in Scientific Manpower Commission, *Manpower Comment* (March 1975), Vol. 12, No. 3, pp. 18–19.

[15] Data relate to children ever born per 1000 women for white women ever married with 4 or more years of college. 1967 data from Bureau of the Census, "Population Characteristics, Previous and Prospective Fertility: 1967," *Current Population Reports*, (January 26, 1971), Series P-20, No. 211, Table 2, pp. 15–16. 1974 data from Bureau of the Census, *Current Population Reports*, Population Characteristics, "Fertility Expectations of American Women: June 1974," (February 1975), Series P-20, No. 277, Table 17, p. 36. The 1967 figures are estimates because the census reported them on a different age basis than the 1974 figures: for groups aged 25–29 and 30–39 rather than for 25- to 34-year olds. I added to the figures for 25- to 29-year olds one-half of the difference between the children of ages 25–29 and 30–39 to obtain the 1800 in the text. In 1967, 25- to 29-year-old women already had more children than those of ages 25–34 in 1974, despite the extra 5 years for childbearing in the latter group. Data on participation of college women with children under age 6 in U.S. Bureau of the Census, 1960 Census of Population, *Educational Attainment*, PC(2)-5B, Table 5, p. 71 show 21% working in 1960 compared to the 30% reported for 1970 in the text.

college graduate women and their potential male mates. As Figure 29 shows, there was a marked change in the attitudes of first-year college men and women toward the allocation of the time of women to work and home activities. As late as 1967, virtually one-half of first-year college women and two-thirds of the men believed that "woman's place is at home"; by 1974, barely one in five women (but 40% of men) still looked at the household as the appropriate place to be. Both groups wanted to discourage large families more than in the past. Moreover, there was an enormous change in the importance

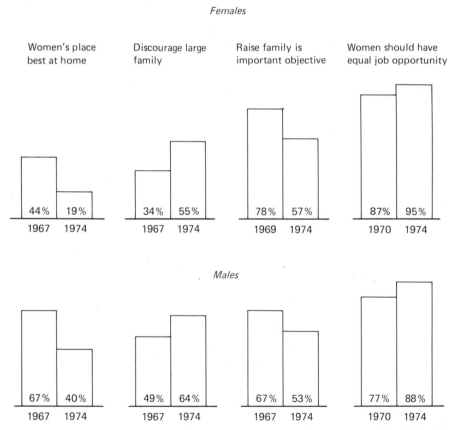

Figure 29. Changes in attitudes of first-year college men and women toward female activities, 1967–1974 (from American Council on Education: "National Norms for Entering College Freshmen, Fall 1967," Vol. 2, No. 7, pp. 19, 27; "National Norms for Entering College Freshmen, Fall 1970," Vol. 5, No. 6; "National Norms for Entering College Freshmen, Fall 1969," Vol. 4, No. 7, p. 27, p. 35; and with UCLA *The American Freshman: National Norms for Fall 1974, pp. 24, 36.*

attached to raising a family. The fraction of women regarding the family as a "very important or essential goal" in life fell from 78% in 1969 to 57% in 1974—a rate similar to that for men. Even more dramatic, the fraction of female students at one college who said they would "like to be a housewife with one or more children" plummeted from 65% in the class of 1964 to just 31% in the class of 1970. At Stanford, 70% of the female students in 1965 reported that they would leave the work force during the time that their children were under the age of 6; in 1972 the proportion was down to 7%! Of the graduates in 1972, only 19% mentioned the role of wife and mother as part of their plans for the next 5 years. Virtually none expected to be a full-time housewife in that period.[16]

The activities of the woman's movement, the antidiscriminatory laws, the decline in birthrates, and the change in attitudes are intertwined parts of a major societal change—whose causal connections cannot be readily pinned down. The impact of these changes on the job market for college-trained women and on the educational and career paths of young female Americans could, however, be seen by the mid-1970s. Much like black college graduates, women graduates were making job market and educational advances—advances that counterbalanced the effects of the declining market for the highly educated, at least in part.

THE ECONOMIC GAINS OF COLLEGE WOMEN

As might be expected on the basis of the "active market" argument of Chapter 1, the most impressive evidence of improvement in the job market for college-trained women is in the position of new graduates. As Figure 30 illustrates, the starting salaries of female baccalaureates working in business rose more rapidly than that of men in the period of market decline, almost keeping pace with inflation. In some specialties, the gains to women were such that they obtained a slight premium. Starting female B.S. chemists, for example, were reported by the American Chemical Society to be earning $10,000 per year in 1974, compared to $9800 for men,

---

[16] These figures are reported in Carnegie Commission on Higher Education, *Opportunities for Women in Higher Education*, pp. 21–22.

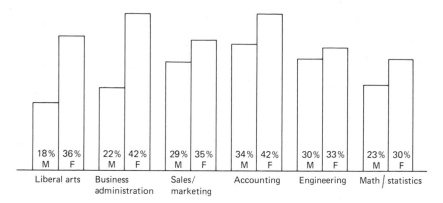

18%	36%	22%	42%	29%	35%	34%	42%	30%	33%	23%	30%
M	F	M	F	M	F	M	F	M	F	M	F
Liberal arts		Business administration		Sales/ marketing		Accounting		Engineering		Math / statistics	

Figure 30. Percentage increases in the starting pay of college graduates in business, by sex and discipline, 1969–1975 (from F. Endicott, *Trends in Employment of College and University Graduates in Business and Industry* [Evanston, Ill.: Northwestern University, 1969, pp. 4–5 and 1975, p. 4, 61).

while starting female engineering, business administration, mathematics—statistics, and liberal arts specialists in business earned from $36 to $312 more than men, according to the Endicott placement survey. By contrast, 6 years earlier there were differentials favoring men of up to $1200 per year. Salary figures for other fields, however, and from a different survey, that of the College Placement Council, show men still receiving somewhat higher starting salaries.

Job placement records show a similar pattern of improvement for college women. Between 1969 and 1975, the proportion of new hires who were female in the companies in the Endicott survey doubled from 10% to 20%. Companies reported "more women engaged in college recruiting" and an increased number of job offers to women. In 1973 the companies in the Endicott sample offered 3064 positions to women and obtained 1451—a ratio of 2.1 offers per new hire compared to a ratio of 1.9 offers per male new hire. A study in the *Journal of College Placement* reported that more recruiters at one major Southern university regarded female graduates as having an advantage over males than vice versa. Nearly one-half believed that the fact that the graduating student is female "may" (39%) or "will significantly" (7%) enhance her career advancement, while only one-third regarded female gender as "possibly limiting" (21%) or "significantly limiting" (3%) her career. Analysis of the position of doctoral graduates by UCLA's Higher Education Research Institute revealed that for the first time new female doctoral graduates obtained jobs as good as those of their male peers in various fields. According to the study, the percentage of new female doctoral graduates hired by institutions equal or superior to those granting their degree was approximately equal to that of men in the academic year 1972–1973. Among new doctoral graduates employed as college teachers, for example, 20.6% of the men and 23.8% of the women were at institutions equal or superior to their degree-granting institution.[17]

The earnings of all female college graduates also improved relative to that of male graduates, though more moderately. Between 1968 and 1974, the income of women with 4 years of college employed full-time and year-round increased by 49% compared to a 33% gain for men. Among those aged 25 to 34, the differential gain for women was 37% versus 24%. Even with these advances, however, women with 4 or more years of college employed full-time and year-round had only 55% as high earnings as men with the same schooling, and those aged 25 to 34, only 67% as high.[18]

While the economic position of women graduates appears to have held up better in the depressed 1970s than that of men, there was noticeable deterioration in some dimensions. Between 1969 and 1974, the ratio of the income of year-round, full-time employed college women aged 25 to 34 to that of their high school peers dropped from 1.42 to 1.29. The fraction of all women graduates working as professionals fell from 81% (1969) to 69% (1974), with much of the decline due to the reduced likelihood of obtaining a teaching job (which dropped from 49 to 43% in the period). On the other hand, however, the ratio of college to high school incomes dropped much less sharply among all women than men: The female ratio fell by just 5 percentage points compared to an 18 percentage point dip in the

[17] The studies are H. Brookshire and H. Lunsden, "Women, Jobs & Mobility," *Journal of College Placement* (Spring 1975), Vol. 35, No. 3; A Cartter and W. Ruhter, *The Disappearance of Sex Discrimination in First Job Placement of New Ph.D.'s* (UCLA, Higher Education Research Institute, 1975).

[18] In 1969 female graduates had mean incomes of $6680; those aged 25 to 34, $6664. In 1974 the comparable mean incomes were $9975 and $9126. In 1969 male graduates had mean incomes of $13,554; those aged 25 to 34, $10,961. In 1974 the comparable incomes are $18,081 and $13,582. These data are from the U.S. Bureau of the Census, "Consumer Income," *Current Population Reports*, Series P-60, No. 66, Table 41, pp. 94–101, No. 101, Table 58, pp. 116–123.

Table 14. Increasing Proportion of Women in Male-Dominated Professions

Occupation	1960	1970	1974
Professional	38.4	39.9	40.5
Accountants	16.5	26.2	23.7
Architects	2.1	3.6	–
Engineers	0.8	0.6	1.3
Law	3.5	4.9	7.0
Life and physical sciences	9.2	13.7	15.9
Pharmacists	7.5	12.0	–
Doctors	6.9	9.3	9.3
Editors and reporters	36.6	40.6	43.6
Teachers, college and university	23.9	28.6	30.9
Managers	14.8	16.6	18.5
Salaried managers	13.9	16.1	18.4

Source: Data for 1960 and 1970 relate to experienced work force as given in U.S. Bureau of the Census, 1970 Census of Population, *Detailed Characteristics*, U.S. Summary, PC(1)-D1, Table 221, pp. 718–719. Data for 1974 are from U.S. Bureau of Labor Statistics, *Employment and Earnings* (June 1975), Vol. 121, No. 12, Table 1, p. 7.

male ratio.[19] More importantly, perhaps, for the first time in many decades, women began to move—as Table 14 shows—into various male professions.

From 1960 to 1970 there was a moderate growth in the female share of workers in several important traditionally male occupations. In accounting, in particular, the share of women jumped by 59%; in law, by 40%, in college teaching, by 20%. In the early 1970s, the movement of women into these "new" occupations accelerated. The proportion of engineers who were women more than doubled, while the proportion of managers increased by 11%. All of these percentage gains are, however, from low initial bases, and they still left enormous differences in the types of jobs held by college-trained men and women. Nevertheless, after having deteriorated from 1930 to 1960, the labor market position of college

[19] The income data are from U.S. Bureau of the Census, "Consumer Income," *Current Population Reports*, Series P-60, No. 75, Table 47, p. 105 and No. 101, Table 58, p. 120. The employment data are from U.S. Bureau of Labor Statistics, Special Labor Force Reports, *Educational Attainment of Workers*, No. 175, Table I, p. A-18, No. 125, Table I, p. A-28.

women relative to men did improve in the 1960s and 1970s. Progress was being made.

While a detailed study of changes in various professions and degree programs is needed to pin down the locus and cause of these changes in the returns to female investments in college, it seems plausible that the overall gains are due to the improved market for college women resulting from the activity of the woman's liberation movement and federal affirmative action. The extensive effort by female academics and professionals to alter conditions for women in the job market may have begun to bear fruit in the early 1970s.

ECONOMIC RETURN TO FEMALE COLLEGE GOING

The economic value of college training to women and thus the monetary incentive to enroll in higher education can be analyzed from two related perspectives. In terms of the job market, one can compare the earnings of college and high school graduate female workers, following the procedure used in Chapter 1 for men, to obtain the rate of return to the 4-year investment. Alternatively, however, because of the importance of the income of husbands in the financial position of families, one can examine the effect of attending college on the marital situation of women and their overall family rather than personal income. Historically, going to college has substantially increased the probability that women marry college men and thus obtain a share of the return on the male investment. In 1970, there was a 63% likelihood that a married female college graduate's mate was a male degree recipient, compared to a bare 10% likelihood that a married female high school graduate's mate had graduated from college. In 1973, the husbands of college women earned $15,950 compared to $12,256 for the husbands of high school women (see Table 13), implying that the college women obtained $3694 higher family income, all else the same, from their marriage. Of course, all else is not "the same," because college-trained women come from better family backgrounds than their high school peers, have higher IQs, and so forth, which also raises the probability that their mates would be college men or high wage earners. Even so, the crude statistics indicate that the enhanced

Table 15. Income of White Women and Husbands of White Women with College and High School Degrees, 1973

	Income of women working in 1973	Income of married women	Income of husbands
All women (18- to 64-years old)			
College graduate	6093	3883	15,950
High school graduate	4187	2326	12,256
Difference	1906	1557	3694
Young women (25- to 29-years old)			
College graduate	6374	4544	12,178
High school graduate	4012	2039	11,377
Difference	2362	2505	801

Source: Calculated from U.S. Bureau of the Census March 1974, *Current Population,* Computer Tapes. Data in Column 1 are means weighted by the census sampling weights; data in columns 2 and 3 are not. This creates only a modest difference in the figures. The figures in Column 1 are lower than those in U.S. Bureau of Census, *Current Population Reports,* Series P-60, No. 97 because I include 18- to 24-year olds.

probability of marrying college men yields a substantial economic return to female college-going.[20]

Does the economic return from the marriage market exceed that from the labor market? Measured solely in penuniary gains, do female investments in 4 years of college pay off largely in terms of their own earnings or in terms of those of the men they marry?

The evidence in Table 15 suggests that in the past at least the economic gains from marriage have exceeded those from the job market. Column 1, which compares the income of white women aged 18 to 64 with 4 or more years of college who worked in 1973 to that of white female high school graduates who also worked shows that the college-trained obtained $1906 more in the labor market. Column 2, focused solely on married women (including those outside the labor market), reveals a smaller differential of $1557. These differentials are roughly half as large as the differential in the income of the husbands of college and high school women, suggesting a much greater gain from marriage than from working. Further analysis, decomposing the differentials into that part resulting from differ-

[20] The marital data are from the U.S. Bureau of the Census, 1970 Census of Population, *Marital Status,* PC(2)-4C, Table 14, p. 269. The income data are tabulated from the March 1974 *Current Population Survey* tape.

ential likelihoods of marrying college men and that due to differences in the income of husbands having the same level of education, suggests that most of the gain from the marriage market is due to differences in the likelihood of obtaining a college mate. If husbands of female high school graduates had the same income as the husbands of female college graduates with the same education the differential in husbands' incomes would be $2864. Hence, 78% of the economic return of female college-going via marriage is attributable to the enhanced likelihood of marrying a college man (and interactions between the two).[21]

The changing job market for female and male graduates of the 1970s can be expected to alter the traditional pattern of incentives for female investments in college. The deterioration in the income position of young college-trained men relative to young women ought to raise the return to female college going from the job market relative to the return from marriage. The evidence in Table 15 on the income of 25- to 29-year olds in 1973 is consistent with this expected development. In sharp contrast to the situation among all women, 25- to 29-year-old female college graduates earned a much greater premium over their high school peers from working than from marrying husbands with high incomes. In the future, as the 25- to 29-year olds age and as many leave the job market to bear and raise children, the economic gain via husbands' incomes will, to be sure, increase relative to that from own labor market activity. Even so, the comparison in the table makes clear the direction of change: an increase in pecuniary rewards to college going from work relative to marriage.

FEMALE COLLEGE GOING

Although female students are generally less economically and vocationally oriented than male students, the changing job market

---

[21] To calculate the income that the husbands of high school graduates would have if they had the same income at each educational level as the husbands of college graduates, I have simply taken a weighted average of the incomes of the husbands of college graduates with varying levels of education. The data come from the U.S. Bureau of the Census, March 1974 *Current Population* data tape. The incomes of husbands with given years of schooling are quite similar, and the interaction term quite small supporting the interpretation in the text.

induced substantial changes in the educational and career decisions of young women. Because the market opportunities and return to schooling for women did not deteriorate as much as for men, the female share of students and graduates rose substantially (Figure 31). Whereas in the 1950s and early 1960s women constituted about 45% of

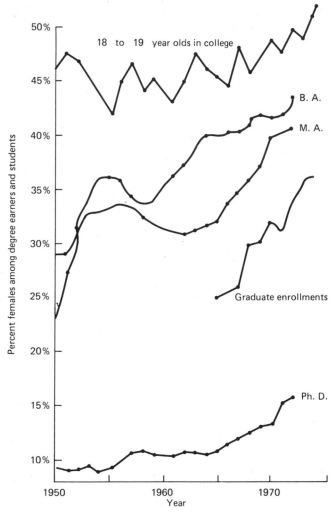

Figure 31. The proportion of students and graduates who were women, 1950–1974, (data on enrollments, 18- to 19-year-olds, and graduates, from U.S. Bureau of the Census, "School Enrollment," *Current Population Reports* Series P-20, 1950–1974; data on degrees, from U.S. Office of Education, *Earned Degrees Conferred*, 1950–1971, with 1972 updated from data provided by the Office).

18- to 19-year old enrollees and only 35% of bachelor's graduates (a differential due to the greater likelihood of dropping out), by 1972, they made up over one-half of enrolled 18- to 19-year-olds and 45% of bachelor's recipients. From less than one-third, the female share of master's recipients increased to 41% by 1972, and the share of Ph.D.'s from about 10% to 20% by 1974. The proportion of graduate students who were women also rose sharply. In medical schools, just 7% of entering students were women in 1959–1960 compared to 13% in 1971–1972 and about 22% in 1974–1975. In law schools, the female share rose from less than 5% in 1966 to 16% by 1972. In graduate engineering, the number of female students rose to 3.4% of the total by 1974.[22]

The increase in the female share of students in the depressed market was accompanied by a significant shift in fields of study and career plans. As Figure 32 illustrates, in a variety of traditionally male fields the proportion of bachelor graduates who were women rose in the late 1960s and early 1970s. In 1960 only 3% of architecture graduates were women, compared to 12% in 1972; in 1960 women made up 4.3% of accounting majors, compared to 10% in 1972. Similarly in geology and physics the female share of degree recipients increased notably. In what is perhaps the most male-dominated field, engineering, only 1% of degree recipients were women in 1972 (up from 0.4% in 1960) but enrollments in the entering class of 1974 promised a large increase to the end of the decade: 6.5% of first-year engineering students in 1974 were female.[23]

The career plans of first-year college women who were in the process of choosing an occupation in the 1970s tell an even more striking story (see Figure 33). In the class of 1978, the "relative probability" that women would enter certain traditional male fields—"relative probability" being defined as the ratio of the proportion of females planning on the field to the proportion of males—rose sharply. When the relative probability is one, the two genders evince

[22] The medical school data are from AMA, "Medical Education," *JAMA* (Supplement, January 1975), Vol. 231, Table 11, p. 18, with 1974 reported in Scientific Manpower Commission, *Manpower Comments* (September 1974), Vol. 12, No. 8, p. 14. Law school data are from, S.R. Bysiewicz, "1972 AALS Questionnaire on Women in Legal Education," *Journal of Legal Education* (1973), Vol. 25, pp. 503–511. Engineering figures are reported in Scientific Manpower Commission, *Manpower Comments* (June 1975), Vol. 12, No. 5, p. 18.

[23] Engineering figures from *ibid.*

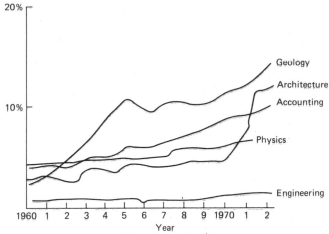

Figure 32. The proportion of bachelor's graduates who were women in primarily male fields (from U.S. Office of Education, *Earned Degrees Conferred*, 1960–1971, with 1972 updated from data provided by the Office).

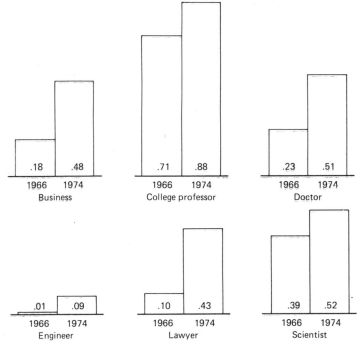

Figure 33. The relative probability that freshman women would enter primarily male occupations: ratios of female to male probabilities of being in the career (calculated from data in Table 2).

the same likelihood of selecting the field; when it is below one, males are more likely to choose it; and conversely when it is above one. Between 1966 and 1974 the relative probability that women would become business executives, doctors, engineers, lawyers, scientists, and college professors rose sharply, in several cases from minuscule to fairly sizable numbers.

All told, female students—like their male peers—were aware of the changing college job market and responded accordingly. The "push" of the falling market for schoolteachers and the "pull" of more favorable demand for women graduates in positions previously filled almost exclusively by men substantially altered long-standing patterns of career and education decisions.

BLACK FEMALE GRADUATES

Since college-trained women earn less than men, and blacks less than whites, one might expect persons with both sex and race "handicaps," to fall at the very bottom of the college job market. Surprisingly, this does not turn out to be the case. Black women with college training earn more than their white peers and tend to hold jobs that are about as good. In 1973 black women with 4 or more years of college earned $1000 more in annual earnings than similarly educated white women.[24]

Why have black college women fared comparatively well in the job market? The principal reason is that, as noted in Chapter 6 compared to white women, black woman graduates work more hours and are less likely to withdraw from the labor force when they have family and child-rearing responsibilities. In 1970, 80% of black female graduates were in the work force, compared to 58% of their white peers. Upward of 77% of black women with 4 years of college and children under the age of 6 worked, compared to just 34% of similarly situated white women. Among professional women with work experience in 1973, 68% of black, compared to 56% of white women worked full-time year-round. The greater commitment of black female graduates to the job market has two effects on their

---

[24] Incomes from U.S. Bureau of the Census, "Consumer Income," *Current Population Reports*, Series P-60, No. 97, p. 129.

earnings: It raises annual income because of the greater time expended at work, and it raises wages by giving them more experience, seniority, and "on-the-job" training.[25]

Underlying the job market orientation of black female graduates are two factors—the lower earnings of black than white husbands and the much higher frequency of female-headed homes in black than in white America. Faced with the option of having husband and wife work full-time to attain middle- or upper-middle-class incomes and escaping inner city slums or keeping the wife at home at greatly reduced family income and living standards, many black families choose the former. The "cost" of this option is that black female graduates have the lowest birthrate of any significant demographic group. In 1970 black women, aged 35 to 39, with 4 years of college, averaged 2.0 live births compared to 2.5 live births among comparable whites.[26]

One additional factor has also contributed to the relatively strong job market for black woman graduates in years past—the segregated school system of the South, which created a special demand for black woman teachers.

The labor market responsibilities of black women have made black female students more economically motivated and attuned to job market opportunities than all female students. In 1974, two-thirds of black women compared to just 35% of all female freshmen checked "high anticipated earnings" as a major factor in their choice of career; 70% and 56% of black women regarded availability of job openings and the chance for rapid advancement as very important, compared to 52% and 30% of all women.[27]

Presumably as a result of this economic orientation, black female college students appear to have responded especially rapidly to the new opportunities for women in the 1970s. By 1974, 15% of black female freshmen (versus 8.5% of all female first-year students)

[25] U.S. Bureau of the Census, 1970 Census of Population, *Employment Status and Work Experience*, PC(2)-6A, Table 9, pp. 99, 101; *Educational Attainment*, PC(2)-5B, Table 6, pp. 125, 129. 1973 data are from Bureau of Labor Statistics, Special Labor Force Report No. 171, *Work Experiences of the Population, 1973*, Table A-5, p. A-4.
[26] U.S. Bureau of the Census, 1970 Census of Population, *Fertility of Women by Education and Family Income for the United States*, PC(51)-51, Table 36 and 37.
[27] American Council of Education and University of California, Los Angeles, *The American Freshman: National Norms for Fall 1974*, p. 32.

planned to enter business, 4.1% (versus 3.5%) intended to make a career in medicine, and 3.5% (versus 2.3%), in law.[28]

While the dual disadvantages, race and sex, do not appear to cause black women to suffer in the job market, they still earn only one-half as much as white male graduates. Their economic position appears strong only when compared to that of white female graduates.

MARKET CHANGES AND THE FUTURE

This and the preceding chapter present an impressive picture of changing employment opportunities and responses to change by black and female graduates in the period of overeducation. Through the early 1970s blacks and women fared better than white men in the depressed college job market, presumably because federal affirmative action and other social changes raised demand for their services relative to that for white men, counterbalancing some of the effects of the overall relative oversupply of graduates. Both groups proved responsive to new opportunities, moving from traditional to new fields and areas of employment. For black men, the improvement relative to white men is, I believe, likely to be maintained into the near future. For women, black and white, however, the situation appears more problematic, for there will be increased downward pressure on the market for college women as the demand for schoolteachers declines in the late 1970s and 1980s. Whether demand in traditionally male fields will increase by enough to offset this pressure is by no means clear. There is, as yet, insufficient experience with the changing demand for female graduates to make a definite judgment.

[28] The freshmen data refer to freshmen in black colleges. They are from American Council of Education, *The American Freshman*, p. 32.

The Functioning of an Overeducated Society

Throughout this book I have stressed the economic aspects of college education—the return to college in the form of salaries and jobs, and the behavioral response of invididuals to this return. If the analysis and forecasts are reasonably on target, the decade of the 1970s will prove to be a significant turning point in the job market for the highly educated. The relation between education and the economy will be different in the future than in the past, with ramifications for the overall functioning of the society. In this final chapter, the major findings of the book are briefly summarized and the potential broad societal implications of the changing economic value of higher education are considered, albeit speculatively.

SUMMARY OF FINDINGS

The purpose of this book has been threefold: to analyze the dimensions of the new depression in the college job market; to explain the reasons for the collapse of the market and the differential experience of various professions and groups; and to peer, cautiously, into the future. Our major findings can be summarized briefly:

1. The college job market underwent an unprecedented downturn at the outset of the 1970s, with young graduates just beginning their careers most severely affected. Real and relative earnings of graduates dropped, employment prospects and occupational attainment deteriorated, and large numbers were forced into occupations normally viewed as being below the college level. For the first time in recent history, the economic value of an investment in college education fell, though with considerable variation among professions and groups.

2. In response to the depressed market, the proportion of young men enrolling in college dropped substantially, reversing the long-term upward trend in educational attainment. The decline in enrollments relative to the population of eligibles occurred in all social strata but was most marked among the lower middle class. However, the enrollment of black youngsters, whose relative position in the college job market improved and the enrollment of women, whose position improved in some respects and worsened in others, did not decline but rather leveled off. At the graduate level, there was also a fall in the proportion of the relevant group enrolled, particularly for degrees in the sciences.

3. Student career decisions were substantially altered by the changing economic fortunes of the various high-level occupations. Where the market was extraordinarily depressed, as in physics, enrollments dropped precipitously; while, in occupations that fared relatively well, applications (as in medicine) or enrollments (as in law through the early 1970s, engineering in the early 1970s, and business administration) rose. Overall, the shift was from the academic and scientific to the traditional professional, and business-oriented specialties.

4. Despite the market downturn, black college graduates fared reasonably well—the result of affirmative action and related antidiscriminatory activity. Corporations, which first began to recruit on black college campuses in the mid-1960s, continued seeking out and hiring black graduates, particularly in engineering, accounting, and the technical fields. Starting black graduates obtained roughly the same salaries as whites and, in response to new opportunities, moved increasingly out of traditional professional services into management and business-oriented majors. The rate of return for blacks investing

in undergraduate and graduate education rose to exceed those for whites.

5. The job market for women graduates did not deteriorate significantly, save in the case of teachers. The salaries of female graduates in business and the employment of women in traditionally male occupations increased in the late 1960s and early 1970s, while the overall premium for female college graduates fell only slightly. As a result, the proportion of college students and graduates who were women rose, and an increasing number of them elected to enter fields dominated by men. Sizable differences between male and female college earnings and occupational attainment remain, however. The future economic position of college women will depend on the net effect of declines in demand for schoolteachers and increases in demand for women in traditionally male areas. Which of these forces will dominate is not clear.

6. Four major factors determine the dynamic functioning of the college job market: the responsive supply behavior of the young; the long working life of graduates, which makes total supply relatively fixed in the short run; the concentration of graduates in certain sectors of the economy and moderate substitutability between college-trained and other workers; and the cobweb feedback system, which leads to recurrent market oscillations, as high salaries and good job opportunities induce many students into fields, producing a flood of graduates 2 to 5 years later, and, all else the same, a relative surplus that in turn reduces salaries and employment opportunities, depressing enrollments, and so on.

7. The downturn of the 1970s was caused by slackened growth of demand, due to reduced expansion of industries that employ many college-trained workers, and continued increases in supply. In education, a critical employment sector, the number of schoolchildren began to fall, lessening the demand for teachers. In many high-technology industries, the reduction of federal R&D and defense spending and of the space program led to a contraction of employment relative to total employment in the economy. On the supply side, there was a sizable increase in the number of graduates seeking work, as the large cohorts of the post–World War II baby boom reached the labor market, their entry having been delayed by the tendency to invest in postgraduate training. Because the number

of young persons in college far exceeds the number of persons of retirement ages with college training, relative supply will continue to increase in the 1980s, despite the fall in the fraction enrolled.

8. The decline in the college market was most severe in the teaching and research professions, and least in business-oriented specialties, reversing the pattern of the 1960s. Elementary and high school teaching was one of the hardest hit professions, and it is likely to continue to suffer from a weak job market through the mid 1980s. Specialists with doctoral degrees also experienced an extreme market downturn, substantially cutting the pecuniary value of the degree. Within the research and teaching areas, however, the market experiences of different professions varied greatly: the economic position of physicists plummeted, that of biologists did not; new high school teachers in English and in foreign languages had smaller chances of obtaining jobs than those in mathematics. In response to the job market, proportionally fewer students elected academic fields in the mid-1970s. As for the future, the depressed market is likely to be maintained in most academic areas, with some of the fields that still had strong markets in the mid–1970s experiencing declines at the turn of the decade. In others, however, such as physics, market equilibrium may be overshot, generating reversals of current relative surpluses.

9. By contrast, graduates with degrees in business specialities, including those in accounting and business administration especially at the master's level, in medicine, and in engineering fared reasonably well in the falling job market. These fields had not expanded so rapidly in the booming sixties, nor were they heavily dependent on education and research spending (save for engineering). In some, cyclical "cobweb" adjustments caused distinct market conditions. Engineering, for example, enjoyed a cobweb upsurge in the mid-1970s, which strengthened the economic position of new engineers relative to other graduates. Law, on the other hand, underwent a similar boom at the turn of the decade and began a downswing in the mid-1970s. As more students switch to business and engineering, however, the decline in the market will be diffused more evenly among college fields.

10. Federal policies exacerbated rather than ameliorated both cobweb and longer-run adjustment problems. Federal R&D spending, which increased greatly in the early and middle 1960s and fell

relative to GNP thereafter, was a major contributor to the sixties boom and seventies bust. Fellowships and scholarships encouraged "overproduction" of master's and doctoral graduates in the 1960s and discouraged enrollment in the 1970s. The high variability of federal spending and the demand for high-level manpower, often responding to short-term crises, was the "squeaky wheel" in the market, inducing cyclical ups and downs and the uneven production of graduates.

11. While the income and occupational attainment of college graduates began falling in the 1970s, college-trained workers continued to have higher earnings and better prospects than their high school peers. Indeed, in some white-collar jobs, as in the sales, managerial, and clerical areas, the relative surplus of college-trained workers appears to have made it more difficult for high school workers to obtain positions. Moreover, there is no indication that less value is being placed on the other, less tangible, rewards of a college education. The continued, though diminished, value of the degree in the job market and the continued nonpecuniary rewards suggest that, for many, college remains a good investment.

12. Forecasts of the state of the college labor market using the recursive adjustment model indicate that the economic position of new bachelor's men is likely to remain depressed through the end of the 1970s, will improve moderately in the early 1980s and rapidly in the late 1980s, though not to the boom conditions of the 1960s. The major force improving the market will be a reduced supply of new baccalaureates. The proportion of young men choosing college will stabilize in the mid-1970s, after having fallen from the peak of the late 1960s, and rise in the 1980s in response to the market upturn. Because the population of college age will be small in the 1980s, however, total enrollments will still drop, which will act to depress the market for Ph.D. and master's graduates until the late 1980s.

While the position of new graduates will improve, that of older graduates, including the classes of the 1970s, may not. The supply of all graduates will grow relative to the working age population until the end of the 1990s, so that supply pressures for reduced economic rewards to the college trained will remain, despite smaller numbers of new graduates. Throughout the period, however, various professions and social groups are likely, as in the past, to fare very differently in the job market, with some graduates doing relatively well and others relatively poorly. Overall, the period of severe "overeducation" is likely to last for about a decade, to be followed by a period of market balance at a lower plateau. In contrast to the past, higher education will be a "marginal" investment, not a sure "guarantee" to relatively high salaries and occupational standing, whose expansion will reduce its benefits.

SPECULATIONS ABOUT SOCIAL IMPLICATIONS

What are the likely impacts of the ongoing and forecasted changes in the economic value of college education on a society in which college has traditionally been a major route to economic progress and social mobility? How will a society in which higher education has a smaller economic payoff, in which further expansion of college training reduces economic rewards, and in which colleges and universities are no longer a leading growth sector function in comparison to societies where education is a much scarcer resource? What actions may improve the position of the overeducated American?

The declining economic value of education can be expected to have direct and indirect impacts on the functioning of the economy and the social system. It is likely to alter the degree and form of social mobility, the distribution of income, the rate of economic growth, and the link between schooling and work. In addition, the spirit or ethos of the "overeducated society" may differ significantly from that of the recent past.

Social Mobility and Income Distribution

Paradoxically, perhaps, the fall in the economic value of college training is likely to have opposite effects on the extent of social mobility and the distribution of incomes. With respect to mobility, the drop in the material rewards to education and stabilization in the fraction of persons choosing the investment implies the end of education as a means of upward mobility in society as a whole, though some groups, such as blacks, may continue to advance via schooling. However, the decline in mobility via education does not mean that the social structure will become more rigidly stratified. Assuming that financial access to colleges and universities remains open to those from poorer backgrounds, there will continue to be movement up the socioeconomic ladder by the school route, accompanied, however, by some intergenerational downward mobility. For the first time in American history non-negligible numbers of young persons will obtain less education than their parents.

In response to the decline in the value of education, individuals and society are likely to search for alternative routes of economic advancement. Training and promotion policies within firms may attain greater importance than in the past. Competition for income and status may come to center more on place of employment and the job market than on the school system.

The reduced role of schooling in social mobility could, depending on the type and efficacy of alternative routes of upward movement, lead to greater class consciousness and conflict. With the potentiality of exiting from one social stratum to another by formal education reduced, individuals may accord greater "loyalty" to their social group. The importance of college as a social melting pot, yielding contacts and friendships across groups, will be diminished. More importantly, if, as some believe, education has served as a "safety valve," helping to maintain social stability in the same manner as was alleged of the frontier years ago, the narrowing of the valve may diminish an important force for stability. The discontent of individuals and families experiencing downward generational mobility and of those from the lower strata who looked upon schooling as their "ticket to the middle class" could have destabilizing political consequences.[1]

At the same time, however, income distribution is likely to become more egalitarian as a result of the relative surplus of the educated. With the number of persons having various levels of education fixed, reductions in the economic value of higher education necessarily creates more equality in labor incomes. With the number going to college falling, relative to current levels, while the total number of graduates continues to increase, the situation is more

---

[1] The "exit–loyalty" terminology is taken from A. Hirschman, *Exit, Voice, and Loyalty* (Cambridge, Mass.: Harvard University Press, 1970).

complex, because income distribution depends not only on wage differentials but on the number of persons in various categories. While detailed calculations are needed to measure the impact, inequality in incomes among workers is likely to diminish. This could ameliorate or counterbalance the deleterious effects of the reduction in mobility.

Economic Growth

Unless new areas of investment are found to replace education, the growth rate of the economy will slacken in the period of overeducation. In the context of standard growth accounting, which makes the effect on growth of a factor depend on its share of income and rate of change, the lower education premium and diminished flow of new college graduates implies a smaller increase in the share of the educated, both in income and in the work force, than in the recent past. As a result, the once sizable contribution of schooling to increases in income per head—estimated to be from one-quarter to one-third of total growth—will drop greatly.[2]

Schooling and Work

The deterioration in job opportunities and occupational attainment for over a decade will create a sizable group of dissatisfied educated workers whose position will be incommensurate with their training and aspirations. The way in which they adjust to the new status of the educated and the way in which society, particularly employers, adjust to their position will be important factors in the social fabric of society. Lacking, in a weak market, the "exit" option of quitting for better jobs, some of the highly educated in non-college-level jobs may resort to political protest and related modes of expressing discontent. Many, however, may come to accept a sharp

[2] Denison's calculations provide a variety of possible estimates, depending on time period and treatment of various factors. The increase in national income per person with economies of scale isolated and allocated among other sources was 1.54% in 1929–1969 and 1.18% in 1929–1948. Education improved labor inputs by 0.41% in the former and 0.40% in the latter, giving relative contributions of 27% and 34% in the two periods, providing the bounds given in the text. See E. Denison, *Accounting for United States Economics Growth 1929–1969* (Washington, D.C.: The Brookings Institution), Table 9-7, p. 136.

break between schooling and work, viewing their education more as a consumption than as an investment activity. They will relinquish the belief that college has clearcut vocational consequences and seek satisfaction from its nonoccupational benefits. The extent to which those with dashed aspirations accept the new reality or seek to change it may turn out to be an important element in the political future.

On the job side, employers can be expected to alter the organization of work to use the newly available educated workers most efficiently. Changes in the nature of work could reduce the division between blue-collar and white-collar workers, permitting greater upward mobility at work places and greater autonomy and responsibility in nonprofessional, nonmanagerial jobs. It could also, however, lead many to concentrate on nonwork leisure activities, with jobs reorganized to reduce their "disutility" by requiring less time, rather than to reduce undesirable features. Traditional promotion patterns and supervisory responsibilities are likely to come under attack and possibly be changed. With declining numbers of young college workers in some fields, the normal transition from professional to administrative or managerial work over the life cycle may be difficult. There will, after all, be fewer young graduates to supervise. More importantly, the young whose promotion and career paths are blocked by older persons in a declining market are likely to be discontented, creating potential intergenerational conflicts at the work place. A major burden is going to be placed on employers to adjust to the new availability of college graduates for jobs that have traditionally been held by the less educated and to the distorted age structure of the college work force.

HIGHER EDUCATION

Colleges and universities will face especially severe pressures and problems in the era of overeducation, as they switch from a growing to a declining economic setting. While my analysis foresees a smoother, more gradual decline in enrollment than standard forecasts, as a result of responsive supply behavior, the situation will still be difficult. Some institutions will close or be absorbed by stronger schools. New sources of students will be sought and offerings changed to increase demand. Some institutions are likely to seek additional older persons by focusing on retraining and vocational programs, possibly mimicking for-profit proprietary schools, which have long sought to attract part-time older students by tailoring programs to their needs. Others may concentrate on nonvocational cultural programs similar to those in many adult education centers. Overall, two divergent patterns are likely to be found on campuses: among students who continue to use schooling as a route for economic advancement, greater seriousness, greater specialization in occupation-oriented fields, greater vocationalism; among those who see little chance of their interests yielding salable skills, a concern solely with the consumption aspects of education, possibly on a part-time basis.

The demographic composition of the student population is also likely to differ from that of the past, with more woman and black students and, depending on policies of financing, possibly fewer from the lower middle class. In addition, because some specialties will be more affected by the falling job market than others, students are likely to choose different majors. More students can be expected to enter business-oriented fields and independent professions, at the expense of academic and research occupations, changing the areas of study of the nation's future leaders, with possible consequences for decision making. Departments faced with declining enrollment are likely to stress the vocational value of their training and offer more job-oriented courses. Because demand will be especially limited in the education sector itself, many graduate programs will undergo a major reorientation, from the preparation of teachers to the preparation of business and government employees, which will require changes in the content and subjects taught.

Changes in educational offerings are unlikely to come smoothly. The traditional mode of adjusting the distribution of faculty to new educational needs—by new hires—will be seriously hampered by no-growth or declining-growth conditions. Substantial attacks on the major element of rigidity in the educational system, tenure, are to be expected, though with uncertain prospects for success. Because there will be a sizable supply of highly qualified young Ph.D.'s seeking work at relatively low salaries in the 1970s, schools that have not locked themselves in by giving tenure to many in the past or by union contracts could significantly raise their standing in academia.

Several new centers of excellence are likely to be created as a result. If other institutions can find ways of reducing older tenured staff, the relative surplus of Ph.D.'s could lead to a widespread improvement in the academic qualifications of university personnel.

If academia is unable to find adequate positions for bright young Ph.D.'s and other researchers and scholars, there could be a major shift in the locus of intellectual effort. Research centers and government and business research groups can be expected to upgrade the quality of their staff, thus becoming intellectually more competitive with higher education.

The weakness of the academic market will alter the relative power of faculty, administrators and students. For better or worse, administrators are likely to attain greater power relative to faculty in the next decade. Teaching and contributions to the institution may, accordingly, become important criteria for academic success, relative to publications and related professional activities. For better or worse, competition for students will give students greater power within colleges. Such competition may reduce the relative cost of higher education for the more able, with scholarships once again given widely for ability as well as need. These changes in power will undoubtedly be resisted and lead to conflicts on campuses, though of a very different nature than those experienced in the riots of the late 1960s.

OPTIONS FOR INSTITUTIONS AND INDIVIDUALS

There are several alternative strategies or changes in modes of behavior that institutions of higher education and individuals may find beneficial in the era of overeducation.

Colleges and universities might ameliorate some of the problems of declining enrollments by linking liberal arts to vocational non-academic training, such as for union crafts, possibly through new degree offerings and operating procedures. By bringing together vocational nonacademic and liberal arts programs, the opportunity for blue-collar workers to undertake artistic and intellectual pursuits unrelated to their careers could be enhanced.

It may also be desirable to alter tuition charges to better reflect costs of different educational programs. For example, graduate programs are often subsidized by undergraduate tuitions, suggesting that graduate tuitions are too low. Such changes will tend to limit graduate enrollments, an effect that is not inconsistent with the anticipated lower demand for Ph.D.'s in many areas. If such price changes are not possible, it may be desirable to limit certain graduate programs even beyond the size determined by student choice. University policies should be such that educational prices or allocation decisions reflect true social costs, no matter who pays.

A third possibility is to reduce the amount of time required for studies, by operating full-time during summer and vacation periods. The present 4 years needed for the bachelor's degree could be reduced, with considerable saving of forgone income to students and at no serious loss of educational quality. All else the same, the reduction in the time needed to obtain a degree, from 4 to 3 years, would cost a student four summers of work at low pay and gain him or her 1 year of work as a graduate at higher pay, raising the economic value of a college training. While in the past the desire for summer leisure may have made a concentrated course of studies attractive to only a few, in the changed market more students are likely to find this option desirable. At the least, experiments in altering the time period of courses and the operations of academia should be made to learn the best ways to deal with the new market reality.

Because the American higher educational system is, despite its flaws, generally superior to that in the rest of the world, attention should be given to the possible expansion of foreign student enrollments, particularly from the newly rich oil countries and such developing countries as Brazil, Mexico, and others, whose human resource demands are likely to outstrip the capacity of domestic universities. Already, Venezuela has initiated a major program to "export" thousands of students to the United States for higher education. We have a comparative advantage in producing college training, it could be "sold" overseas, taking up some of the slack in domestic student enrollment.

As for individuals, while there are no panaceas to a declining market, students can improve their employment prospects in several ways. First, they can undertake earlier and more careful career planning than in the past, giving close attention to the different opportunities within broad fields: to the greater likelihood of obtaining a teaching job by specializing, say, in mathematics, rather than in foreign languages; to the better opportunities for civil, rather than aeronautical, engineers; to the greater demand for applied, rather than pure, mathematics and so forth. Second, lemminglike rushes into particular areas, such as into law in the late 1960s, and doctoral science studies in the early 1960s, should be avoided. When more and more students are flocking into an area, that is a good indication of possible cobweb surpluses in the future. Third, for those concerned with long-term careers, job searching should not be concentrated in the East Coast and West Coast areas, where the demand–supply imbalance is most severe. Teaching jobs are scarce all over, but they are far more difficult to find in New York and San Francisco than in small towns in the interior of the country. Architecture positions are hard to come by in Boston but not so hard to find in Houston, and so forth. College graduates need not, like the unemployed coal miners of the 1960s, worsen their chances for good careers by being geographically immobile. Fourth, women and blacks—who have good chances for positions in some nontraditional fields—should not be deterred from these careers even when, as in, say, physics, overall job prospects look bad. While the market for academic faculty will be weak in the future, unless affirmative action disappears the relative paucity of qualified blacks and women means that there are good chances for these groups in academia. Fifth, those with arcane interests may find they have an advantage when competing for specific kinds of jobs, for example, a specialist in Slavic literature is likely to have a better chance for a job with a firm likely to do business in Eastern Europe. It is probably better to follow specific "odd" courses of study, rather than standard majors that fail to distinguish a student from his peers. Finally, even students with strong liberal arts interests should take some vocationally oriented courses, such as computer programming, which will help obtain jobs.

As for the graduates of the early and mid-1970s, who have already experienced weakened labor market prospects, the forecasted upturn of the 1980s holds some promise. To take advantage of the potentially improved market, these graduates should seek to maintain college-level skills, preserve career options, and prepare to move into better jobs in the 1980s. Some may find it fruitful to undertake retraining in colleges to restore atrophied skills when the market begins to improve.

RESPONSE OF THE GOVERNMENT AND BODY POLITIC

How will the political system respond to the period of over-education? There are several possible government reactions to a continued depression in the college market. Governments could "let nature take its course" by permitting the natural market adjustment processes to operate in the manner described in Chapter 3. Such a laissez-faire policy does not mean that the government will not influence the market but that any effects will be the by-product of other policies and not of specific actions to aid the depressed college graduate. Alternatively, the national government could seek to lessen cyclical fluctuations in the college market just as it currently seeks (unsuccessfully) to ameliorate the fluctuations in the business cycle. Dampening cobweb ups and downs might involve "countercobweb" scholarships and aid to education—leaning against the wind in order to maintain programs and yield more steady supplies in the future. Specialists in such technical areas as physics, where possible increased manpower demands and the long period of training make shortages conceivable in the next decade, might be "stockpiled" by awarding longer postdoctoral grants or by other forms of nonpermanent employment that would maintain research skills, in much the same way as we have stockpiled certain natural resources, including agricultural commodities. Policies designed to reduce the shortage—surplus cycles will require additional manpower analyses and planning, possibly as part of overall national economic planning of the type that some have recommended to Congress.

Under pressure from college-trained workers and their families, governments might also try to increase the demand for graduates directly. One reaction to a surplus of teachers would, for example, involve expansion of early childhood education, as the AFT and NEA would like. Through the political system we could opt for a society that is overeducated in relation to the labor market, rather than one that is undereducated in relation to human potential. Because the college trained continue to have better incomes and job prospects than the less educated, however, I do not believe that special "aid to the educated" programs are desirable.

Moreover, on the basis of past governmental behavior and responses in the early 1970s, ranging from federal fellowship cutbacks to state educational policies, these prospects seem unrealistic. Despite the political power of higher education and its clients, the government is more likely, if anything, to overreact to the market depression by reducing support for the college and university systems as part of the general rejection of higher education as having "failed" to live up to the promises of the 1960s

ETHOS OF THE OVEREDUCATED SOCIETY

A society in which higher education has a reduced economic value and is marginally rather than highly desirable is likely to have a very different spirit than traditional societies, where education is a scarcer resource. On the positive side, there may be a substantial decline in the formalistic use of schooling as a credential or screening device. New roles will be filled by educated persons, and the structure of economic achievement and progress will be less closely tied to classroom performance than in the past. Some of the social distinctions between college graduates and other persons, and the national obsession with degrees are likely to decline, especially if relatively many persons from better family backgrounds choose alternative career patterns. Individuals are likely to seek out new routes for socioeconomic progress, with potentially fruitful outcomes, depending on the form of institutions created.

On the negative side, because the value and prestige attached to education and high-level jobs is at least partly due to high salaries, the overall social evaluation of schooling is likely to fall in the period of overeducation. Contrary to the hopes of Galbraith, the "scientific—education estate" will face hard times, in terms of prestige, income, and power, due to its skills no longer being very scarce. Knowledge is power only if most people do not have it. More dangerous, perhaps, the failure of relatively many educated persons to achieve their career goals and the possible failure of others to find ways of improving their position outside of the educational sector could lead some to political extremism.

THE REST OF THE WORLD

There is some evidence that other developed "Western" countries, ranging from Japan to Sweden, are also on the verge of an era of overeducation. In Japan, the relative income of college graduates appears to have fallen sharply, though rapid economic growth maintained significant real absolute differences in income through the 1970s. Ulrich Teichler and Yoko Teichler-Urata of the Max Planck Institute of Germany have found, for example, that the ratio of university to high school graduates incomes in Japan dropped from almost 2.5 to just 1.5 to 1.0 between 1955 and 1971.[3] OECD reports suggest some waning of the job market for graduates in Western Europe. In Great Britain it was reported that "the 15% margin of difference enjoyed by the degree-holding graduate in 1967 (was) cut by about half" through 1975.[4] At the same time, however, there remain enormous premiums to the educated in less-developed countries with, in some cases (Venezuela, the Arab oil states, Iran, Ecuador, and Brazil, among others) college workers having potentially higher salaries than in the West. If political circumstances permit, this could lead to the migration of college-trained Americans overseas to obtain the graduate-level jobs and salaries they cannot find in the United States—a reverse braindrain. The outflow of highly educated workers from Great Britain could be a harbinger of the future.

FINAL PROVISO

An economist is not trained either to analyze or to forecast the broad social consequences of such far-reaching developments as long-run declines in the economic value of college training and of slack-

---

[3] See U. Teichler and Y. Teichler-Urata, *Die Entwicklung der Beschäftigungsmöglichkeiten für akademisch ausgebildete Arbeitsdräfte in Japan*, (Göttingen: Schwartz, 1975).
[4] *N.Y. Times* (18 Feb, 1976).

ened growth in higher education. Even for those elements of reality for which his training is suitable—namely, the quantitative dimensions of change in supply, demand, employment, and salaries—the history of forecasts is replete with failure. Accordingly, the preceding discussion of the period of overeducation and its possible characteristics must be viewed as speculative guesswork that merely points the way for more detailed analysis and thought by other social scientists.

Appendix A
College-High School
Income Differentials
and Rates of Return[1]

The rate of return estimates given in Table 1 of Chapter 1 are based on tabulations of data from the March 1969 and March 1974 Current Population Survey (CPS) of the U.S. Bureau of the Census. The basic statistics used in the calculations are given in Table A–1, which records the mean earnings of four-year college graduate and high school graduate white men by age. Because earnings during school and at the outset of the working life are critical in rate of return computations, the figures in the table are presented by year for ages 18–22, with the data for college men from ages 18 to 21 limited to those in school and that for high school to those who have, in fact, graduated. Because incomes refer to the previous year, the ages at which these men actually earned the reported amounts are 17–21. What is perhaps most striking about the observed fall in the position of graduates is that the drop in the relative position of graduates occurs almost exclusively among the young, as the "active market" hypothesis described in Chapter 1 would predict. In 1968, college men aged 25- to 29-years old earned 17% more than high school men of the same age; in 1973, just 6% more. By contrast, relative incomes at other ages show only slight changes.

[1] For a more detailed analysis, see R. Freeman, "The Decline in the Economic Rewards to College Education," *Review of Economics and Statistics* (forthcoming).

Table A-1. Current Dollar Incomes of White Men from Current Population Reports Survey Tapes, March 1969 and March 1974

	1968		1973	
	College	High school	College	High school
Age				
18[a]	1132	2600	1244	3907
19[a]	1224	3930	1523	5188
20[a]	1332	4260	1824	6100
21[a]	1392	4654	1963	6954
22	4641	5606	6107	7265
25–29	8591	7320	10,242	9702
30–34	11,390	8512	15,113	11,618
35–39	13,219	8987	17,684	11,827
40–44	12,868	9101	18,265	12,680
45–49	13,433	9005	18,806	12,945
50–54	13,491	8893	18,194	12,315
55–59	13,875	8487	19,459	12,059
60–64	12,840	8372	14,356	10,860

[a]College incomes for ages 18–21 refer to men in school.
Source: Tabulated from CPS tapes. Income defined as the sum of wage and salary and self-employment income.

The concentration of the decline in the relative income of graduates among the young, with a resultant "twist" in cross-section age-earnings profiles raises problems for the calculation of discounted future incomes and rates of return. To what extent are the 1973 cross-section profiles, in which the least experienced have especially low relative incomes, reliable indicators of possible future cohort gains? Will the young "recoup" the relative losses of the late 1960s and early 1970s or will their incomes follow historic cohort patterns from lower initial positions?

If the relatively lower income of young male graduates resulted from greater investment in on-the-job training, rapid income gains in the future might be expected. The evidence on occupational position and on other aspects of labor market performance, such as unemployment given in Chapter 1, is more suggestive, however, of reduced rather than greater investment in skills. Similarly, if the job market for graduates improves in the near future and if those suffering in the early 1960s share the improvement, they also may recoup at least some of the relative losses of the 1968–1973 period. Evidence of the impact of the depressed market on the position of older male graduates does not, however, make such a scenario seem highly likely. The problem raised by the changes in the 1970s relates to the fact (as noted in the text) that rates of return and expected dis-counted incomes are *forward-looking* concepts, which require im-plicit (as in the case of the usual cross-section income analysis) or explicit forecasts of future possibilities. In the past when the job market for college graduates was strong, cohort and cross-section profiles were quite similar,[2] the problem could be "finessed." With the depressed market for the young of the 1970s, however, dis-counted present values and rates of return will differ (in ways they did not in the past) depending on postulates about future income profiles. The 1973 cross-section profile will yield relatively high estimates of rates of return since it, in essence, postulates that the young will recoup the losses of the past quinquennium and enjoy more rapid growth of income as they age than previous groups.

LIFETIME INCOMES AND RATES OF RETURN

Table A-2 reports the results of estimating discounted present values of lifetime income and internal rates of return from 1968 and 1973 under five alternative assumptions about future income streams. The assumptions are designed to provide a reasonably com-prehensive set of possibilities ranging from those in which graduates recoup much of the losses of the early 1970s to those in which they do not. Line 1 gives results using the 1973 cross-section income profiles for 1973 and the 1968 cross-section for 1968. Line 2 gives similar estimates using actual 1968–1973, 1963–1968 and 1963–1973 cohort income gains to forecast future income possibilities. In each case the income profiles were generated by applying the rele-vant change in incomes to the incomes of 25- to 29-year olds in 5-year intervals. That is, I estimate the income of 30- to 34-year olds by multiplying the income of 25- to 29-year olds by the life cycle growth over 5 years and then take that figure, multiply it by the life-cycle growth from ages 30–34 to 35–39 to obtain the next

[2] J. Mincer, *Schooling, Earnings and Experience* (New York: Columbia University Press, 1974), pp. 77–79.

Table A-2. Alternative Estimates of Private and Internal Rates of Return, 1968–1973

	Approximate rates of return (to .5%)	
	1968	1973
Assumed income path		
1. Actual cross-sections with 1.5% growth	12.5%	10%
2. Applying 1968 cross-section to 1973 initial conditions with 1.5% growth	12.5%	8%
3. 1963–1973 cohort changes	11.0%	7.5%
4. 1968–1973 cohort changes	10%	7.0%
5. 1963–1968 cohort changes	13%	9.0%

NOTES: Lifetime income streams obtained:

Line 1: Using actual CPS cross-sections, with incomes interpolated by 5-year intervals from age group 25–29 and 1.5% annual growth.

Line 2: Using 1968 cross-section, with 25- to 29-year-old incomes in 1973 as starting point for life-cycle gains and 1.5% annual growth.

Line 3: Applied 1963–1973 cohort changes to 25- to 29-year-old incomes in 1968 and 1973.

Line 4: Applied 1968–1973 cohort changes to 25- to 29-year-old incomes in 1968 and 1973.

Line 5: Applied 1963–1968 cohort changes to 25- to 29-year-old incomes in 1968 and 1973.

After tax incomes for private returns, obtained by adjusting incomes by tax liability reported in U.S. Bureau of Census, *Statistical Abstract 1973*, Table 631, p. 395 with interpolations between income classes. I used the married couple, independent income tax liabilities. Private cost of college obtained from U.S. Bureau of the Census, Current Population Reports, "Income and Expenses of Students Enrolled in Postsecondary School: October 1973," Series P-20, No. 281, Table F, p. 4. I took a weighted average of the median educational expenses for full-time students in these institutions as weights using the same table. This yielded an estimated cost of $1250 per year. For simplicity, this cost is assumed to hold for each year of college. To get a figure for 1968, I calculated the percentage change in tuition and fees from 1969–1970 to 1974–1975 in U.S. Office of Education, *Digest of Educational Statistics, 1974*, Table 128, p. 113, weighting the public and private figures by the proportion of college students in these types of institutions in 1973 as given in *ibid*, Table 87, p. 75. Applying the resultant percentage change (53%) to the $1250 estimate for 1973 yields an estimated cost in 1968 of $817 per year.

figure, and so forth.[3] In intermediate years, I interpolated by simple linear procedures. For comparability, except in line 1, I apply the same income profile to both the 1968 and 1973 groups of graduates.

To take account of the years in school, the income of men, by individual year, in school and out of school, as given in Table A-1

[3] Recall that the actual ages during which earnings are received are one less than the figures given in the text.

was used. For the age 22 (when college men presumably work part year) they are both given the income of out-of-school men. Incomes at ages 23, 24, and 25 are obtained by extrapolating the change in income from ages 25–29 to 30–34 from the income in the midpoint year 27. The actual reported incomes during school are roughly equal to the one-fourth assumed in most previous computations. Private benefits are obtained by applying tax rates to incomes, and private costs from a recent census publication as described in the table footnote. To focus on the effect of the postschool labor market changes on the return, I keep the same cross-section profile estimates for the years 18–24. This can be modified in the cohort calculations to obtain a better fix on either historic returns or potential future returns. Finally, the cross-section estimates are adjusted for potential increases in real income in the future by a growth factor of 1.5% per annum. Larger or smaller growth will alter the estimated present values and returns but are unlikely to affect the substantive results. Since cohort incomes are based on actual income gains, no such adjustment is made in lines 3–5.

The computations show that the compression in the college premium among the young and increased cost of college reduced the internal rate of return under all of the postulated future income streams. The smallest drop occurs in Line 1, where it is assumed that the young graduates of the 1970s obtain exceptional cohort income gains in the future to attain the premiums of older generations in the 1973 cross-section. Even here, however, the rate of return falls by about 2.5 percentage points. Under the other—and potentially more realistic—assumptions, the return is estimated to fall from 3 to 4.5 points. If the 1963–1973 decadal cohort change in income is taken as the "best" estimate of possible long-run developments, the rate is estimated to fall from 11% to 7.5%. In these cases, the young do *not* recoup the loss in relative income of the 1970s.

All of the calculations in the table are to be viewed as rough order-of-magnitude estimates based on alternative future possibilities. Whether de facto any of these rates turns out to be correct depends on future economic developments which are difficult to foresee.

As for the period from 1973 to 1975 the most recent data on the relative position of young college men, from the starting salary series of the College Placement Council and Endicott Surveys, suggest that the relative position of college graduates declined more modestly, in the 1973—1975 period, in part because high school graduates were presumably more adversely affected by the downturn. Data from the May CPS surveys, which ask questions about "usual weekly earnings" rather than annual average earnings tell a similar story. According to these data, between 1973 and 1975 the premium income of college graduates 25- to 29-years old dropped from 12% in 1973 to 8% in 1975. On the other hand, however, data on yearly incomes by years of schooling for 1974 show a larger fall in the position of male college graduates (a drop in the income of 25- 34-year-old college men) relative to high school men of 7 percentage points.[4] Since the direct cost of college has continued to rise,[5] the return has presumably dropped further in the 1973-1975 period, perhaps by 1 additional percentage point.

[4] U.S. Bureau of the Census, "Consumer Income," *Current Population Reports*, Series P–60 No. 97, p. 122 and No. 101, p. 116 for 1973–1974 changes: in 1973 the ratio of the income of full-time, year-round college to high school men aged 25 to 34 stood at 1.23; in 1974, at 1.16. I tabulated the usual weekly earnings figures from the computer tapes for the May 1973 and May 1975 *Current Population Surveys*.

[5] U.S. Office of Education, *Digest of Educational Statistics, 1974*, Table 128, p. 113.

Appendix B
Forecast Model

he forecasts used in Chapter 3 are based on the following three-equation model of the job market for college graduates:

1. *Supply of freshman males to college* (period covered: 1951–1973)

$$FRSH = -2.02 + .88 \text{ POP} + 1.31 \ [CSAL-ASAL] + .21 \ FRSH \ (-1)$$
$$(.21) \qquad (.26) \qquad\qquad (.16)$$

$$R^2 = .987 \qquad SEE = .049 \qquad d.w. = 1.79$$

2. *Dependence of graduates on number of freshmen* (period covered: 1954–1973)

$$BA = -.63 + .71 \ FRSH[-4] + .29 \ FRSH[-5]$$
$$(.20) \qquad\qquad (.20)$$

$$R^2 = .976 \qquad SEE = .061 \qquad d.w. = 0.55$$

3. *Determination of college salaries* (period covered: 1951–1973)

$$CSAL = -2.25 - .15 \ BA(-1) + 1.1 \ DEM + .31 \ ASAL + .45 \ CSAL(-1)$$
$$(.02) \qquad\quad (.51) \qquad (.24) \qquad (.11)$$

$$R^2 = .994 \qquad SEE = .018 \qquad d.w. = 1.51$$

where:

FRSH = number of first-degree, credit-enrolled males, as reported in U.S. Office of Education, *Digest of Educational Statistics 1974*, Table 91, p. 77.

POP = number of 18- to 19-year-old men, as reported in U.S. Bureau of the Census, *Current Population Reports*, "School Enrollment," Series P-20, various editions.

CSAL = a weighted average of college starting salaries taken from the annual survey of F. Endicott, "Trends in Employment of College and University Graduates in Business and Industry," (Placement Center, Northwestern University). The weights are .05 for accounting, .35 for engineering, .20 for general business trainees, and .40 for sales. They are designed to reflect the approximate distribution of college graduates in engineering and related sciences, accounting, bachelor's of business administration, and "other fields," assuming that "sales" jobs reflect nontechnical opportunities in other fields. Since the salaries move together, in general, alternative fixed-weight indices yield similar results.

CSAL is in 1967 dollars, deflated by the Consumer Price Index as given in U.S. Department of Labor, *Handbook of Labor Statistics 1975*, Table 123, p. 314.

DEM = index of demand for college graduates, calculated by taking a fixed-weight index of employment in 46 industries. The weights are the proportion of men in each industry with college degrees in 1960, as given in U.S. Bureau of the Census, 1960 Census of Population, *Industrial Characteristics*, PC(2)-7F, Table 21. The employment figures are from U.S. Department of Commerce, *Survey of Current Business* (July ed.).

BA = number of male bachelor's graduates, from U.S. Office of Education, *Earned Degrees Conferred*, various editions with 1972 from xeroxed sheets provided by the Office of Education. Where available, I used the figures that relate to bachelors only, not those that include first professionals. To estimate the number of baccalaureates' net of first professionals for the years preceding 1961, when the Office of Education first differentiated the figures, I subtracted the number of degrees in medicine and other health fields, theology, law, and architecture from the bachelors and first-professional degree data to obtain a second series and spliced the two with

1961 as the overlap year. The major adjustment involves subtraction of medicine, law, and theology degrees from the bachelor series.

ASAL = average annual earnings of full-time workers in the U.S., as reported in U.S. Department of Commerce, *Survey of Current Business* (July ed.). It is in constant 1967 dollars.

Numbers in parentheses after variables refer to the time lag for the variable, with (−4), for example, reflecting a 4-year lag. Numbers in parentheses below variables are standard errors; *d.w.* = Durbin-Watson statistic; *SEE* = standard error of estimate; R^2 = percentage of variation explained by the equation. All variables are in logarithmic form. The years chosen for the regressions are dictated by data availability, with the immediate post–World War II period deleted from consideration due to the "extraordinary" enrollments that resulted from the "backlog" of demand from the war and the G. I. bill. The unavailability of degree figures for the years after 1972 dictated that the period end in 1973; estimated degrees were used for that year.

Equation 1 is the basic supply equation of the model, linking the number of men enrolling in the first year of college to the relevant population and to the differential between the income of starting male college workers and of all fully employed workers in the society, which is to be viewed as a rough index of the college income premium. The lagged number of freshmen is introduced to reflect lagged adjustments in the context of the usual partial adjustment model. The equation is a rough, first-order approximation to the underlying "true" relation between economic incentives and enrollment in college. It ignores, largely because of the lack of adequate time-series data, tuition and fee charges. While this undoubtedly creates some problems, it is unlikely to bias seriously the results, because most of the costs of college occur in the form of forgone income, not tuition and fees.[1] The equation uses the ratio of college starting to average salaries as the measure of salary incentive rather than the more appropriate rate of return, whose calculation would require time-series figures on lifetime incomes that are not available on a year by year basis. The population data relate to

---

[1] G. Becker, *Human Capital* (New York: Columbia University Press, 1964), p. 75 estimated that forgone earnings made up 75% of the full cost of college, a statistic that, has fallen, at most, moderately in recent years.

18- to 19-year olds, who constitute about 60% of freshmen.[2] In a correctly specified model in which POP reflects the entire relevant group on "potential" students, the coefficient on population should be unity; in the context of the lagged adjustment model, the coefficient divided by 1 minus the coefficient 1, the lagged term should be unity, as it is.[3] While Equation 1 is imperfect, it suffices to provide a rough "test" of the hypothesized behavioral link between the job market and college enrollments and estimates of the relevant parameters.

Equation 2 simply relates the number of bachelors graduates in a given year to the number of freshmen 4 and, because of delays, 5 years earlier.

Equation 3 makes the starting salaries of college graduates an inverse function of the number graduating and a direct function of the index of demand and of alternative salaries in the economy. The coefficient on *BA* measures the effect of a 1% increase in the number of graduates on salaries. The *ASAL* term is introduced to show the effect of economy-wide increases in wages on college salaries due to the shift in demand toward graduates when the wage of other workers rises. The lagged college salary variable, $CSAL(-1)$, measures the adjustment process in the market in the context of the usual partial adjustment model.[4] In this model, the short-term effect of independent variables on the dependent variable is given by the regression coefficients; the long-term effect is given by the coefficients divided by 1 minus the coefficient on the lagged dependent variable. The major weakness in this equation is the failure to treat the impact of the number of older college graduates and women on

[2] U.S. Bureau of the Census, "Social and Economic Characteristics of Students" *Current Population Reports*, (October 1973), Series P-20, No. 272, Table 15, p. 54.

[3] In this model, a variable moves toward its equilibrium value by some proportion (0 $< \lambda < 1$) of the difference between the equilibrium and past value. Formally, if X is the variable and $\bar{X}$ the equilibrium value we have

$$\Delta X = \lambda[\bar{X} - X(-1)]$$

or

$$X = \lambda\bar{X} + (1-\lambda) X(-1)$$

where $X(-1)$ is the value in the previous period. For long term equilibrium $X = \bar{X}$. The coefficients on factors that determine $\bar{X}$ are thus divided by 1 minus the coefficient on $X(-1)$ to obtain their long-term impacts.

[4] See preceding Footnote 3.

the starting salaries of men. In the absence of quantitative information about whether older and younger graduates are complements
or substitutes and the extent to which women and men will compete
in the same markets in the future, I eschewed analysis of these
interrelations. While the good "fit" of the equation indicates that
concentrating on the relation between male *BA*s and starting salaries
was not grievously wrong in the past, this problem with the structure
of the equation may mar the forecasts and should, as stated in the
text, be considered in evaluating them.

The three equations form a recursive system which is particularly amenable to forecasting.[5] The system is, to be sure, small,
relying on very few variables and relations and thereby ignoring
certain potentially important aspects of the world. While more complex and detailed models, along the lines of national econometric
models or input–output models of the structure of the economy,
would enhance our knowledge of the college market and illuminate
the economics of the system, the present model suffices to indicate
possible future developments.

The forecasts given in Figure 14 were calculated on a base of
1975. I calculated the change in college salaries for 1975 from the
Endicott surveys for 1975 and 1974, using the predicted salaries.[6]
The change in alternative salaries was estimated by the change in
average hourly earnings from June 1974 to June 1975.[7] The change
in first-year enrollments in 1974 was obtained from the Office of
Education, while the change in 1975 was calculated by the model.
Forecasts of changes in the population of 18- to 19-year olds were
made from data on the age of men by single years, as given in the
1970 Census of Population.[8] I assumed that alternative salaries
increase at its long-term trend rate of 2.4% per annum in the future
but that the growth of demand for college graduates increases at its
1970s pace of 0.5% per annum, as opposed to the pre-1970s rate. As
noted in the text, more "optimistic" assumptions about the growth

[5] H. Wold, *Econometric Model-Building* (Amsterdam: North-Holland, 1967).

[6] F. Endicott, *Trends in Employment of College and University Graduates in Business
and Industry*, (Northwestern University, 1975, p. 4 and 1974, p. 4).

[7] U.S. Department of Commerce, *Survey of Current Business* (Aug. 1965), p. S-15.

[8] U.S. Bureau of the Census, 1970 Census of Population, *United States Summary*
Section 1, Table 50, p. 265. I added the single years figures to obtain 18- to 19-year olds
comparable to the figures in the regressions.

of demand for graduates yield forecasts that follow roughly the same time path as that in the figure but with a more pronounced upward trend in the 1980s. I experimented with other forms of recursive three-equation models and obtained results also comparable to those in the figure: moderate decline in the job market for graduates through 1977–1978, followed by a gradual upturn in the late 1970s and early 1980s, and an ensuing boom in the late 1980s, followed finally by a leveling and modest decline in the early 1990s. Lest any of the forecasts be taken too seriously, I restate the text warning that they provide only a rough notion of how certain factors are likely to affect the situation of graduates and can be readily invalidated by unforeseen shifts in demand due, say, to unpredictable structural changes in the economy, new technologies, government programs, wars, or depressions. Experiments with related models at the MIT Center for Policy Alternatives have shown that failure to foresee sharp shifts in exogenous variables has led to sizeable divergencies between simulated and actual patterns even though the basic model provides a good "fix" on behavioral and market realities.

Index

Expectations
as determinants of enrollment decisions,
54–56
income, 12, 13

F

Fellowships
graduate cutbacks, 23–24
for minorities, 153
Fertility rates
drop in 1960s and 1970s, 167
and years of schooling, 30
Feuer, Lewis, 30
Fields of study
changes brought about by collapse of
college manpower market, 39–42
of women, 175–179
First National City Bank, college courses
offered at, 47
Frankfurter, Felix, 124

G

Galbraith, John Kenneth
power of the scientific estate, 81
technostructure, 3
Government, 7
affirmative action, 97–98
Civil Rights Act of 1964, 137, 146, 165
dependence of college market on, 62, 79
impact on supply and demand in the
labor market, 62–63
Medicare and medicaid, 119
possible overeducation policies, 196–197
R&D expenditures, 100–102
Great Depression, 4, 7
college graduate unemployment, 28
increase in income since, 3

H

Harris, Seymour, 1940s labor market prediction, 79
Harvard University
black enrollment, 155–156
Business School: graduate success, 132
faculty reduction by attrition, 45
Harvard College job opportunities, 28

Law School: career choices, 128
top law graduates, 127
High school graduates (18- to 19-year olds
enrolling directly in college, recent
trends, 34–36
Human capital, 15
Humanities
enrollment, 21
salaries, 12, 154
unemployment, 21

I

Income
distribution, 188–189
expectations, 12, 13
and relative education levels, 13–15, 24

J

Job opportunities
for college graduates, 19–21, 27–28
defined, 10
for language students, 92

L

LaGuardia Community College, courses
offered at First National City Bank,
47
Lawyers
American Bar Association, 124
and the cobweb cycle, 124–129
enrollment, 125–129
market structure, 124, 128
quality of applicants, 128
salaries, 126
Leontief, Wassily, input–output table for
U.S. economy, 62

M

M.D., see Physicians
Massachusetts Institute of Technology
black enrollment, 150
Center for Policy Alternatives, 6, 52, 115
early retirement of senior faculty, 46